D0354246

PRAISE FOR WALID PHARES AND *FUTURE JIHAD*

"Phares understands the language of Jihadism and analyses Arab Islamic politics authoritatively. He is a leading educator to the public and an eye opener to decision makers. Right on the subject and says it like it is."

—*Dr. Jacob Keryakes, NBC Arabic Translator and Linguist*

"Dr. Walid Phares is an experienced expert whom the media trusts to provide accurate and timely insights on the nature of jihad and Islamic-based terrorism. His book is a 'must read' on the threats we face in the future."

—*Andrew Cochran, Founder & Editor, The Counterterrorism Blog*

"Dr. Phares' comments and analysis are always insightful and provide a cultural 'insider's view' of the Middle East and the global jihad movement."

—*Rick Hahn, Former FBI Terrorism expert. MSNBC Counter Terrorism analyst*

"Dr. Phares has an unmatched knowledge of the Middle East with its tightly interwoven tapestry of language, religion, history and politics. He can bring an inter-disciplinary approach to complex security issues. Unlike so many analysts, he can convey his encyclopedic knowledge of the Middle East in multiple languages."

—*Colonel Kenneth Allard, USA (Ret.), Former Dean,*
National War College and NBC Defense Analyst

"Walid Phares' precise, 'pulls no punches' analysis of an extremely complex and difficult issue should be required reading in the counterterrorism community."

—*Col. Rick Francona, Retired intelligence officer, CNBC News analyst*

"Walid Phares is a uniquely perceptive expert on radical Islamism, terrorism, and related issues."

—*Cliff May, President, Foundation for the Defense of Democracies*

"Walid Phares' academic analysis of the politics of Jihad ideologies and movements and their perception of international relations is unique. His book, Future Jihad, is pioneering in the new field of post 9/11 clash of ideas. His deep understanding and equal of Arab and Western political cultures enables him to tell the story entirely as he frequently does in writing but also on al jazeera, al Hurra, and the many Western networks such as NBC, CNN, Fox News, CBC, and BBC."

—*Dr. Franck Salameh, Professor of Arab Culture, Boston University*

MORE PRAISE FOR WALID PHARES AND *FUTURE JIHAD*

"Walid Phares' expert analysis on Jihad terrorism and its future possibilities is unparalleled. His depth and breadth of knowledge on Jihad terrorism and its historical roots is essential to understanding the enemy we face. His arguments that we must know and understand our adversary in order to confront it are extremely convincing. Phares' analysis is fundamental to defeating the Jihadis and their ideology. His book is a must-read for students and policy-makers around the world."

—Stephen Shellman, Ph.D., Co-Director,
Workshop on Teaching about Terrorism and Professor, College of William & Mary

"Walid Phares is the ultimate 'connect-the-dots' analyst. Where others see a blur disconnected facts, he sees a picture, and he is a master at describing what he sees to audiences as diverse as college students, federal courts, and the viewers of CNN. If you want to know who the jihadist enemies of America and the West are, what they are doing and why, and what must be done to defeat them, there is no better guide than Walid Phares."

—Dennis Hale, Associate Professor, Boston College

"The concept of 'jihad terrorism' presented by Dr. Walid Phares puts the West on notice as to the true nature of the enemy and the parameters of what is, essentially, a total war between competing and incompatible worldviews."

—Earl Tilford, Professor of History, Grove City College

"Walid Phares is a daring historian. He plays towards the Arab and Muslim world the role of Russian thinker Andrei Amalrik towards the Soviet Union: Speaking the truth."

—Dr. Jean Aucagne S.J, Saint Joseph University, Beirut

FUTURE JIHAD

Terrorist Strategies against America

WALID PHARES

FUTURE JIHAD
Copyright © Walid Phares, 2005.
All rights reserved. No part of this book may be used or reproduced in any manner
whatsoever without written permission except in the case of brief quotations embodied in
critical articles or reviews.

First published 2005 by
PALGRAVE MACMILLAN™
175 Fifth Avenue, New York, N.Y. 10010 and
Houndmills, Basingstoke, Hampshire, England RG21 6XS.
Companies and representatives throughout the world.

PALGRAVE MACMILLAN is the global academic imprint of the Palgrave Macmillan
division of St. Martin's Press, LLC and of Palgrave Macmillan Ltd. Macmillan® is a
registered trademark in the United States, United Kingdom and other countries. Palgrave is a
registered trademark in the European Union and other countries.

ISBN 1-4039-7074-2 hardback

Library of Congress Cataloging-in-Publication Data
Phares, Walid, 1957–
Future Jihad : terrorist strategies against America / Walid Phares.
    p.   cm.
  Includes bibliographical references and index.
  ISBN 1-4039-7074-2 (alk. paper)
   1. Terrorism—United States.   2. Terrorism—Islamic countries.   3. Terrorism—
Religious aspects—Islam.   4. Jihad.   5. Qaida (Organization)   6. War on Terrorism,
2001–   7. Anti-Americanism.   I. Title.
HV6432.P493   2005
363.32'0973—dc22

                                                                                        2005049892

A catalogue record for this book is available from the British Library.

Design by Letra Libre, Inc.

First edition: November 2005.
10 9 8 7 6 5 4 3 2 1
Printed in the United States of America

CONTENTS

ACKNOWLEDGMENTS

This book is the result of a lifetime of observation and analysis. Its findings were drawn from decades of reading and research and patient listening to opinions expressed in a variety of forms. The birth of the book has to be credited to an endless number of people I have met in my long journey across the world.

My first acknowledgment must be to my readers, audiences, and faithful participants in the many forums to which I have made presentations. I must thank everyone who over the years had encouraged me to put these thoughts into writing.

My second acknowledgment is to Cliff May, the president of the Foundation for the Defense of Democracies in Washington. I owe Cliff for his continuous support for my projects, and, along with my colleagues at the Foundation, I thank him for hosting me as a senior fellow and for deeply understanding the importance of my work and promoting it.

My third acknowledgment goes to the team to which I owe the publishing project. Lynne Rabinoff, my very patient agent, never lost hope in this book, even as I postponed my decision for two years. She relentlessly encouraged me to take the step and make this book a reality. Airié Stuart, my editor, editorial director at Palgrave Macmillan, understood the message and importance of the book and guided me through the publishing process, strategizing with me and editing. I thank her for championing this book. I would also like to thank Bruce Murphy and the editors for their valuable comments on the manuscript, and also thank the production and marketing teams for their efficiency.

My fourth acknowledgment is directed toward those who have influenced my thinking and methods. I hold a special regard for those instructors who impacted my intellectual evolution in my formative classroom years. My thanks also go to all the various editors, network producers and administrators, journalists, publishers, anchorpeople, writers, and intellectuals on three continents who valued my remarks and my work and made it possible for me to share it with the public for over a quarter of a century. But, above all, I owe my thought process to my older brother, Sami, who decades ago opened my eyes. He was my mentor in the adolescence of my research life, and I cannot thank him enough for the light he shed during those early years.

My final acknowledgment extends toward those in my personal life, those who have been affected by the time taken away from them and instead focused on this book. I must thank my loved ones and family, who stood by me during the hard times and shared the burden of a life filled with difficulties. I know my work would make them proud. My particular thoughts go to my mother and my sister, witnesses to my sacrifices. My strength comes from their understanding of my dedication to my work.

And beyond the frontiers of life, I owe to my late father my constant desire to bring truth to people. He taught and convinced me that truth brings justice; he used to say: "Bring knowledge around you, that's your mission."

LIST OF ILLUSTRATIONS

INTRODUCTION

W HEN THE SECOND JET SLAMMED INTO THE NORTH World Trade Center
Tower in Manhattan, I immediately told students standing next to me,
"It's a jihad *Ghazwa* . . . they have chosen the Yarmuk option." The eyes of a
few students around me opened wide. That Tuesday morning the world was
changing at a record rapid pace—and yet in a sense it was moving in slow motion for most Americans. During that agonizing half hour from 8:45 A.M. to
9:15 A.M., my students, my colleagues, and I belonged to two different worlds.
In the corner of the campus where I was teaching on that day of infamy, I felt
very much alone: What I had known, researched, and watched building year
after year was finally here, ravaging my new homeland. I was as shocked as
anyone, but unlike many I was not surprised. What had come to pass was
something I had studied and tried to warn others about for more than two
decades. It made me more determined to impact the future of what I knew was
coming from that point on.

Across America, people's eyes were fixed on the smoke, the firefighters, the
debris, the faces covered with blood and dust, and the gestures and declarations of America's leaders. Americans felt like lost souls. People around the
world—supporters of peace and democratic ideas, at any rate—felt that the
losses could easily have been their own. Many of their leaders said they felt they
were Americans during that tragic day.[1] Spreading outward like a wave from the
events of September 11 was a terrible new reality that enveloped the minds of
an entire nation and perhaps the world.

TV crews rushed into the conference room of my building one hour after
the massacre. I had been analyzing the jihad phenomenon for twenty-five years,
yet as the technicians were setting up their cameras, I found myself wondering
what to say. If I told them what I knew, they would simply not understand my
logic. After all, it had taken me a lifetime to understand. If I did not try to explain it, I would be allowing America's enemies to win on another day in the future. Other colleagues around the country faced a similar dilemma. Those few
of us who knew about the danger and had tried to warn about it had been
voices crying in the wilderness (often against enormous personal and institutional hostility); now our time had come. But the public vision was too blurred,
the systems of knowledge were blocked, and the government had been failed by
those charged with providing it with the truth.

The first question I took from the journalists was, of course, "What happened?" Twenty-two years earlier I had published my first book, followed by a plethora of other books, articles, and hundreds of lectures, all addressing the clash to come.[2] And it had finally come. How could I describe what had just occurred to the American people, and who had done this to them? When al Qaeda launched its mujahidin to bleed America in the early 1990s, very few in this country had projected a future jihad. By 2001, we were, in fact, already at war with an enemy unknown to most American citizens. The war was at least a decade old, but our media, elite, government, diplomats, and educators did not acknowledge this until the tragedy of September 11. Meanwhile, some of us had spent careers, lives, and resources studying this holy war and its strategies, tactics, and achievements; we had watched as it progressed unchecked. How could we explain the horrors of that Tuesday morning in an almost complete intellectual void? I wanted to help set the record straight and begin to unravel what was denied for so many years: the truth.

"This is the Pearl Harbor of terrorism" was my answer to the first question that morning. As I said this, I recognized the gigantic walls that prevented Americans and westerners from absorbing the realities that had been building in the East for decades. I believed that these obstructionist tendencies would continue to block the presentation of what the public needed to understand the tragedy. But at that moment I wanted to explain that we as a nation had been attacked in a war that was already raging. Indeed, in the following years, I continued to remind audiences that the war had been in existence for far longer than had been acknowledged in the West. The United States was not attacked randomly, but as a part of a planned offensive war.[3] This was not a mere lunatic reaction to U.S. foreign policy by a handful of deranged men; the enemies who targeted the United States on September 11 had a plan based on previous successes, all carefully planned, justified, and executed—and certainly it was a prelude to future attacks to come, in pursuit of clearly defined goals. Eventually America would have to understand the historical significance of what was happening, because it would now forever be linked to it.

The terrorists who attacked us that morning had planned their aggression over the long term, had strategic ambitions, wanted cataclysmic results, and did so as a first wave in a much larger, all-out war against America and all it stood for. The closest example that would resonate with the pre–September 11 mind of most Americans was Japan's treacherous 1941 attack. The comparison is not perfect, however. But in an imperfect collective state of consciousness, it was an eye-opener. The pilots who bombed Pearl Harbor were not on their own mission. They were not frustrated individuals who decided one morning that

Washington was evil and had to be punished. They were not an isolated unit but part of an army, and their army was not without political leadership, an ideology, and geopolitical ambitions. They were not a mafia punishing the police, nor a gang retaliating against officials. Likewise, Mohammed Atta and his men were a unit within a network—part of an international terror army, under a global command structure and political organization that was in turn the fruit of an ideology, one that has penetrated many countries and governments and has been calling for a world war against America and western society as a whole. In the West by 2005, we have come some way in understanding this, but we still have a long ways to go.

The war against terrorism should have been in the forefront of public debate and policy at least a decade before the September 11 aggression. So when we contemplate the events that led to the massacre in Manhattan and Washington in 2001, and the subsequent confrontations in Afghanistan, Iraq, Madrid, London, Riyadh, Pakistan, Bali, Istanbul, Beslan, Beirut, and the Sunni triangle, and when we revisit the general reaction to September 11 immediately after the dust settled, then we certainly draw the mother of all lessons: What went wrong? Bernard Lewis has provided a powerful analysis of "what went wrong" in the Muslim world that led to the attacks. I shift the question to failures in the *targeted* societies that led to the hole exploited by the jihadists.[4] In simple terms, what went wrong in America, the West, and the international community? Why were we not ready as we should have been? And are we ready, even now, and after all that has happened, for what is to come?

We might linger a moment over the fact that the first question posed in the media, dizzying the elites and unleashing government soul-searching, was, "Why do they hate us?" How is it possible that a nation at war, as the 9/11 Commission later admitted we were, did not know why its enemies hated it?[5] Who had blocked this knowledge? Historically, when nations are attacked, especially if these aggressions have been prepared for years, and more particularly if previous attacks have signaled this attitude (and given rise to an abundant literature), it is known. The enemy is not a complete surprise.

Regrettably, we must recognize that the fog of misinformation has not yet dissipated. Consider the number of articles, editorials, interviews, panels, books, forums, and discussions that have filled our airwaves and national debates—yet are still unable to say why the perpetrators "hate us"; is America really ready for what future jihad holds? One main objective of this book is to attempt to explain why "they" hate us—if it is about "hate" to start with—and what ingredients we still are not aware of that may be relevant to the future.

Unfortunately, the first question, "Why do they hate us?" was not the only troubling one. In the days, weeks, and months following the slaughter, and as the public inquiry mounted, a whole series of stunning questions followed from many sources. All indicate that the problem of perception adds to the complexity of what we are facing. When we review the questions even now, four years later, they are bewildering. How could America have been so unaware of such a massive threat? I listed the ten most common questions for the National Intelligence Conference on national security, held in Washington, D.C., in January 2005:[6]

1. Who are they?
2. What did they want to happen?
3. Why did they launch the attacks of September 11?
4. Are they at war with us? Why? Since when?
5. What did they want to achieve?
6. Why didn't we know about it?
7. Who obstructed our knowledge of it?
8. Are they planning on future wars?
9. Have these wars already started?
10. What can we do about them?

These are the questions that this book seeks to answer, because I believe that the answers are still not clear and that we are in danger unless we face them.

WHO ARE THEY?

The second question to emerge from the endless writings and talks since the towers collapsed was: "Who are they?" With the exception of a couple of dozen analysts in the very specialized agencies and another dozen experts in the Beltway's think tanks, very few had uttered the words "al Qaeda" before September 11. During hearings of the 9/11 Commission, during the summer of 2004, two secretaries of state, two defense secretaries, and a counterterrorism czar were not able to agree on the birthdate of bin Laden's organization.[7] A sea of experts, publishing at will—*after* the attacks, I might note—pored over the records of the 1990s looking for evidence and pieces of information. An Ali Baba's cave opened up suddenly with a myriad of theories, conspiracy theories, and personal sagas. But despite psychological analysis of the organization's membership, health profiles of its leaders, speculations on the latest move and the potential links, and even rumors, the "Who are they?" question remains on the table. Is al Qaeda a central organization or a federation of groups? Did Osama bin Laden create it, or did it create him? Why didn't most Americans see him, hear him, or understand what it was about? Didn't he declare war against America years before on al Jazeera? Is al Qaeda a product of an ideology? If so, what is it?

WHAT DID THEY WANT TO HAPPEN?

What did the perpetrators' organization want, globally, historically, and ideologically? Was there a worldview behind al Qaeda's action? Its members spoke of jihad, of *kufr,* of *istishad,* of *fatah;* what did they mean by these concepts? They theorized about *dar el harb* and *dar el Islam,* as their domain and ours, respectively. Where are these zones? Where are New York, Washington, London, Madrid, Baghdad, Kabul, Riyadh, Istanbul, Beirut, and Khartoum in their vision—the one that brought them to Manhattan, Fallujah, and Beslan? Why are most Americans unable to answer these questions?

WHY DID THEY LAUNCH THE ATTACKS OF SEPTEMBER 11?

Can we trust the statements explaining their rationale made by Osama bin Laden and his spokesperson, Suleiman Abu Ghaith? Were the real motivations behind September 11 the U.S. sanctions against Iraq's regime, the U.S. support of Israel, and American troops stationed on Arabian soil? Was it true—as many academics, intellectuals, and activists affirmed—that the attacks were a direct response to American foreign policy? Did the terrorists launch the attacks in retaliation for U.S. actions or to trigger reactions? Were the operations opening a war or resuming it? On that Tuesday morning, few Americans were able to answer these questions, not even those in the highest offices of the land. Today, years later, the American people are still confused about the answers.

ARE THEY AT WAR WITH US? WHY? SINCE WHEN?

On February 22, 1998, Osama bin Laden proclaimed a world front for jihad and declared war against infidel America.[8] He based it on religious edicts. He followed his declaration with twin strikes in August against U.S. embassies in Africa. Since the early 1990s, jihad-inspired attacks had taken place against Americans, America, and other countries around the world. After the 1998 declaration of war, more strikes took place, including against the USS *Cole* in

Yemen. But on September 10, 2001, the United States had not declared war against al Qaeda. During the summer of 2004, we learned from officials who were in charge of counterterrorism that al Qaeda had been targeted as early as 1998; there had been a number of opportunities to address its threats. The 9/11 Commission told us that U.S. agencies and institutions were spending energy, time, and money to bring down al Qaeda and its leaders; other groups were monitored for fundraising and other actions in support of terrorism for years. Yet: Were we or were we not at war with those who were at war with us? On the surface this question seems simple, but is in fact extremely difficult to answer. From all that ensued after September 11—before and after Tora Bora, before and since the removal of Saddam Hussein, and before and after the beginning of the Syrian withdrawal from Lebanon—yes, there is a war against terrorism, that is, "them." And from all that has been uncovered, reassessed by U.S. and western authorities, experts, intellectuals, historians, and debate architects since September 11, we now admit that a war was launched against America years earlier, with a declared agenda and clearly stated objectives.

WHAT DID THEY WANT TO ACHIEVE?

The attacks on the World Trade Center and the Pentagon, most commentators and experts agreed, were highly symbolic. Jihad suicide bombers wanted to destroy America's credibility worldwide. Even the founder of al Qaeda said so on al Jazeera television in the weeks following the strikes. He, scores of his followers, and sympathizers in the Arab Muslim world rushed to conclude that the United States' moral power was shattered with the damage and destruction of the buildings in its two greatest cities. Most debaters on all sides of the divide concluded that ultimately, Atta and his co-executioners had achieved their goals by penetrating U.S. security and destroying in forty minutes Americans' trust in the homeland's security. At first, this seems to be true. But there may have been more to it than scoring a victory with massive bloodshed. What mechanisms did the jihadists want to unleash, and did they succeed? Did they hope to ignite more than the suicidal attack of nineteen men? Were the objectives the ones announced, or were their objectives planted deeper—under the skin of our nation?

The questioning unleashed that Tuesday morning in September 2001 never stopped in my mind, even though it had hardly begun in the public realm. For the next list of questions was even more disturbing—though it took two more years before a high body in government would try to address them.

WHY DIDN'T WE KNOW ABOUT IT?

Hindsight is a psychological impediment to clear analysis. The collective ex-perience of Americans since September 11 makes it hard to realize that most of what has been learned since the attacks was not known before. Because of the rush to action by government since, the overseas military engagements, and the exhaustive public debate during these wars and throughout the presidential election, the public tends to now believe that it always knew about the dangers and the threats. But harsh historical reality says otherwise. In fact, most Amer-icans did not know that a malevolent foreign force had declared war against their country and had no knowledge of that enemy; most segments of the po-litical and intellectual establishment were unaware of the existence of such organizations; if they knew about them, they did not know about their ideolo-gies or consider them a national security threat. The main question, of why we as a nation were unaware, remains. Why didn't our national leaders address their public, the legislative branch, or the media during the ten years before the attacks, as strikes and operations were taking place from (at least) the early 1990s on? Why didn't the president address Congress after the August 1998 attacks against the embassies and ask for powers of war? Why wasn't the Tal-iban removed that year, instead of several years and thousands of lives later?

These questions cannot be wished away. In the 1990s the essence of pub-lic debate about terrorism was focused on the root causes of violent groups and in most cases was tied to U.S. foreign policy mistakes. There was no govern-mental mission driven by resources aimed at fighting this war. There was little or no analysis of the roots of the jihadist movement worldwide, let alone its strategic articulation of aims and plans for campaigns. Even as the smoke of the disasters was still hanging in the skies, educational and information systems around the world were still focusing the public's attention in other directions.

A few hours after the attacks, al Jazeera aired stories of all sorts to divert at-tention from the real perpetrators. One release accused the Japanese Red Army "in retaliation for Hiroshima and Nagasaki"; another fingered the "American Indians"; Internet reports were circulating about Mossad's responsibility. Not only had Americans been mis-educated for years and poorly informed; the rest of the world had, and when the massacre took place, final attempts to continue blurring our vision were in place.[9]

WHO OBSTRUCTED OUR KNOWLEDGE ABOUT IT?

But who would obstruct this much-needed knowledge, and why? At what stage did the misinformation occur? Was it a deliberate effort to mollify America and distract its attention from the aggressor in order to strike at will? Or was it indeed a failure of the systems that were supposed to educate, inform, and mobilize the nation? These are tough questions indeed—but for someone who spent the 1990s observing and analyzing the creeping spread of the jihad networks and culture into the nation's systems, they cannot be dismissed as the result of hindsight. In comparing my analysis of jihad tactics during the 1990s to the findings of the 9/11 Commission, one conclusion emerges: An obstruction of knowledge took place.

Consider this: The 9/11 Commission released a tape, recorded a few minutes after the tragedy in Washington, in which a fighter pilot rushing to the scene over the Pentagon exclaims: "Gosh, the Russians got us!" Ten years after the end of the cold war, the Russians were still being seen as the "strategic enemy," not the jihadists who had been attacking America and Americans for over a decade.[10]

If we go back to newspaper articles, columns, op-eds, documentaries, and round tables for the decade between the fall of the Soviet Union and September 11 and tabulate all that we find on the jihadi threat worldwide, it is clear that, on the whole, the media establishment was unaware of the growing realities of world politics. A few pieces investigated some suicide bombers in Israel; a few lines reported violence in Algeria, or the machine-gunning of tourists in Egypt's Luxor. But the media missed the greater phenomenon: the growing spread of Islamic fundamentalist units and activities in various countries and specifically against the United States. It is not that the fundamentalists were operating in secret. Their abundant literature, disseminated across continents, should have been enough to trigger academic attention, research, and advice. In fact, it did—but for over a decade the dominant academic elite simply dismissed the threat and called jihad a myth.[11]

WHOSE FAILURE?

I argue that the root of the denial was a full-scale cultural one, because I witnessed that denial firsthand throughout the decade preceding September 11. From day one after my arrival in this country in the fall of 1990, I noted the mechanism (the series of activities) that led to the tragedy. This is not to say that I knew where and when the attack would come, or that others should have. No one could have predicted the year, the day, and the hour, nor the instruments and the results. But those in government charged with identifying threats were blinded by a deceptive fog. In retrospect, the 9/11 Commission tried hard to connect the dots and come up with an answer as to why it happened and how. The criminal investigation mapped out the road to the strikes, and the political inquiry found out that shortcomings were universal and occurred at all levels of government and under multiple administrations. But the commission did not catch the bigger failure. In his fiery testimony to the commission, former counterterrorism czar Richard Clarke said: "I failed you, your government failed you."[12] But he did not say who had failed the government. The three branches of government and their agencies are not just buildings and papers; they are a chain of men and women with limited—sometimes extended—knowledge in particular fields. As any political scientist knows, government is a related set of human teams, responding to each other and feeding each other with data and resources. The question thus is: Who failed the machine of the government? The hearings of 2004 provided us with a glimpse. A highly sophisticated group of commissioners tackled the question thoroughly, but at the end of the day stopped short of completion. On the day they offered their findings to the American people, two members of the commission addressed a select number of former officials and experts via a conference call. I was privileged to have been included in their briefing. The final conclusion of the 9/11 hearings shattered many taboos and released many old interdictions. The report finally spoke of jihad, jihadism, Islamic fundamentalism, and the litany of organizations involved. It retraced the decade-long history of their actions and attempts to hurt the United States and other nations around the world.

By comparison with the previous era, the report was a revolutionary text. It named names. While most world governments are still stuck with public diplomacy and "diplomatic" language, never crossing from the concept of "terrorism" to the "j" word, the commission told us there is another "world" out there, a space ruled by ideologies and terrorist strategies aiming at our cities, towns, countries, laws, peoples, and cultures. But the commission landed on its "Normandy" and stayed there. Now we know that there is a "universe" of jihad out there, totally at odds with the norms of international relations and not abiding by the modern era's agreements on world politics. That reality was not officially acknowledged before September 11, but it is now.

But how did we fail to see that universe before? That question is very important today, as it may help us not only prevent a new tragedy from happening, but may allow us to win the war on terrorism. If we can understand how we "failed" to see it coming back in the 1990s, perhaps we can avoid new jihads. The commission concluded that "it was a failure of imagination."[13] In the final analysis, the bipartisan group reasoned that as Americans, we failed to imagine such a thing happening, and so could not fathom it even as it happened. After hearing this conclusion during the prebriefing on the commission's findings, I exclaimed, "Yes, it was a failure of imagination, but it was caused by a failure of *education*."

Had we been educated, our imagination would have been wider and greater. Had we been taught what jihad was, we could have predicted its drive. Had we been warned about jihadism, we could have devised a resistance to it. Had we been informed when the war first started, we could have defended ourselves thereafter. Education failed the public and the government. The question then is: Was this a deliberate attempt by the education community to hide the truth?

ARE THEY PLANNING FUTURE WARS?

It would take a whole decade to understand our failures and the missteps that led to September 11. But that is not a luxury America and other countries around the world have. The raids on New York and Washington were not the end of an era but the beginning of one. Historians will certainly consume much time in filling out the greater tableau. They have the time, but America's national security doesn't, nor does world peace. The "world"— people, movements, ideologies—that caused September 11 did not go away. True, the geopolitical map has certainly changed with the rise of homeland security in the United States, the removal of the Taliban, the uprooting of Saddam Hussein, elections in Afghanistan and Iraq, and the ongoing popular uprisings in Lebanon and the Middle East. But Osama bin Laden is still at large, as are thousands of his followers; so is Ayman Thawahiri, his number two. The neo-Taliban still have an influence in the Muslim nuclear power, Pakistan. Al Zarqawi roams the Sunni triangle of Iraq, and al Qaeda's chapters are increasingly threatening Saudi Arabia and the region.

Madrid's judges arrested many terrorists after the Spanish government withdrew its troops from Iraq.[14] But there are still plenty of Islamic fundamentalists on the Iberian Peninsula. Britain, France, and Germany have stepped up their counterterrorism measures, but those countries are in fact two decades, not one, behind. The Netherlands is discovering what has grown up inside its political culture. Russia has been hesitant on Iraq and sold weapons to Syria and nuclear material to Iran—only to see Beslan's horror unfold. Indonesia has made arrests, but its jihadists have survived. The London bombings, a year after the Madrid train attacks, opened yet a wider battlefield in the war with jihadism. The terrorists proved their intentions to thrust jihad into Europe's geopolitics and intimidate it's populations as a prelude to submission to jihad's "diktat."

The war on terror is proceeding, but the jihad wars are proceeding as well. In fact, what we are seeing is two planets colliding at a great speed.

HAS THE FUTURE OF JIHAD ALREADY BEGUN?

To put it bluntly, yes, future jihads have already started. Now the United States and the international community have an opportunity to win the battle of "foresight" after they have realized in hindsight what was missed in the 1990s. By looking forward, I will attempt to analyze al Qaeda's (and other offshoots') strategic thinking with regard to future wars against the United States and its allies. There has been a fundamental misunderstanding about al Qaeda's ultimate goals. Strategic questions, such as what the jihadists want to achieve for the next decade or what al Qaeda's long-term plans are, are yet unanswered. Is the "international army of holy war" seriously aiming at conquest of the West or at rebuilding what was lost in the past? Do jihadists really want to restore the caliphate that ruled the Islamic world (and significantly, parts of what we now call the West) for over a thousand years? An inquiry into such questions would help determine what the United States and its allies need to do to win this war.

In the text that follows, I attempt to answer such critical questions as: What are al Qaeda's future strategies against the United States? How long will this war last? Is the United States secure on the inside? Will it have to engage the jihadists worldwide in multiple campaigns, and if so, where? Do al Qaeda and its nebulous allies—including potentially non-Sunni groups such as Hezbollah—have a world strategy to defeat the United States? How is victory defined by jihadists? What are the critical components of U.S. victory?

I show that the jihadist strategies include a deep infiltration of America's government, defenses, and its youth. Jihadi doctrines do not rule out the acquisition and the possible use of weapons of mass destruction.

The war is expected to last more than a decade. I argue that the United States is mobilized domestically for this war but is not yet fully secured. It will take mass cultural adaptation to fight jihad. America must win the war of ideas—it must capture the minds of the women, youth, and elite that form the foundation of the future. Americans must learn a higher, more difficult truth about the terrorists—and also about what and who allowed the jihadists to be successful until September 11 and beyond—so that they can begin the actual resistance. Washington's perception and planning for the global war on terrorism is only beginning. Many aspects of our response to and understanding of the jihadists need to be changed or developed: our national education, our justice system, our intelligence agencies, our political alliances around the world, and our spending policies. Some myths will have to be broken, and many realities must be unearthed.

A U.S. policy on jihad will have to be shaped; it will have to have its own men and women dedicated to it, and it must be fought at all levels worldwide. We can compare America's position today to the end of 1942. We have declared war against the new enemy and made some initial inroads, but the tide has not reversed. From their centers, the enemies are still waging global war against the West and the United States. In sum, major sacrifices are still ahead of us, and gigantic efforts and events are yet to occur. The high point of the conflict is yet to come.

The last four years created a major breach in how Americans and westerners look at world politics and international relations. The latest presidential election showed how issues of security, insecurity, and uncertainty prey on the minds of voters.

Images from overseas have changed the perceptions of viewers and readers: Beheadings, mass graves, and the statements made by the vast networks of jihadists and other radicals have brought home the weighty question of future holy wars against the United States and the West. Americans are now preoccupied by two wars: the jihad that has been launched against them and the war on terrorism that has been directed at the jihadists. Collectively we are searching for the answer as to which one shall be successful.

The answer is that al Qaeda has a world strategy—but it is not what we have thought or been led to believe it was. It is shaped by intellectual forces wider than the membership of the organization and far older than the cold war. The "system" at war with America is in fact centuries old and cannot be defined solely in terms of countries, regimes, or leaders. I call this system the "mother ship." I have seen its mechanisms at work, its complexities, and its long-term vision. The jihadists' vision of defeat has not yet been understood by the West. Jihadists do not see the death of Osama or loss of Fallujah as a defeat. Neither do westerners correctly understand the jihadists' vision of victory. In jihadists' view, Allah determines both victory and defeat.

So then, why and how did the jihadists establish the basis for the new war against the United States? It is crucial to analyze bin Laden's thinking, which can be done only from a jihadist perspective.[15] As will be shown in this book, the vision of a 9/11 attack was one decade old, but the ideology that led to it stretches far into the past. Osama built his vision upon sources that have also to be examined.

Reading, listening, and absorbing Islamic fundamentalist literature for over twelve years has enabled me to understand the mindset of Osama bin Laden and therefore the strategic planning of his organization. One of the least understood chapters of the war on terror is what can be considered the "thinking mode" of al Qaeda and other jihadists: What do they factor into their planning? How deep is their penetration of the western system, and since when? Who helps them from outside the organization? Was their assault on Manhattan and Washington only a raid? Or was it a trigger to a wider chain of events they thought would happen? From reading their declarations, websites, and chat rooms, the deep and strategic goals they had in mind are beginning to surface. From this knowledge base we can learn lessons about their future strategy and also plan our own.

Another important dimension of the struggle is al Qaeda's reaction to U.S. reactions, especially in the 1990s. From a jihadist perspective, what was the meaning of the first attack against the Twin Towers in 1993? When was the decision for this first assault made, and why? Why were there attacks against targets in Saudi Arabia and against the Khubar Towers in the mid-1990s? Was al Qaeda the sole attacker?

Then, in 1996 and 1998 came the jihadist formal declarations of war against America—incredibly, an event hardly noticed by the western media. I will demonstrate that this declaration was the watershed that set the September 11 attacks in motion. Who were the clerics behind that move? The attack on the USS *Cole* and the millennium plot moved the plan forward, but these attacks were only the tip of the iceberg. Based on my careful analysis of the video- and audiotapes aired on al Jazeera and on other media, I assert that al Qaeda's plan was and remains more comprehensive than what is commonly believed. English-only analysts are at a big disadvantage when dealing with information from the Arab world. Not all of what was said in Arabic was translated, and not all of what was translated was understood in context.

Bin Laden had a plan, a substitute plan, and a counterplan. This book unveils them all. Al Qaeda strikes, but it then analyzes the subsequent reactions of its enemies. It has a long-term vision, but can revise its tactics as necessary. This book shows the real al Qaeda; I will also show how the dominant political culture in the West has helped to obfuscate it.

TEN QUESTIONS FOR THE FUTURE

A better understanding of the past leads us to a clearer analysis of future trends. Such analysis opens up the way for a series of critically important questions. To recap:

1. Do they wish to destroy the enemy (us) or absorb it?

2. Do they want to attack the West and the United States before they accomplish their goals in the Muslim world first? (A crucial question, leading to many others.)

3. Will it be possible to conclude peace with the jihadists? What would doing so entail?

4. What are al Qaeda's priorities in the struggle against the United States?

5. What weaknesses and holes do the jihadists see in America and the West, and how would they use them?

6. Are the governments in the United States and other western nations ready for these future wars?

7. What would the next generations of Americans, today's children and youth, have to face in these wars?

8. What should the United States and the West do to avoid future jihads?

9. Why wasn't it already done in the past?

10. Are the jihadists alone, or do they have the backing of other powers and states?

My goal in writing this book is to help answer these questions. My first objective is to show that the future is very much about the past. The future of America depends on our understanding of the historical roots of jihadism. This is not a war with an enemy with whom governments can sign peace treaties or establish new frontiers. We are facing forces that link directly to ancient and modern history. Their ideology was born decades ago, but was inspired by doctrines from the Middle Ages. America has never engaged in a conflict with deeper roots in the past. Today's terrorists see the world with different eyes and minds from all Americans—and from most communities worldwide. To fully understand their mindset, we must learn about the terrorists' history and their reading of history. The future of U.S. national security, international relations, and world stability lies in the hands of those who are first to learn about the terrorists' relevant history. That is the key to their code, but it is not a secret one; it was simply hidden for too long by our own elite, which denied the public this fundamental knowledge. By severing the historical roots from contemporary conflicts waged by the terrorists, and by camouflaging their real long-term intents (which are also linked to their vision of history), our elite blurred or even blinded our vision.[16]

In this book I make the case that a central obligation in the war on terror, waged since the fall of 2001, is education of the public: the American public first, but international public opinion as well. The outcome of the conflict will be decided by how well citizens understand the threat. The Islamic fundamentalists' jihadist strategies are not fully centered on classical state warfare. The resources of regimes have been merged with the capabilities of networks. The jihadists' presence is fluid and their actions are stealthy until the final stages of an operation. But ironically, jihadists emerge, grow, and develop almost entirely in the open. If we look at their public manifestations and thinking, whether in chat room conversations or media like al Jazeera, we can begin to understand their objectives. And if we learn about their past and deeper history, we can understand their current and future strategies.

Many among us wonder about the global strategy of the jihadists. In this book, I not only show the existence of a global jihadist strategy, but I also uncover its several different components. Not only are the terror plans frightening; they are already underway on a global level. I show that terrorist and jihadist strategies against the United States and the West started earlier than most of us generally think, that terrorists have been more successful in infiltrating than we expect, and that they are readying themselves for far larger strikes than they have mounted in the past.

My aim is to participate in the global effort to educate the West about past mistakes in judgment that led to the terrorist advances. But more important, I hope to convey an urgent message to the reader: From what we now know regarding what really happened, and from what we know could have happened, comes a terrifying picture of what *could* happen around the world if the appropriate policies and measures are not taken.

Chapter One

THE HISTORICAL ROOTS OF JIHAD

WHEN THE PRESIDENT OF THE UNITED STATES delivers speeches about "them," he calls them "terrorists." When they address the world, they call themselves "the men of jihad." Are the terrorists waging a war whose name we do not want to accept, or is the international community waging a war against terrorism while ignoring its goals and its ideology? This is more than a question of semantics. When asked about "jihad," many diplomats and scholars used to dismiss it as irrelevant in world politics. Today, however, we have to ask whether in doing so we are just ignoring a name or whether we are also turning a blind eye to the enemy's aims, deepest beliefs, and the wellspring of its will. If we do this, are we actually mobilizing against the instruments of terror rather than against the roots of its creation?

To understand who the jihadists really are and what they ultimately want, we need to examine the complex history involved in the term, the ideology behind it, its evolution, and its effect on individuals. We need to understand the historical alliances of jihadists as well as their ideological enemies. Without understanding this past, we can never fully understand our enemy and what the future might hold.

We first need to absorb then later we need to get familiar with the origins of jihad as a word and as an ideology in order to develop an understanding of who the ideological and political users of this concept are today. Osama bin Laden, Ayman Thawahiri, al Zarqawi of al Qaeda, and Hassan Nasrallah of Hezbollah all invoke jihad; we cannot afford to ignore or dismiss the concept and its history.

Among the many important questions that have to be answered are: Why is there a debate about the concept of jihad? Does it have a single meaning or

multiple ones? When did it arise, and why? Who has used it and for what pur-
poses? What is the relationship between jihad and the "infidels"? What is the
connection between jihad and peace?

WHY IS THERE A DEBATE?

The first time I read about jihad was in middle school, in my native Beirut,
Lebanon. I attended classes in more than one school in different parts of that small
multiethnic country. At the time, there was no major media debate about jihad, as
everyone had just one understanding of what it was. It was part of history, part of
the dominant culture, and so it was never questioned. Decades later, after I relocated to the United States in 1990, I had my second encounter with the word. But
this time it was in the center of a public debate and the object of much intellectual
and academic wrestling. In the sophisticated elite establishment of America, the
term "jihad" brought unease, even before September 11, 2001. But the concern
was not about what jihad might mean for the future. High-profile professors, respected journalists, and political activists were trying to diffuse the tension sur-
rounding the word and deflect its historical sense. In most literature, scholarly
articles, public lectures, and lobbying and social efforts related to Middle East politics, as well as religious studies and interfaith activities, there was a constant attempt to portray jihad as a spiritual phenomenon that could be and was abused by
extremist ideologies and radical political factions who were making it into something it really was not.[1] In the early 1990s, I was stunned to read and hear the western establishment making these tremendous efforts to convince audiences and
readers of the benign character of jihad; in the Middle East, for the most part, the
term retained its age-old, unreconstructed meanings. Jihad is not benign, and the
West's denial of that fact was terribly ironic. By instinct and as a result of my personal and professional background, I realized the enormity of what was happening: The United States was paving the way for its own defeat, by blurring its vision,
confusing its mind, and moderating its reactions to the early danger signs, not to
mention the terrorist strikes to come. It was clear that the nation turned a blind eye
to the historical definition of jihad, the one that would really come to matter.[2]

ONE MEANING: OR TWO?

In my classrooms, in the books I read, on the radio, and on the black-and-white
television programs of my childhood and school years, jihad was simple and
clear. It was a word that had meant one thing for the last thirteen centuries. It
was part of the history of many peoples and of a gigantic region, and was un-

derstood by all parties—those whom it was applied against and those who applied it—as *a call for action*. The concept of jihad was so widespread and so
deeply rooted in the culture of the region that many—even non-Muslims—used
it as a name for their children. A cousin of mine and other children in my own
village shared the name jihad. It was used as commonly as the word "crusade"
in the West. In all Arabic stories, legends, and even in cartoons, jihad was omnipresent. No one was trying to hide it, camouflage it, or moderate its meaning.
From Morocco to Afghanistan, the word meant only one thing.[3]

In the United States, however, political and intellectual forces were mobilizing to insert a new meaning into the concept and inject that new and reshaped concept into mainstream American thinking. The question is: Why?
Why would lobbies want to blur the meaning of jihad in the West, while those
who called for jihad east of the Mediterranean had no intention of redefining it?
This question can be answered only after we have investigated the various
strategies developed by the jihadists and the efforts made by their apologists inside the United States and the West in general.

To understand the ideology of the jihadists, or those who call themselves
jihadiyun or *mujahidin* (and thereby extrapolate their policies, strategies, and
future actions), one must first understand the full definition of the word. This
is not as easy as you might think, for several reasons.[4]

First, the word itself: Arab linguistics are very complex; furthermore, the
field is dominated by schools that are malleable to political pressures. It seems
prudent to say that, in addition to mastering the Arabic language, I have also
been trained in comparative cultural analysis, the next step after linguistic translation. While you do not need this level of education to understand and interpret
the term "jihad," it is the level of knowledge you need to be able to identify the
influences and permutations that can exist in Arabic over one single word. My
unique perspective provides me with the advantage of a strategic cultural analysis, but at the same time makes it more difficult to relate findings to either western or arab society. That is to say, it is very difficult for a genuinely bilingual
person to explain an alien culture and its cultural history to a monolingual society, and vice versa. Linguistic translation is one thing, cultural explanation is
something else. Among Arab speakers, for example, the concept of jihad comes
naturally. In western or non-Arab, non-Muslim societies, serious academic effort
is required to explain the term. And herein lies the challenge. The "translator"
may neither be able nor willing to convey the fundamental meaning.

We in the West have been at the mercy of those who where supposed to
translate and explain an entire ideology but instead sanitized it and camouflaged it. The same applies on the other side. In western culture, democracy is

being taught in the classroom, but it is a historically understood concept. The intellectual translation into Arab Muslim culture depends on the "translating party." In those cultures, its real meaning has been complicated and altered in the *madrassas* (Islamic religious schools) or when taught by antidemocracy teachers.

A second difficulty is the fact that jihad as a concept has actually mutated to some degree over time. In the early seventh century A.D./C.E., jihad meant a unified set of values in full adherence to what was then the ambient political vocabulary of the time. Jihad was a dual religious and political theme at its very first inception. Centuries later, as the stages of Arab Islamic statehood and doctrines developed, the jihad concept would be reinforced by what was achieved by the Islamic state and the related worldview. In other words, it was strengthened, not weakened. But with the modern age, the rise of international secular ideas, the development of international law, and the surge of different strategic interests among the Islamic ideologies, jihad developed different meanings in different intellectual settings as a way to satisfy various interests. Hence, what was universally accepted in the seventh century or commonly understood in the seventeenth century has become more complex at the beginning of the twenty-first century. Therefore, one has to use the term "jihad" carefully, while remaining faithful to the popular and historical perception of it.

THE LINGUISTICS OF JIHAD

A short lesson in the linguistic history of the term is necessary to further understand its complexity. "Jihad" comes from the root word *Jihd*, but is not synonymous with it. *Jihd* means "effort." From that root many other branches were developed in ancient Arabic, depending on the action, context, and the historical meanings that developed as a result of linguistic mutations.

In Arabic syntax, the word "jihad" (Jehaad) means *haalat al Jihd*, or "a state of *jihd*." In analytical linguistics, "jihad" transliterates into "a state of permanent efforts." The word was constructed to launch a particular vision. It came from a specific situation, at a specific time, and espoused the need of that time but has continued to develop since. In essence, it was created to change with the relevant historic situation.

Many in the scholarly community in the West admit that the word "jihad" had an initial meaning, but not all interpretations are alike. Some believe the word first had only one sense, while others affirm that it always had two senses. In Arab Muslim culture, the consensus on the meaning of jihad is much larger. It definitely draws from historical accounts and religious citations. But yet again, even in the culture of origin, ideologies and schools produce their own versions. Some stress its intangible meaning; others widen its sense into alternatives and shades. But the comprehensive and widely understood content of "jihad" is universal. It was born during the early stages of the Islamic expansion and developed for centuries as a state and religious concept, before being redefined by an ideological movement at the onset of the twentieth century.

HISTORICAL BIRTH

Because of its implications for international politics, the question of war and peace, and most recently its connection with terrorist movements, which have adopted it fully in their lexicon, the concept of jihad has dramatic importance in today's world. Regardless of its ancient use, jihad as practiced by terror networks such as al Qaeda and Hezbollah and regimes such as the Taliban or Iran's mullahs is in conflict with all types of secular and human rights–based laws. But since its users—the radical organizations—and modern doctrines refer to jihad in the most historicist dimension, we are forced to investigate it historically. In other words, even if great powers used the term "jihad" in the past as a tool of war and peace, it nevertheless deserves a historical understanding since the jihadists of modern times fully adhere to its past roots (or so they claim).

Jihad as a concept was initially advanced by the early Muslim leaders at the onset of the establishment of the Islamic state, *al dawla al Islamiya.* The first recorded use of the concept of jihad as a political word goes back to the early military efforts made by the followers of Prophet Mohammed during their struggle with the Meccan establishment (seventh century A.D./C.E.). According to Islamic history, this occurred after the migration of the faithful from Mecca to Medina in what Muslims believe was the beginning of the *Hijra* era, or emigration. In fact, the Islamic era starts then, and the foundation of the political entity of Islam can be traced to the Medina era.[5]

The debate about the identity of Islam as a religion and a state has had many streams. Historically, the early Muslims formed a state around their religion. *"Al islam deen wa dawla,"* said the founding fathers: "Islam is a religion and a state." Hence at the time of the inception, theology and politics were molded in one. While I intend to bypass the theological discussion on Islam, it must be noted that, according to historical accounts of both secular and Muslim historians, the Islamic movement was political as much as it was religious. In comparative religion, one could compare it to the biblical march of the ancient Hebrews or the movement of Christian empires. The divine was part of the sociopolitical. The early movement of Muslims, first under their Prophet and later after his passing, advanced both religion and political dynamics. In addition to the five tenets of faith, the organization of the community was centered on structures, movements, decision-making systems, and political agendas.

The five pillars of the faith are (1) witness *(Shahada);* (2) prayer *(salat);* (3) pilgrimage *(hajj);* (4) alms *(Zakat);* and (5) fasting *(sawm).*[6] All of these articles of faith are entirely spiritual and in some ways comparable to elements from the previous monotheist religions, Judaism and Christianity. Muslim theologians believe that Islam is the last expression of Abrahamic revelations that started with Adam and Eve and ended with Mohammed. But many secular historians and sociologists argue that early Islam was influenced by Jewish and Christian teachings. This debate will remain in the realm of comparative religions as it deals with metaphysical beliefs and messianic revelations. The question of Mohammed's prophetic character is comparable to the question of Jesus' divine nature and of the Hebrews' covenant with God. It was, is, and will remain a question of faith, above and beyond international relations. The question of jihad, however, is qualitatively different.

Jihad was declared by the early Muslim leaders as *a sixth unofficial pillar of Islam.* It was conceived as an "instrument of Islam," a sufficient but not a necessary condition for the spread and defense of the religion. In its pure logic, jihad was needed if things were not going smoothly. To simplify, for one to be a Muslim, he or she had to perform the five duties mentioned above. But if the conditions requiring jihad were not present, one could still be a Muslim. What were the necessary conditions for jihad?

From historical accounts, including (but not only) religious texts and references, jihad was a state of mobilization in the interest of the Muslim *umma* (nation) as it developed its military and strategic dimensions. When Muslims fled Meccan oppression at the hands of Mecca's pagan political establishment, they defined themselves as an *"umma."* As they settled in Medina, north of Mecca, the followers of Mohammed organized themselves into a political and military institution. They decided to overrun Mecca's ruling institution and replace it with a *dawla,* a state. It was to become the *dawlat al Islam:* the state of Islam, soon to become the Islamic state. That theologically grounded choice to establish a government for the new religion was the basis on which the ruler— first the Prophet himself, then his successors—granted themselves the right of sovereignty to manage the affairs of the state for the nation. The protection of, expansion of, and management of the *dawlat al umma* (the state of the Muslim nation) led logically to the buildup of instruments of governance for war and peace. Jihad, as per all theological and historical references, is a state of *juhd:* a state of effort at the service of the *umma,* the state, and Allah. It is a call to mobilize the resources, energies, and capabilities of individuals in the service of the higher cause. Jihad is the sum of all *jihds,* or efforts. It is triggered by an order given by the legitimate authority. It has a theological force that cannot be canceled except by a legitimate authority.[7]

Nida' al jihad, or the call for jihad, is the highest injunction to gather the forces of the community in the service of the Islamic *umma.* Originally there was no jihad for one's personal interests. Jihad outside the global effort prescribed by the *umma* does not exist. Personal efforts to enhance jihad are part of communal jihad. Many analysts and scholars in modern times presented jihad as either personal-spiritual or as collective-political. Muslim scholars' distinction between *al jihad al akbar* (greater internal and spiritual strife) and *jihad fi sabeel al umma* (at the service of the community) force modern scholars to draw political conclusions. In fact, Muslim scholars conceive all levels of jihad to be at the service of the global jihadic effort for the advancement of the community.

Personal jihad is at the service and in preparation for the wider, ultimate jihad. Many western writers and apologists for modern jihad have tried to portray personal jihad as a "spiritual experience on the inside," almost like yoga. Such efforts can only blur the public's vision and its grasp of the real dangers emanating from the modern use of jihad.

Since jihad was an obligation *(wajib)* to act, the next questions are why and what for? Why did the early Muslim leaders invent, develop, and use jihad as an instrument of struggle? Historians have done significant work in this regard; what is commonly accepted as a tradition in the Arab and Muslim world is that collective jihad was launched under two conditions: The first condition was when the *umma* was in physical danger of being attacked. There was a pre-Islamic precedent for this. In seventh-century Arabia, the main mobilizing power was the tribal one. Before Islam, in what Muslims call the era of *Jahiliya* (pre-Islamic era of ignorance), most Arabs, including urban and nomadic ones, were organized into tribes. The head of the tribes called for military mobilization for "tribal" causes.[8] But after Islam was established, the new "community" bypassed the individual tribes and had to legitimize the call for mobilization under supreme religious values. Hence jihad was to become the legitimate call for mobilization and action and ultimately war. But the second condition for jihad was not defensive but offensive: to promote, propagate, and conquer *for* Islam. The *umma* was not static in its geography. The essence of its initial marching order was to expand universally. By comparison, the divine marching order received by the Jews was to head toward the Promised Land. The equivalent in early Arabian Islam was to expand outward to the world.

Hence jihad cannot be oversimplified as either defensive or offensive only. From the outside, it may look as if it were a mechanism at the disposal of the rulers of the *umma* if attacked, or when they decide to march forward.[9] From the inside of the concept, it is an all-out doctrine that legitimizes an action on behalf of the ruler. The legitimate leaders, civilian or religious, have the duty of performing jihad when possible and at their discretion. Hence, even though jihad may overlap with other principles of law, such as legitimate defense or struggle for national liberation or resistance, it has a different doctrinal source and must be articulated under the Islamic set of laws known as *Sharia,* not other laws. This debate, begun in the seventh century, was renewed in the twentieth century and is today, fourteen centuries later, at the heart of the fundamentalist ideology. Like any weapon, it could be used to defend oneself or to attack, but why did the early leaders of the community "need" jihad per se?

The first assembled Muslim community was in a state of war within Arabia against the dominant establishment in Mecca and eventually against non-Muslim tribes as well. The founder, Prophet Mohammed, was among other things a military commander.[10] After the retreat from Mecca, the army of followers had to rebuild their strength in Medina and move forward. The decision was to wage war against Mecca until it surrendered. This point in history marks the first comprehensive jihad. Had early Muslims not decided to form an army to conquer the de facto capital of the peninsula, and had they decided to reduce their call to individual preaching only, jihad may never have been put in place. But the "need" for a military doctrine to mobilize the community above the tribal level produced a duty for all adherents to offer their resources, even up to the ultimate sacrifice of their lives. With jihad instituted as a duty, it became practically a sixth tenet of the religion. If the five articles of faith were acts of personal commitment to particular beliefs, jihad became the engine to shield as well as expand the community of believers. In other words, the people of faith were granted a tool to preserve and advance the faith, beyond personal commitment to their religious beliefs. In simple words, because jihad was developed as a religious duty fourteen centuries ago, modern-day radicals refer to it as such. And since Islamic religious authority has never refuted holy war, and no such reformation has yet taken place, it is difficult to prevent the use of religion to legitimize today's "jihadist" warfare. Organizations such as the Sunni al Qaeda and the Shiite Hezbollah skillfully take advantage of that fact.

The Mecca-Muslim war was the first geopolitical jihad. After that, all battles became holy; all encounters with the enemy were inscribed as part of religious duty. Somewhat parallel to the biblical wars that were considered to be sanctioned by God, the early wars in Arabia were perceived as religiously in-

spired. These wars enabled the Muslim armies to defeat Mecca's rulers and declare Islam as the only religion in Mecca. From there on, the successes were
lightning-quick; historical accounts show a rapid progress in all directions
within the peninsula. Many tribes came to join the movement; others fought it
and lost; and some were ejected from Arabia. The war for Arabia was the very
first victory for Islam and was owed to jihad. By the time of the Prophet's death,
most of Arabia had been unified under the banner of Islam. The next stage for
jihad was after the passing of the *Rasul* (i.e., the Messenger of Allah). His companions and commanders had the choice between confining themselves to Arabia or resuming the jihad outside the realm of Islam's birthplace. They chose
the latter.

THE FATAH: CONQUEST

The conquest of the outside world was a choice of historical dimension. After
the death of Mohammed, his companions met in a council, a *mejliss*. This
council became the first institution after the passing of the founder. The leadership made important decisions. The first, which would affect all of Muslim
history, was to agree on the principle of succession to the *nabiy* ("Prophet" in
Arabic). Succession is *khilafa*. Successor is *khalifa*, from which the westernized equivalent is caliph. The institutional successor would inherit the divine
inspiration from the Messenger of Allah and at the same time his power to
guide the *umma*. That passage from the Prophet to the caliphate made Islamic
history possible. Had the companions not decided to establish a caliphate, no
one would have guaranteed that the Muslims would be successful in marching
onward. The next step would affect the history of the world.[11]

After they decided to create an institution that would succeed the Messenger and take into its hands the affairs of the Islamic state, the *mejliss* made another decision that was to impact the entire destiny of the caliphate, the Arabs,
and the evolution of Muslim politics for the following thirteen centuries. It was
about the actual frontiers of the Islamic state. Where should they be drawn,
around Mecca and Medina, or should they be limitless? Again, leaving apart a
discussion of the initial five articles of faith, the historical geopolitical fact of
what happened in the seventh century and after was that the decision to expand
was taken—meaning the territorial expansion of the Islamic state. While religious conversion and evangelism may be matters of theology, state expansion is
primarily military. It is interesting to note the differences between Arab and
Muslim history textbooks compared to modern western and American academic texts with regard to these crucial developments. In most cases, the latter

skillfully dodge the question of military conquest and talk about "propagation" of Islam between the seventh and the ninth centuries. Traditional Arab and Muslim books, however, faithfully relate the facts: The Muslim "army" undertook a comprehensive, openly acknowledged series of military campaigns from Arabia to Spain in the West and to India in the East. Later on, the expansion of the religion of Islam went beyond the sovereignty of the caliphate: Both in Africa and in Asia, different types of conversions took place. But as the big sorties from Arabia began, the caliphate devised a doctrine of conquest so that religion and the *umma* would both expand, rationalizing that expansion with the concept of establishment of religion, or *Iqamat al deen*. Here again, future militants would base their action on past realities. It is striking to see, a millennium later, jihadi groups such as al Muhajirun in Great Britain calling for a resumption of the conquests and referring to precisely this early stage in Muslim history.[12]

The logic was impeccable: Since the caliphate is the supreme institution of the Islamic state, and since the state is responsible for the future of the *umma*, and since the *umma* has a mission to expand so that the religion will be established around the world *(Iqamatu eddine)*, the mechanics must come together. The principle was to expand religion, and the means was the Islamic state. And therefore the state (the caliphate in this framework) had to devise the techniques, the reasons, the arguments, and the doctrine for the expansion. Unlike the Huns or the Vikings, who marched at will with no self-explanation for conquest, the Arab conquerors were intellectually sophisticated. They wanted to achieve state expansion goals under a sound religious doctrine, and so they constructed one.

DAR EL HARB

At first, the scholars of the caliphate depicted the world to their followers as divided in two. In this worldview, on one side was the area where the Islamic state reigned and the *Sharia* of Allah was sovereign. It was called *dar el Islam.* Literally it translates to "house (or abode) of Islam." This "zone" overlapped with but did not correspond completely with the areas of Muslim settlement; it matched the borders of Islamic state control. In the area of Islamic *dawla,* Islam had legal authority. It was also called *dar el salam,* meaning "house of peace." The idea was that wherever the Islamic state is found, peace will be prevalent and guaranteed. On the other side of the equation, there was *dar el Harb,* which translates simply as "house of War," or, technically, War Zone. It did not mean specifically that war was the dominant social-political reality in those areas. It meant that outside the *dar el Islam,* there is no real peace. Many historians argue that *dar el Harb* was an area at the discretion of *dar el Islam:* The caliph would decide, depending on his judgment and on circumstances, if the Islamic state should advance into *dar el Harb* and how. Modern-day jihad warriors picked up this division from ancient times. Drawing legitimacy from these old unreformed concepts, radical groups in Sudan, Indonesia, Lebanon, Chechnya, and other areas claim they are reestablishing the *dar el Islam* and waging campaigns against the other side, with full conviction that they are resuming an unachieved mission.

Hence the caliphate created a unilateral dynamic of moving forward. There is to be no reversal of the geography of the Islamic state. On the contrary, there is only one way open: onward and upward. This doctrine was called *al fatah,* translated literally as "the opening." In simple geopolitical terms, *fatah* was the conquest of non-Muslim lands. It was the legitimization of the expansion of the state. It was not called occupation. It was perceived as a divinely authorized march into the land outside the state. "Invasion" has a name in Arabic: *ejteyah.* "Occupation" has another: *ehtelal.* Both have negative connotations, which would invite legitimate reprisal from the conquered peoples. Hence, the inventors of the word *"fatah"* were proposing a new term that means, practically, both invasion and occupation, but without saying it. It was often connected to a higher aim—such as at the service of Allah, religion, or the *umma*—a connection that both rendered the concept legitimate and provided an emotional component to its adherents. To perform *fatah* in the seventh century was perfectly legitimate in the eyes of the followers of the caliphs, as if the lands of *dar el harb* were awaiting the "liberators." Fatah was *mubah*—permissible if conducted by the proper authorities, which in those days meant the supreme commander of the believers, the caliph.

Conquest was not a unique characteristic of the Islamic expansion or of Arab invasions. At different times many nations simply conquered others and settled their own populations on foreign lands. That is the core of world history. But the uniqueness of studying the *fatah* today is that many historians, not only in the Arab world but also in the West, continue to deny that those armies marching out of the Arabian peninsula were simply conquerors. It would be the equivalent of stating that the Roman Empire spread by convincing the Mediterranean peoples of the justness of Rome, or that Spain talked the South American Indians into accepting its colonial rule, or that Britain used lawyers, not battleships, to build its empire. All of these empires, too, furnished themselves with ideas—from the Pax Romana to the "white man's burden"—that morally justified their conquests in the eyes of their followers.

The move to invade the outside world was the single most important geopolitical development (triggered by Arab Muslims) in world history, along with the European settlement of the Americas. After the death of Mohammed, the council selected Abu Bakr al Siddiq (632–634 A.D./C.E.) as his successor. He resumed the campaigns of integration of all Arab tribes. These early companions of the Messenger of Allah were known as the wise caliphs, or *al Rashidun*. Today all Muslims consider them to be Islam's founding fathers. Some later saw them as the precedent to follow, or the *salaf*. They attended to the newly formed "nation" and proceeded with the unification of the Arabian tribes across the peninsula, a task never before achieved in the history of the Arabs. At his death he was replaced by Caliph Umar (634–644), then by Caliph Uthman Ibn Affan (644–656). Caliph Ali ruled from 656 to 661 A.D./C.E. The Muslim forces were disciplined by religion, which motivated them by transcending the limits of tribes. The other Arabian tribes were divided and of different religious affiliations. Most of them worshipped a variety of deities, but some tribes were Eastern Christians, mostly in northern Arabia, while others were Jewish, particularly in Yemen and around Yathrib and Medina. The unification of Arabia was mostly by way of direct military subjugation, but in many cases occurred by tribes rallying the Muslims. The conversions into the new religion were fast, and often tribes attempted to reject Islam and return to their deities. But the Islamic state would not allow what it called *ridda,* or return to a previous religious belief. In such cases, there was a clear injunction for physical elimination. After the death of Mohammed, there took place the *hurub al ridda,* or wars of reinstating Islam among tribes that decided to quit it. These military campaigns were very bloody. The *dawla,* or state of Islam, was at stake: A domino effect might erode the demography of the new *umma.* In later times, and especially in the twentieth century, the ideology of jihadism would refer to these wars as a reason to attack any Muslim who would divert from religion or change faith. Cases of jihadist execution of former Muslims or of converts to other religions are widespread at the hands of the modern-day radicals. The terror unleashed by the contemporary jihadi reached missionaries in Lebanon, Africa, and Iran and civilians engaged in outreach to Muslims. Here again, the use of ancient history has had dramatic consequences.[13]

Some would argue that the *ridda* wars were the reason for the conquests. According to this theory, the *fatah* march into the *dar el harb* was intended to unite the converted tribes and offer them a way to expand outside Arabia. Instead of internal wars among Arabs threatening the new Islamic state, outside wars to open new lands and opportunities were the logical path to ensure unity.[14] But historians who draw from analysis based on political economy believe that the *fatah*—although inspired by the powerful doctrine of jihad—was essentially a solution to the socioeconomic needs of Arabian tribes. This analysis merits some consideration. Insulated and isolated for centuries, the inhabitants of these vast deserts were structured around nomadic traditions and centered on Mecca's supremacy. When the Islamic state was established as a sort of transcendent power across their known world, the promise of a higher power had to be translated into enlarged boundaries. In short, because the Bedouin norms were disrupted and the hopes for a better life were raised very high, the caliphate of the *Rashidun* sought expansion. The theories are abundant, and not all explored. This is one problem with Middle East studies. But whatever the speculations of research, according to all accounts the march of the *fatah* was nevertheless a hurricane.

After the death of Uthman Ibn Affan, two candidates for the caliphate were considered: Ali, the younger cousin and son-in-law of the Prophet, and a bright and handsome *qaid*, or commander of the armies; and Umar, older companion of the Messenger of Allah. An arrangement was made to select Umar and to have Ali take over later. This would be the first seed of a historic internal dissention among Muslims. But under Caliph Umar, the world of antiquity changed. For the first time in known history, a unified Arab army marched out of the peninsula under the banner of Islam. One of its greatest generals, Khalid Ibn al Walid, moved north toward the Syrian plateau and met the then sophisticated and large Byzantine army. The *fatah* took place in an unprecedented context. Barefoot nomads, with no advanced weapons and no experience in classical warfare, were taking on the two largest empires of the time: the Byzantine Roman Christian Empire to their west and the Persian Zoroastrian Empire to their east. Comparatively speaking, it was like a force coming out of the Arabian desert during the Cold War to attack the Soviet Union and the United States simultaneously. Outnumbered Arab Muslims, with little experience and almost no technology, marched head-on to meet two imperial armies with numerical superiority, better technology, and backed by dozens of wealthy cities. How did the Arab jihad win such a war?

Historians argue and counterargue but I find four reasons to be sound.

1. In the mid-seventh century A.D./C.E., the two "superpowers" had already been at war for a few centuries, which had weakened their economy, military forces, and determination to fight.
2. The Arabs were motivated, mobilized by the doctrine of jihad, and had nothing significant to lose in Arabia. The green prairies, water, and cities of light lay ahead of them.

3. The dense content of the jihad promises, including visions of the hereafter—which I will review later—eliminated or diminished the fear of death.
4. The fact that the Byzantines and Persians had scant knowledge about the new invader worked in the latter's favor. The imperial elites had not prepared the peoples and the rulers for the advent of the *fatah* armies.

These reasons, in addition to other geopolitical ingredients of the times, made it possible for a small but determined fish to devour a pair of large but ailing whales. We will see later that other reasons allowed the Arabs to maintain their conquests after they obtained them.

The single most important date in Arab-Islamic military history, a date that has changed the face of the planet, is August 5, 636 A.D./C.E. This is the day the armies of the *fatah* won the crucial battle of Yarmuk against the Byzantine army. A plateau situated next to a small river by the same name, Yarmuk is technically on the southern hills of the Golan Heights, between Jordan and Syria. Khalid Ibn al Walid moved his forces swiftly to face off with Heracles' Roman legions, in a battle scene similar to those in *The Lord of the Rings*. The accounts of this vast battle are impressive by military history standards, but its consequences are too important not to analyze. The battle of Yarmuk is in every Arab textbook, including the ones I have used in my classrooms. It is central to the collective reading of history, at least in the Arab world. Yet unlike the battles of Troy, Carthage, Waterloo, and Normandy, it is not mentioned in western textbooks.[15]

By the end of the day, and after a sandstorm (which has been laden with religious interpretations), the men on camels and light horses had destroyed the Byzantine army with all of its heavy armor. From that day on, no power was able to stop the forces of the *fatah* and the jihad energy that had exploded. Allah was on the side of the soldiers of the caliphate and rewarded their commitment against superior forces with a victory of biblical dimensions. Within one year, Palestine and the city of Jerusalem fell to the conquerors. The year after, Damascus, Syria, and lands all the way to Asia Minor were in the hands of the marching jihad forces. To the east, the equally crucial battle of Qadissiya (or Nehavend) resulted in the defeat of the large Persian army and their retreat from Mesopotamia, which fell to the commanders of the *fatah*. The victories were so stunning, the captured lands and cities so vast and populated, that the march resumed immediately. Unlike previous conquests by the Egyptians, Assyrians, Greeks, Romans, and Persians, the Arab-Islamic invasions were fast, decisive, and unstoppable.

If you read the jihadists' contemporary literature or listen to their online chats, you will understand how they portray their future victories as reflective of Yarmuk and the subsequent advances of the Islamic army.

FATAH'S OPEN FIELDS

Under the guidance of Caliph Umar and the command of Khalid and the other leaders of the conquest, the invasion expanded west and east simultaneously. The speed of the *fatah* exceeded that of any known invasion in ancient history, except for that of the Huns. The marches, battles, and thrusts into empires, kingdoms, and principalities deserve entire treatises. The conquerors swept into new cultures. One after another, fortresses, towns, and villages came under the control of the caliphate. Garrisons were established, local commanders were appointed, and more tribes were brought from the peninsula to populate strategic locations. Meanwhile, the vanguard was crossing into new lands and clashing with new monarchs. The *fatah* of the seventh century onward can be compared with the astounding march of Alexander the Great, with one difference: The Macedonian Empire was lost after the emperor's own death. In contrast, the caliphate survived individual caliphs for centuries. That was the endless source of power to the new *dar el Islam.* From federated tribes inside an isolated desert to a world empire, the jihad devised to defend and expand the *umma* became a *fatah* with incalculable effects.

These tableaux from ancient times are very much alive in the minds of modern-day jihadists. When indoctrinating recruits, the radical Islamists link today's battles to seventh-century successes. The roots of al Qaeda's and Hezbollah's vision of victory—despite technological realities—go back not only to ideology but also to real historical events, such as the early conquests.

After their domination of the Fertile Crescent from Mesopotamia to Jerusalem, the jihad armies crossed the Sinai Peninsula into Egypt. Under the command of Amr Ibn el A'as, the *fatah* soldiers defeated the Byzantines and established a province along the Nile River. At the same time, Arab Islamic forces invaded Persia through what is now Afghanistan. In North Africa, the invasion reached Cyrenaica, today's Libya, followed by Numedia and Mauritania, today's Algeria and Morocco. After subduing the native Berbers, the Arabs pushed forward toward Christian Europe through the maritime passage into Iberia in 715 A.D./C.E.

"THE SEA IS BEHIND YOU"

There then occurred another benchmark moment in the history of the caliphate. The commander of the conquest, Tariq Bin Ziad, originally a Berber, stood up in front of his troops and said: "*al Bahru min waraikum, wal adu min amamikum.*" One of the most remembered calls to jihad in Arab memory, it translates to: "The sea is behind you and the enemy is ahead of you." Tariq, from which name came Jabal Tariq, the Tariq Mountain (Gibraltar), epitomized the ultimate *fatah* and jihad: Landing on foreign lands, thrusting into the *dar el harb* (house of war) and attacking head-on, under a classic mismatch of forces. The night before, Tariq ordered his own fleet, which had carried the expeditionary force from the Maghreb, to be burned. He was producing the ultimate jihad: nothing to lose, always move forward. You commit to sacrifice, and Allah will provide victory. Tariq's speech, which has been taught in schools for centuries, is very revealing in the study of jihad. It was the ultimate, purest expression of the conquest doctrine. Jihad into Spain meant crossing waters into a third continent, thousands of miles away from Mecca and Medina. The successes in the North African campaigns by earlier caliphs emboldened the marchers into invading north, all the way to France. These images of victorious, unstoppable *mujahedin fi sabeel Allah* (jihad fighters for Allah) taking city after city, grabbing one kingdom after another, are part of the *fresque* of the *fatah* and are attributed to the power of jihad.

By the late eighth century, the Arab armies had reached south of Paris and the edge of the Leman Lake in Switzerland and had already conquered Sicily, while also raiding Constantinople and the Adriatic coasts. This first *fatah* may have overrun western and southern Europe had not Frankish commander Charles Martel broken the Arabs' advance in Poitiers. (Some call it the battle of Tours.) To the east, the caliphate occupied Persia and pushed its invasions into northeast Central Asia, close to China's borders. Arab armies encountered Indian principalities along the Hindus River. In a few decades, an empire was born, greater than all ancient empires combined, stretching over three continents. In *Lord of the Rings* imagery, this was jihad conquering Middle Earth. The huge transformation raised a gigantic question: Why were the Arabs invading these lands and dominating these peoples? The Islamic state's answer is instructive.[16]

THE OTHERS: INFIDELS OR *KUFFAR*

Is there a doctrinal foundation for the *fatah?* In simple terms, why would Arab Muslim armies head out of the peninsula and invade the upper Middle East? Why conquer Syria, Mesopotamia, and Palestine, or Egypt and Persia? According to all recorded history, no significant powers had occupied Arabia for centuries. The *fatah* was certainly not a response to an occupation or to an outside invasion. It is clearly a conquest by the Arabs of "others" and an occupation of their lands in an endless tide. How did the leaders of jihad—the men who were in charge of the Islamic state—explain it to their followers and legit-imize their order to attack foreign peoples and lands unilaterally?

At first glance, one would certainly lump together the Arab-Islamic inva-sions with innumerable other wars and conquests in the history of the world. Almost all nations, in all times, have launched such campaigns. But each case had its own logic in addition to its own needs and interests. In the case of the Arab *fatah,* two underlying analyses of the world and humanity mobilized the foot soldiers of jihad. One was theological, the other geopolitical. Both have been extracted and reinstated by modern-age jihadists.

THE THEOLOGICAL WEB

Drawing from theological texts including verses from the Qu'ran, references in the Hadith (sayings and practices of the Messenger of Allah), and speeches by the companions of the Prophet, scholars and political leaders of the Islamic state declared a distinction between Muslims and all others. They described the non-Muslims at large as *kuffar,* a term later translated in European lan-guages as "infidels." The Arabic word *kuffar* (plural *kafir)* comes from the root word *kufr,* which means "aggression against the right path." Theologically, it derives from the concept of *kafaru billah,* or those who did not accept Allah as God, or did not accept his message or the injunctions of his prophets as the true path—in short, *kuffar* were those who had not converted yet. In the case of jihad and *fatah* at their inception, the *kuffar* (also translated as "authors of blasphemy") are in a state of aggression against the divine and therefore against the *umma.* Hence, the *kuffar* are the theological enemies of the state.

But the distinctions were more complicated. First, all non-Muslims were qualified as *kuffar,* including Jews and Christians. But because of theological and historical reasons, Jews and Christians were placed in a special category as a subclass of infidels. They were given the rank of "People of the Book." They were basically offered a transitional ground; Jews and Christians were special *kuffar,* because of the Abrahamic link. The question then arises of how "Peo-ple of the Book" *(Ahl al Kitab)*—who are accepted in the holy scriptures of Islam—can be infidels at the same time. What is the relationship between "Peo-ple of the Book" and the infidels? Aren't they the same people? Yes and no.[17]

The drive of the *umma* was to entice the "People of the Book" ultimately to convert. Quotes from the Qu'ran stated that non-Muslims should not be forced into religion: *"La Ikrah fil deen."* But the superceding goal of the *umma* remained *Iqamatu eddine,* or the establishment of the religion world-wide. Aside from the special theological question of Jews and Christians, all non-Muslims were infidels. This attitude toward the *kuffar,* drawn from many religious sources, became institutionalized within the evolving caliphate. One can see the differences between treating the infidels individually if they fall under the Islamic state and the general policy of converting them and, when possible, subjugating their areas. The relationship with the infidels was complex on the theological level, but the trends were clear: They were given partial status as *Ahl al Kitab* but ultimately, because they were *kuffar,* they were to be converted. Most religions view outsiders with suspicion—consider the Jews and the Gentiles, the Christians and the pagans; the historical question was the actual way of dealing with the other in the very real realm of geopolitics.

Centuries later, future generations of militants would take over concepts from the seventh century and adapt them to their current political agenda.

THE GEOPOLITICS OF THE INFIDELS

As noted, the founders of the early Islamic state divided the world into two zones: *dar el harb* and *dar el Islam.* Infidels could be found in *dar el Islam* under the rule of the caliphate. Their fate was to be determined by the Sharia or at the discretion of the commander of the believers. Beginning with the rule of Caliph Umar, Christians and Jews who fell under the new regime were granted a special status. But infidels who remained in *dar el harb* were "sovereign" *kuffar,* and the relationship with them, according to the documents of the Islamic state, was dependent on the discretion of the Muslim rulers. In principle, they were an open target, when the balance of power allowed, or when the caliphate decided to resume the *fatah.* The fate of *dar el harb* was totally linked to the caliphate's capacity to wage jihad.

This explains how twentieth-century ideologues, such as Sayid Qutb in midcentury and Sheikh Yussef al Qardawi a few years before the attacks of September 11, 2001, would inform their followers that the decision to move into *dar el harb* is at the discretion of the ruler. Hence the right to take on the "other side" was not abrogated despite a thousand years; it was reaffirmed under right authority.

SULH: INTERIM PEACE

Intriguingly, the rulers of *dar el Islam* offered treaties and peace agreements to both past and future enemies. It was called *sulh,* which can be translated as "a momentary peace"; from it came the word *musalaha,* or act of reconciliation. The concept of peace had its own words and logic. *Salaam,* which means "permanent peace," was a state of plenitude reached via the rule of the Islamic state. *Salaam,* or true peace, was to happen within the caliphate or when it decided so. *Sulh,* or interim peace, was a diplomatic tool at the disposal of the supreme commander, to be employed until the political balance again became favorable to the state. Thus, the logic of jihad—a statist logic par excellence—was to wage *fatah* when possible, conclude *sulh* when needed, and go back to jihad when conditions were right again. Implacably, methodically, and relentlessly, the doctrine of jihad fueled the *fatah* for centuries. But the caliphate and its doctrinaires were extremely careful to legitimize their strategies. Unlike the Mongols, the Vikings, or the Goths, they built a platform of legitimization for their policies.

While the decision to wage jihad and to order more *fatah* was unilateral and based on geopolitical calculations, the public argumentation was always refined. Despite the fact that the Islamic state systematically lacked legitimacy during most of the jihad wars for a thousand years, its historians, clerics, and rulers feverishly invoked grounds for unilateral offensives. The most interesting reasons came at the onset of the conquests. The argument ran as follows: The caliph sends delegates to an infidel city calling on its monarch and inhabitants to convert. They are given the option to do so and maintain their power structure in the city. This is the peace option. If they refuse to join the caliphate, they are "breaching" the peace and are considered to be on the path of war. This is the jihad option. Ironically, some historians sliced off the first step and argued that the caliphate was a peacemaker because it constantly offered peace treaties. The so-called Middle East experts did not put the offer in its original perspective, that is, "You will have peace if you surrender to my rule." This very fundamental root of caliphate colonial policy was similar to but more subtle than the Pax Romana. The Romans directly asked for surrender, because they did not have a state religious agenda. They were interested in taxes and global domination. The caliphate wanted the same, but aimed ultimately to transform the conquered peoples and absorb them into the identity of the conqueror.

Armed with this powerful political philosophy, the Arab dynasties expanded their borders, arguing that their neighbors had not accepted their proposal of peace. Conquering them brought the dynasty into contact with new neighbors, who also failed to accept peace, and so on. That is how tribes from Yemen, the Hejaz, and Hadramut found themselves fighting wars in Ninive, Jerusalem, Byblos, Persepolis, Alexandria, and ultimately on the northern slopes of the Pyrenees. Certainly they were not migrating for jobs, nor were they part of a preaching brotherhood. To the contrary, the elites of the newly founded state claimed that they were called on to wage jihads in remote lands

for the satisfaction of Allah. For centuries, the jihad machine presented and con-
solidated the arguments for *fatah* as "defensive." Under this logic, launching a
military offensive across the Strait of Gibraltar into another continent was a
move to protect the Maghreb from the infidels—just as invading the Maghreb
had been to defend Egypt. Invading Egypt had been necessary to shield Syria,
and to start with, conquering the whole Fertile Crescent was to deter Byzantium
from marching into Arabia. When the soldiers of the caliphate were chasing after
Hindu villagers thousands of miles to the east of the peninsula and raiding cities
in the middle of France thousands of miles to the west, the arguments never wa-
vered. It was always because of an aggressor to be retaliated against. In fact, in
simpler terms, infidel land was an open field. In the final analysis, the *fatah* was
yet another colonialist enterprise, but much more sophisticated, successful, and,
above all, compelling for its followers than those of its historical sisters.

Later chapters will analyze how modern-day jihadists have borrowed from
ancient jihad while neglecting the transformations of international relations. Al
Qaeda, the NIF of Sudan, the Taliban, Hezbollah of Lebanon, and others often
position themselves as "defensive," even though their operations are strategically offensive.

DHIMMIS

The next question on the menu of jihad was the status and fate of conquered
populations. If tribes or cities would surrender willingly and convert, not only
would they be treated equally, but they would be part of the next *fatah* against
the neighboring country. However, if the infidel population fell under the new
regime as a result of a military encounter, it would have three options. Assuming that the population survived the horrors of postvictory massacres (a common characteristic of all ancient wars), it would have to choose:

1. To convert to Islam. In that case, the former *kuffar* would be upgraded to
   privileged first-level citizenship in the caliphate.
2. Not to convert to the new religion. In that case, a new status was established
   to manage the lives of those who chose to maintain the old religions. Their
   status would be downgraded to a second-class citizenship under the
   caliphate.
3. To refuse both statuses. In that case, the military solution would be applied,
   ranging from elimination to ethnic cleansing.

The logic of the *fatah* was to enlarge the borders of the Islamic state quan-
titatively and qualitatively. In contrast with the Romans or the later British colo-

nial enterprises, the caliphate expansion was connected to the religious and identity transformation of the conquered peoples. It was a strategic objective to ensure the Islamization of the invaded nations and, if possible, their Arabization. The entire survival of the *fatah* enterprise hung on the assimilation of the conquered masses. The statistics of the times were a powerful incentive. According to most historians, there were about 20 million people living between Persia and the Upper Nile at the time of the *fatah*. The sum of all forces and accompanying tribes that thrust out of the peninsula was around half a million. How would a much smaller number of conquerors absorb a universe of nations, cultures, structures, cities, and civilizations without being absorbed by it? The adventure of Alexander the Great was illustrative of invaders melting into the culture of the invaded. The caliphs opted for another strategy: Instead of being absorbed by the more advanced societies of the ancient Middle East, they would mutate them into the new rising civilization. The second great challenge of the *fatah* was to integrate the large body of the conquered nations into the smaller entity of the conquerors. The *dhimmi* process was the answer.

After the battle of Yarmuk, the Arabs were facing a new reality. They were invading areas with large populations and dominating highly sophisticated cities. A problem that had been simple to address with equally equipped nomadic tribes in the *Jazeera* (the Arabic name for the Arabian Peninsula) was a different matter when overseeing millions of technologically more advanced peoples. These masses had to be integrated into the Arab-Islamic culture and religion either directly, if they chose to adhere, or slowly and indirectly, if they chose to remain faithful to their original affiliation. Caliph Umar, under whom the early conquests of Syria, Palestine, and Mesopotamia occurred, created the *dhimmi* status, which later was called *al Shurut al Umariya,* or the "Umar conditions."

But when Christians and Jews chose to (or were forced to) become *ahl al Dhimma*—that is, to live under the *dhimmi* status—their world changed radically. Indeed, a minority of subdued peoples, especially in urban areas and cities, preferred to retain their religions even if they thereby became second-class citizens. Before the outside *fatah,* the Islamic state drove all Christian and Jewish tribes out of the peninsula. Many jihadists refer to an alleged statement made by Prophet Mohammed asking his generals, just before he died, to evacuate the infidels from the peninsula. According to them he said, "*Ukhruju al mushrekeen min Jazeerat al Arab*" ("Evacuate the apostates from the Arabian Peninsula"). Without dwelling on the veracity of the statement, it was largely accepted by the successors as a real one. Hence, after 636 no Christian and Jewish Arabs were left on the peninsula. All the Christian tribes of Arabia, including Taghlib and the Ghassanides, were converted to the new religion. The question of how Yemen's Jews survived will not be discussed here.

Understandably, a majority of the conquered peoples entered the process of Islamization and Arabization. They formed the bulk of the new citizenry of the caliphate. From them and their resources, future *fatah*(s) drew their strength. Ironically, most of the men marching in the conquest of Egypt were Arabized soldiers from the Fertile Crescent of Syria and Mesopotamia. Islamized populations of Egypt and Libya fought their ethnic cousins, North Africa's Berbers, under the flag of the caliphate. And as noted earlier, when the armies of jihad crossed to Gibraltar, their commander was an Arabized Berber. The second and third generations of "assimilated" peoples were more efficient than the original tribes of the peninsula in marching forward, in the knowledge of other cultures, and in their closeness to the local environment.

Some of the *dhimmi* stipulations were inspired by Umar's interpretation of the Qur'an and the Hadith; others were tailored to meet the realities of the *fatah*. The caliphates established a new legal status for non-Muslims under the Islamic state. If they accepted the sovereign rule of the caliphate, Christians and Jews (based on religious affiliation, not ethnic and national identities) would have a "protected" space inside *dar el Islam* and "under" the Islamic state. In recent years, this status has been strongly debated both in the Arab Muslim world and in the West. Many Muslim scholars—but not all—argue that the *dhimmi* status is evidence of tolerance by the caliphate. According to this explanation, the Islamic state at least erected a space for the preservation of Christians and Jews. Other scholars, particularly those from *dhimmi* or eastern backgrounds, responded that the "protection" was initially from the Islamic state itself. They argue that the *dhimmi* peoples were nothing but occupied nations put in legal "reservations" at the discretion of the rulers. They question the logic of "protection"; apologists for the caliphate present it as a "gift."[18]

According to the Umar conditions, the *ahl al Dhimma,* or *dhimmis,* would adhere to a pact with the Islamic state, a sort of contract. They would lose all rights of sovereignty (or self-determination), such as forming autonomous or independent states. They would be forbidden from high offices in government and from the armed forces, and would have to submit to a special way of life. Among the many signs of distinction: They were to walk on the left side of roads, wear special clothing, were banned from riding horses, had to live in special areas, and were not to raise their voices in the presence of Muslims. Last but not least, they were to pay an additional, different tax called *jizya* ("penalty"). Assembled in one code, the Umar conditions were designed to squeeze these communities into integration, starting with conversion. Through this mechanism, the *fatah* was able to move forward quickly, while the assimilation machine was absorbing large national and ethnic communities.

Notwithstanding the old historical character of the treatment of *dhimmis,* modern-day jihadi continue to apply the rules in Sudan, Egypt, Pakistan, Algeria, and Indonesia.[19]

RESISTANCE TO THE *DHIMMI* ORDER

Note, however, that the level of implementation or severity in the application differed from one area to another and from period to period. The history of the *dhimmi* is too long to universalize, but it had a common effect on the numbers of its adherents: They dwindled significantly to small minorities scattered across the empire. In some rare occasions and located in specific parts of the region, native resistance to the *fatah* led to confrontations: Copts in the Nile Delta, Maronites in Mount Lebanon, Berbers in the Atlas range, and later on Africans in Numedia. But these cases were too rare and marginal to reverse the process of the regional assimilation. Not all such efforts were fully successful, and not all opposition to the *fatah* onslaught was from non-Muslims. Some Islamized populations and ethnicities developed their own ways of resisting the dominant caliphate power. In Persia, for example, Islamization was accepted but not Arabization. Such was also the case with the North African Berbers, the Kurds, and some African tribes south of Egypt. Even within the larger Arab Muslim nation, internal dissentions would affect the results of *fatah* and, somewhat, the theological unity of jihad.

ISLAMIC CIVIL WAR

As Arab Muslim forces were advancing inside the *dar el harb,* a series of internal wars of succession created the largest divide under the caliphate. By the mid-seventh century A.D./C.E., the partisans of Imam Ali Bin Abi Talib, son-in-law and cousin of the Prophet, wanted him to be the next successor to the Messenger of Allah. Because of jealousies and precarious balances of power inside the caliphate, an alliance of senior leaders refused his candidacy, and after he was selected, they waged war against him. The main leader of the coalition was Muawiya, the Arab governor of Damascus. He and his followers claimed they would abide by the laws *(Sunna)* of Mohammed, not his bloodline. The partisans (in Arabic, *Shiia*) of Ali fought back and claimed that their leader was a caliph by his merits, not because of the House of the Prophet. The ensuing war left Ali and his two sons dead and Muawiya as the new Umayyad caliph, with a

Muslim capital in Damascus. Because of that first "civil war" within the caliphate, two competing views on the governance, theology, and politics of Islam arose: the Sunni majority and the Shiia minority. The divide within the *umma* would affect its future identity and unity, as Shiites formed large pockets in Iran, Azerbaijan, and eastern Arabia, within a wider Muslim Sunni world.[20] The Sunnis followed the institution of the caliphate and became wielders of world power through the various dynasties and empires. The Shiites seceded from the caliphate after Ali, developed their own theology, and formed their own bastions inside the Muslim world. Other smaller offshoots later appeared over the centuries and in various places: Druses, Alawites, Ismaelis, Zaidis, Abathiya, and others. To the orthodox Sunnis, the smaller factions are heretics. To the Shiites, the Sunni institution has usurped the legitimate rights of the people of the House (of Mohammed), or *ahl al bayt.* In general terms, the Sunni-held caliphate would suppress the Shiites and other groups for centuries, while the Muslim minorities would adopt doctrines of simulation, called *takiya,* to escape the wrath of the dominant power.[21]

But did the Muslim civil war stop the *fatah* from progressing in the seventh century? No; the armies of the conquest kept marching on all fronts even as the wars of succession were taking place in Arabia and southern Iraq—in fact, there would later be Shiia generals in the imperial armies of the caliphs. The divisions over theology and the succession and theology failed to create a split in the vision of *fatah* and jihad because the mission of jihad was too powerful to be rejected by the Muslim minorities. They continued to adhere to it, as long as it was not applied against them; similarly, in the case of *fatah,* it was accepted by the suppressed communities if directed against the *dar el harb* and the infidels, although they did not always forcefully back it. Jihad was the policy of the ruling caliphs and they were primarily the ones who practiced it. When powerful enough to do so, Shiite dynasties also practiced jihad.

THE FIRST COUP D'ETAT WITHIN ISLAM

In the first years under the wise rulers, *al Rashidun,* the caliphate was an "untouchable" institution. But the "civil war" among Sunnis and Shiites shook its unified foundations. Since then, there were Muslims—followers of Ali, the Shiites—who did not believe in it. But another political earthquake was to further politicize the institution and diminish its apostolic halo. In 750, a clan from Arabia, the Banu Abbas, plotted against the ruling Umayyad dynasty founded by *Muawiya.* The Abbasids invited the entire Umayyad clan to a social event and slaughtered them. One Umayyad prince fled to Muslim Spain and founded an Andalusian Umayyad dynasty. The new masters moved the capital of the empire to the newly built city of Baghdad.

The Abbasid dynasty ruled for centuries and was powerful enough to dominate lands from China to Morocco. It established the strongest and largest Islamic empire of all time. But as the dynasty aged, its power started to decline, and the *wali,* or regional governors, asserted their independence and even declared local caliphates. By the time the Crusades started in 1099, the empire was highly divided.

THE CRUSADERS

Another ongoing debate on the relationship between the Islamic empire and Christian Europe revolves around the issue of whether the Crusades were a religious war or not. Were they a response to aggression or a colonial enterprise? History is full of complexities and is always in the eyes of the beholder. To Arabs and Muslims, the crusaders were European Christian invaders landing on Arab Muslim shores in Syria and Palestine. To the Europeans of the time, the caliphate was an empire that invaded Spain and southern France after taking control of the Holy Land and was threatening to destroy Rome. In Jewish history, the crusaders massacred the Jews in Jerusalem. To Middle Eastern Christians, the Arabs were the invaders and the Christian Europeans the liberators. These conflicting visions of history will continue until, perhaps, a global and more scientific perception overrides them all.

To the Islamic states of the eleventh century—and they had become many by then—the military expeditions coming from Europe were infidel invasions against the caliphate and Islam. The Crusades were met by jihad, now on the defensive for the first time since the seventh century. After 636 the *fatah* had gone from one offensive to another. By 1099, the tables were turned. Not only were the *kuffar* back on the offensive, but they were winning the battles—at least at the beginning. The Crusades created a massive shock in the Muslim East. How were the infidels able to destroy the achievements of the army of Allah? A theological crisis ensued. The situation worsened when other *kuffars* arrived from east of Mesopotamia: the Mongols in the thirteenth century. Their hordes destroyed the Persian provinces of the empire and burned Baghdad to the ground. It was the lowest point of the Arab caliphate.[22]

However, a dynasty out of Egypt, the Mameluks, repeated what the first *fatah* had achieved in the seventh century. Fighting on two fronts, they defeated the Mongols, before converting them, and the crusaders, before expelling them from the Middle East in the early fourteenth century. The Mameluks adopted a very rigid attitude toward the infidels, both outside their sultanate and within, including extreme intolerance of Christians. Jihad was perceived as the savior of Islam from both the Christian crusaders and the pagan Mongols.[23]

THE SECOND *FATAH:* THE OTTOMANS

As chaos was spreading in the Abbasid Empire, a nomadic ethnic group at the edges of Central Asia converted to Islam: the Turks. With the slow, agonizing decline of Baghdad's power, these Turkic tribes gradually migrated toward the center of the Middle East, first to become part of the Abbasid bureaucracy, then to supply the caliphs with guards, on their way to becoming the second-most important actors in Islamic history. From greater Turkistan to the southern Caucasus, Muslim Turks waged war against the remnants of the Byzantine Empire. Seen from a historical perspective, the Turkish armies (called Ottomans in reference to Othman, their founder) thrust into Asia Minor, which Arabs had failed to occupy. The Ottoman drive, under the banner of Islam, became the second great *fatah.* The Ottomans crossed the Bosporus into the Balkans. Constantinople, the capital of Eastern Christianity, fell into the hands of their sultan.[24] As with their predecessors a few centuries before, nothing could stop their march into Europe. After Greece, Serbia, Bulgaria, Romania, Moldavia, and Hungary, the new *fatah* reached the gates of Vienna, where a coalition of central European princes stopped it. One-third of infidel Europe was under the domination of the Ottomans.[25]

Turning to the Arab provinces in the Middle East, the Ottomans sought the supreme leadership of the caliphate. In 1516, the Turks defeated the Mameluks in Syria, and kept marching through Arab lands until they conquered all formerly Abbasid provinces westward to Algeria. They did not invade Persia, which had meanwhile recaptured its independence as a Shiite nation. The Ottomans' jihad was overwhelming. To top their military supremacy, they declared their sultan as caliph and moved the capital of the caliphate to Istanbul, the new name of the former Christian Constantinople.[26]

The Turkish *fatah* was as stunning as its Arab predecessor had been. In order to project themselves as the new leaders of the Muslim world, the sultans underwent a northbound jihad into the heart of the *kuffar* continent, Europe. The cataclysmic advance in the Balkans and central Europe and the invasion of Ukraine and the entire Caucasus shook the foundations of the classical balance of power between the Christian kingdoms and the Islamic state. The military

successes of the Turks had another effect on the East. After the Crusades, the
Mongol invasions, and the decline of the Abbasids as universal rulers of *dar el
Islam,* the Ottomans imposed themselves as custodians of the faith and of the
umma. The *fatah* in Europe consecrated the Ottoman jihad as supreme and
opened the path for taking over the old *dar el Islam* in the Middle East and
North Africa. Success brings success. For centuries to come, the Ottomans
were accepted as the new rulers, despite the fact that they were not Arabs, because they moved the borders of the *Dawla Islamiya* deeper into the *dar el
harb.* The logic of jihad superceded the logic of ethnic difference between
Arabs and Turks. Hence, the Muslim peoples of the new Ottoman Empire
granted allegiance to the sultans more as caliphs than as emperors. The Ottoman caliphate would last until 1923.[27]

DHIMMI BECOMES MILLET

The Ottoman Empire ruled more Christians, and later on Jews, than any Arab
empire. The *dhimmis* under the Umayyads and the Abbasids were small minorities in the Levant. But with the conquest of Armenia, Greece, the Balkans,
and beyond, the sultans were ruling additional millions of non-Muslims, mostly
Christians. For geopolitical reasons, it was not practical to apply the strict
dhimmi status to the one-fifth of Europe then dominated by the Ottomans. Istanbul mutated the Umar conditions into a more modern status: the Millet. The
Ottoman system, in contrast with the Arab *dhimma,* recognized the character of
"community" experienced by the various Christian denominations, Jews, and
other non-Muslim groups. The new characterization was less a liberalization
based on political development than a practical measure to better organize the
subdued populations. As a caliph, the Ottoman sultan was able to rule Arabs
and other Muslims without challenge to his legitimacy. The master of Istanbul
was, after all, the successor to the Prophet. That theological lineage assured the
sultan of the faithfulness of half of the empire. The other half was populated
with Christians. The *millet* regime was a modernization of the *dhimmi* status.
In some cases it served a bureaucratic purpose. The heads of the *Milla* communities became technically the agents of the sublime porte. They collected the
taxes, kept an eye on the community, and reported to the *wali,* or regional governors. Again, the modern debate in Middle East studies about the *millet* has
followed the same intellectual confrontation. Most Muslim and some western
scholars still insist that the Ottomans liberalized the status of the People of the
Book, while most Mideast Christians, Jews, and some Muslim liberals see in

the *millet* a "collaboration" system that better organized the control of the non-Muslim subjects of the empire.

JIHAD AS A STATE TOOL

From the first jihads in Arabia in the seventh century until the last official jihads conducted by Istanbul in World War I, the exercise of the call for "holy war" (as classical historians portrayed it) was officially a state business. Since its inception, the *Nida' ul Jihad* (literally, call for jihad) was under the prerogative of the Prophet, his successors, and the official representatives of the caliphs. As understood from chronicles, clerics, and historians, jihad is a religious duty per se, but calling for it is only within the purview of the ruler. Thus, from the seventh century until early in the twentieth, jihad could not be proclaimed, ignited, or conducted for personal reasons. Although not every member of the *umma* had the right to declare jihad on his own, each could join the jihad at any time under specific conditions. The legitimate authorities of the Islamic state were the only recognized starters of jihad.

For example, if the caliph wished to conquer Egypt but not Ethiopia, no jihad could take place against Ethiopia, but only against Egypt. And if the state concluded a "peace agreement" with the infidels, no Muslim had a right to perform jihad against the *kuffar*. In short, jihad is not random, and neither is the *fatah*. There are legal, doctrinal, and pragmatic conditions for the conduct of jihad. The question is not what kind of warfare to perform or when jihad is requested or permissible (those questions will be discussed in due course), but who is calling for it and how legitimate it is.

For centuries, the decision to wage jihad was essentially at the discretion of the caliph or his representatives. But the mechanism of declaring jihad was highly organized. There were two requirements.

1. There should be a *fatwa,* or religious edict. Even if the infidels were a permanent category of enemies of *dar el Islam,* the designation of imminent enemies had to be licensed by a senior cleric or a group of religious scholars.
2. Once the religious edict is obtained, often at the request of the ruler, jihad becomes a raw tool of war and state decision-making. At that point, military, economic, intelligence, and other factors are integrated into the process, as with any war strategy.

Jihad could be used in the defense of the empire or of parts of the *dar el Islam* and, depending on the geopolitical ambitions of the caliph, as a tool of invasion, annexation, and conquest (i.e., into *dar el harb*).

CONCLUSION

As we have seen, analyzing a phenomenon like jihad over more than a millennium is not a simple matter. As a state policy, a doctrinal tool, and an instrument with which dozens of wars, invasions, conquests, and resistances were waged, it is part of world history. For thirteen centuries and at least until the fall of the sultanate and the caliphate in 1923, jihad and *fatah* were a public philosophy of the rulers east and south of the Mediterranean. Millions believed in launching them, and millions perished as a result of them. Jihad and *fatah*, like Crusades and *conquistas,* were colonial and imperialist enterprises, even though they were grounded in religion. While the concept of jihad was also applied to inner spiritual struggles adopted by individuals, it remained nevertheless under the overarching doctrine of historical jihad.[28] The inner cleansing, as we discussed earlier, was to better prepare for the jihad in the public sphere. At least until secular modernity developed in many areas of the Muslim world, the real, greater jihad was a state doctrine, designed and applied for the interest of the *umma.*

The history of jihad cannot be summed up easily. But it was developed and pursued with great force and energy in a unified practice and vision for as long as it was in the hands of absolute governments, in the same way as the decision for war and peace rested in the hands of other religiously sanctified states around the world, until they were reformed. The main challenge for jihad, and subsequently for *fatah*, was the ability of post-Ottoman Muslim governments, elites, and clerics to reform the concept or abandon it altogether.[29]

In the years after the collapse of the caliphate, three currents emerged from the ashes of the world official body of jihad: one that rejected it and adhered to international law; another one that ignored the debate while adhering practically to the new international community; and a third, the jihadists, which resuscitated it, reshaped its doctrines, and wages wars and conflicts in its name.

Chapter Two

WHO ARE THE
JIHADISTS?

BEFORE THE SEPTEMBER 11 ATTACKS, very few people in the United States and the West would have known what jihad was much less been able to answer the question: Who are the jihadists? When al Qaeda targeted America, its ideology, roots, and objectives were unknown to most of the public. It is clear that experts like Richard Clarke were aware of al Qaeda's threat but not necessarily its detailed strategy.[1] A few people, such as the CNN reporter Peter Bergen, had begun to unravel al Qaeda and its mission.[2] But it is safe to say that the American public was oblivious to the real danger. In contrast with other enemies in American and European history, such as the Nazis, the fascists, and the Soviets, the jihadists did not make it to the conventional "list" until Mohammed Atta and his mujahidin brought down the two most important towers in world history and the single most powerful military command on Earth. Until then, neither in the classrooms nor in the newspapers, could one sense that jihadism was as threatening a force as it turned out to be.

Four years later, we have still to ask: Where do the jihadists come from? What do they want?

THE ROOTS OF THE JIHADISTS

As I noted in the last chapter, the term "jihad" made a slow entry into western vocabulary, particularly among English speakers. Throughout the 1990s, those who warned of the rising threat coming from the East did so in reference to Islamic fundamentalists, Islamists, radical Islam, Muslim extremists, and other such concepts.[3] While those names are correct if placed in a proper context, a better understanding requires a strong focus on the actual definitions used by the terrorists themselves, which were grounded above all in the idea of jihad. Thus, the most appropriate and correct term would have been, and still is, jihadists.

Al-Jihadiyun, or in English "jihadists," is the term chosen by all those who believe that the concept of jihad is historically legitimate and that they are pursuing the orders of Allah in following this call for mobilization. It is important to understand that the self-proclaimed jihadists believe that their identification as such is part of their commitment to Islam, in their interpretation. Simply, jihadists believe that Islam has ordered them to the realm of jihad. Again, the ideological currents that draw from the jihad doctrine do not project themselves as neo-Muslim or as a new brand of Islam. To the contrary, they firmly believe that they represent the true religion and the authentic civilization of Islam, and therefore are the legitimate heirs of past Islamic history. Going even further, jihadists believe that other Muslims have diverted from the true path of Islam. They constantly affirm their attachment to the letter of their holy scriptures and claim that their vision of Islam is the single acceptable one.

The jihadist sees history as a linear development to be measured in terms of the application of one particular code (embodied in the Qu'ran, Sharia law, and other texts) as accepted by jihadist scholars. In this sense, the jihadists have developed an interpretation of Islam the religion and applied it in the realm of world politics. In simpler terms, the jihadists are twentieth-century terrorists who want to resume the wars unleashed by Islamic empires nearly fourteen centuries ago. But in the absence of an actual unified Islamic "empire" like that of the Abbasids and the Ottomans, today's jihadists have to act on its behalf, committing violence in the name of a whole community and an entire religion, yet without a mandate from the people.

THE LOGIC OF THE JIHADISTS

To understand the worldview of the jihadists and their future plans, one has to enter their minds and understand their reading of history. Here it is in a nutshell.

First of all, like many other religious believers, they believe firmly in the divine authority of the text of the various sources of Islam. On that level, they are like most Muslims of faith and similar to all people of faith from all religions around the world. Jews believe in the Ten Commandments and the Torah, Christians believe in the New Testament, and Muslims consider Mohammed to be the last Prophet and abide by the five tenets of Islam. It is important to understand that the followers of jihadism are part of a religion but adhere to its most rigid interpretations. From that angle, all jihadists have to be Islamic fundamentalists; they are certainly very religious and devoted practitioners. They consider all events that took place in the early phase of Islam's genesis as universally true and explained only by the power of the text, and to have occurred literally as they were described, accounted for, and related by the first companions of the Prophet and their immediate successors[4] (in Arabic they are called the *salaf,* literally the "preceding founders"). But where, if at all, do the jihadists depart from religious dogma and mainstream belief?

The debate within jihad studies is raging. There are many who do not believe that the jihadists are innovating but that they reflect the real religion as it was revealed some fourteen centuries ago.[5] Others think that the jihadists do draw their beliefs from real religion, but that their actions are not authorized or accepted by the common sense of most Muslims today.[6] The debate will continue, but all schools (including the jihadists themselves) agree that they are on a mission to resume what their ancestors began. Put simply, in the mind of the jihadists, there was no rupture in the evolution of the Islamic state since its inception in Medina. No reform has taken place, and therefore the jihadists are in line to fulfill a mission launched centuries ago. Here lies the fine line between jihadists and would-be mainstream thinking within the Muslim world. To make an analogy, in western or Christian terms, no one is saying that the jihadists, by their actions and beliefs, have made themselves "heretics" or "apostates" who no longer belong to the Muslim religion. It is accepted that they base their interpretations and actions on an actual history and legitimate theology; the debate is about whether they should be doing it.

Most Muslims acknowledge the achievements, wars, and civilizational interactions of their long history. Most of them see their history in the same way as Christians and Jews see theirs, and are attached to it. But within the Muslim community a strong group, the Islamic fundamentalists, known also as Islamists, believe that past history and present are intertwined and form the correct basis to engage with the future. While most Jews identify with the biblical accounts of the conquest of the Holy Land, not all of them base their entire outlook regarding contemporary world politics on direct biblical statements. And even if some do, their divine marching orders do not extrapolate to other nations and other lands. Christians generally acknowledge their history, admitting that statesmanship and politics diverted the original peaceful faith into empire building and conquest. The Crusades are part of European Christian history, churches mostly legitimized the settlement of the Americas, and in many ways colonialism was tied into the political cultures of western Christianity. But no significant segments of today's Christian polity voice a desire to resume past conquests or to use medieval theologies to direct modern world politics. This is where the jihadists distinguish themselves not only from other Muslims, but also from most social doctrines.

In essence, the Islamist movements, from which the doctrine of jihadism flourishes, see themselves as a direct continuation of the Islamic state and strive for its reestablishment—including its past expansionist drive. It is true that modern fundamentalists among Jewish and Christian communities also identify themselves as the heirs of ancient divine "marching orders," but significant geopolitical differences exist between the jihadists and the non-Muslim fundamentalists. One is that because no reform has taken place within Islam, the Islamists have wide latitude to mobilize their communities. Another is that jihadists reject international laws and the current international structure. Finally, the jihadists constitute a direct threat to nations and governments in a way that can blaze up into world conflicts.

The jihadist logic is historicist and theological at the same time. In the mind of its authors, leaders, and militants, the initial *rissala* (mission) bestowed on the Prophet, and carried on by the caliphs for more than thirteen centuries, is also theirs. Here lies the central power and enigma of the movement. The jihadists believe that what was initiated in Muslim history ages ago is still moving forward today, just as it was in the beginning. They also believe that Allah is still commanding them to perform these *wajibat,* or duties, without interruption. And they are firmly convinced that the enemies of their ancestors as perceived in those times are still the enemies of today, in a war that has not ended for the last millennium and a half.

For example, al Qaeda's statements in the twenty-first century, before and after September 11, describe the United States and Europe as "crusaders." Osama bin Laden talks about the West as *al Rum,* or "the Byzantines," and all Islamists describe Christians and Jews as *kuffar,* or infidels. The enemies of the jihadists are not who these people really are today, but who the jihadists believe they still are—the same as they were over a thousand years ago. The self-described duty of these militant warriors is to resume the old jihad implacably and relentlessly until the goals of the past caliphs are fulfilled. Those who see the modern jihad followers as mere freedom fighters, or national resistance militants, or even revolutionaries, have totally missed the deep essence of who al Qaeda and other jihadists are. Only those who have understood both jihad in Islamic history and the jihadists' search for renewal of that phenomenon have it right. In movie terms, the jihadists would see themselves as being like characters from *Star Wars:* They participate in a perennial struggle between fixed powers of good and evil and a resurgent call to achieve the goals of the ancient predecessors—same planet, different age. But just how and why did they come to believe in themselves as warriors in an ancient and unfinished battle?[7]

THE MIDDLE AGES: IBN TAYMIYA

"We've lost to the infidels because we've strayed away from the right path, from Allah's path." With this type of assertion, a dogmatic school of thought convinced many Muslims and Arabs in the Middle Ages that the massive defeats at the hands of the enemies of Islam were caused by the failure of the rulers to abide by the guidelines of the founding fathers. The historical context to these concepts explained their frustrations.

The Arab Islamic conquests had reached as far as France to the west and India to the east in the eighth century A.D./C.E. The inhabitants of this empire saw what no previous Arab had ever witnessed: an undaunted, excessive, and expansive power that stretched over three continents. From Bedouins to sophisticated colonialists in less than a hundred years, the settlers coming from the peninsula were as proud as Roman citizens at the peak of their empire, or as the British during the period when the sun never set over their world empire. As outlined in the last chapter, the Arab settlers who reached these remote lands, along with the Arabized population, were convinced that it was offered to them as a reward for their adherence to the new religion and their strict obedience to its tenets, as taught by the founding elite since the early days of Medina. A citizen of the caliphate in the ninth century lived in the greatest superpower of all time. The Abbasid caliphate not only sat on three continents on the largest landmass of any known empire, but it also was the culmination of technological and scientific power. During the days of Caliph Harun al Rashid, Baghdad was New York and Washington combined. An unparalleled power emanated from it, forcing foreign leaders, such as Charlemagne, to sign peace and cooperation treaties with al Rashid and his successors. From the barefoot Arabian nomads who roamed the deserts for thousands of years to the CEO of the largest and most powerful empire of all times, in about a century, the history of the Arabs was aggrandized endlessly. And to ground these achievements in permanent mechanisms and convince the populace to remain faithful to the state, the religious clerics linked the successes and the conquests to the level of adherence to the letter of the religious codes. The more the masses and their leaders abided by the strict law revealed in the seventh century by the founding fathers, or the *salaf*, the more Allah would grant victory and prosperity; officials of the state and clerics constantly affirmed this belief. Certainly, a parallel version existed across the Mediterranean among Christians and across oceans in most other religions.

But, by the end of the eleventh century, the world of imperial Islam was transformed. After centuries of having intimidated all its neighbors, from Byzantium to Rome, into a defensive posture, the caliphate was suddenly the target of devastating invasions and destructions. The peoples of the Arab Islamic empire had lived under the assumption that no force on Earth could defeat the Muslim armies strategically, to reverse the *fatah*, and, worse, to penetrate deep inside the *dar el Islam*. The dominant belief that cemented the popular trust in the commander of the believers was that all conquests, and subsequently all jihads, were not only blessed by the divine but ultimately the will of Allah. For, according to the official version of the state *(dawla)*, without God's intervention, no real victory could have been possible. How could the tribes of Arabia have subdued Byzantium and the Persian empires combined, and reached lands as distant as France and India, without the consent and the command of the heavens? No one from the seventh to the tenth centuries had seriously asked: But what if Allah gives the victory to the infidels instead? How to explain it, and what should be done about it? Such a debate took place in the twenty-first century after the removal of the Taliban and of Saddam Hussein; but even to ask such questions was inconceivable in the tenth century. However, what was about to happen was brutally real and a harsh awakening for the supposedly never-ending power of the expanding Islamic empire. By 1099, Arabs and Muslims living on the east coast of the Mediterranean watched with shock as tall, blond, blue-eyed soldiers marched across the land into northern Syria and from there into Palestine and Jerusalem. The crusaders, under the banner of the cross, crushed one after another all armies sent to meet them by the caliph or the local governors and monarchs. Emerging from Asia Minor and coming ashore from fleets, the heavily shielded Europeans were conquering a Muslim land—a land that itself had been conquered by Muslims in the early days of the *fatah*. How could this happen?

The crusaders, infidels in the eyes of the Muslims, conquered northern Syria, Lebanon, and most of Palestine. On top of it, they took Jerusalem and established Christian states from Asia Minor to the Sinai. This epoch is remembered in Arab textbooks as the worst in history. Not only because the very principle of the *dar el Islam* was reversed by the *dar el harb;* not only because the combined military efforts of the caliphate and the local Muslim powers to push the crusaders back failed for more than a century and a half, but also for a reason that has not been emphasized in most accounts across ages: By reaching south of Jerusalem and the deserts of Jordan and the Sinai, the infidels were about to accomplish the nightmare of nightmares, an apocalypse of biblical proportions—the soldiers of the cross, as referred to by modern jihadists, were at the edges of the Arabian Peninsula. Nothing, no army, stood between them and the province of Hejaz, where Mecca and Medina lay practically without defenses. By the standards of international relations of the times, an advance of the crusaders into the birthplace of Islam would have been catastrophic, and one would think at the time final.

As if the threat from the West were not enough, another perhaps greater threat burst from the East toward the end of the period of the crusader states in the early fourteenth century. A formidable force marched, or perhaps one should say charged, out of central Asia and into the Muslim empire, destroying all defenses in its path and finally reaching the actual capital of the empire. These were the Mongols under Genghis Khan and Hulaku Khan; they left smoking ruins and mayhem from India to Persia, defeating the Muslims on their way. The extreme brutality of the invaders and the fall of Baghdad shocked the subjects of the caliphate. With the European Christians on the eastern shores of the Mediterranean, the Byzantines still in place in Asia Minor to the north, and the advance of the Mongols from the east and the burning of Abbasid Baghdad, the Muslim world was living its greatest tragedy. When the northern provinces of Arab Andalusia fell to the Christian Reconquista of Spain, many thought that the end of days for the Islamic state had come.

In this particular historical environment, the root causes for jihadism were born. Indeed, in many spots in the crumbling world of Islam, and out of the medieval Middle East, a millenary call for jihad emerged. One of the proponents was the scholar and chronicler Ibn Taymiya, an Arab Muslim from Syria. A witness of the great tragedies of his time, he observed the infidel Christians coming from the west and the pagan Mongols from the east in a pincer movement aimed at terminating the caliphate on Earth. In reaction, Ibn Taymiya developed the doctrines of jihad and *takfir,* which have influenced what would become, centuries later, the jihadi and Salafi movements of modern times. From his writings, sayings, and later references grew a radical set of ideas that would in time transform themselves into waves of ideologies, the latest being al Qaeda of Osama bin Laden.

In his works, the illuminated doctrinaire of the thirteenth century postulated:

1. The Islamic state was the result of a commitment by the early founders, including the companions of the Prophet and his successors, the *salaf;* they possessed the only right codes of behavior, which brought about the rule of Allah on the planet. They acted in a way that satisfied the maker of Heaven and Earth. Hence, only the way of the *salaf* was the right way.

2. The first main code was a literal application by Muslims of all periods of the words of the Qu'ran, the *Hadith,* and all components of the *Sharia.* Any change in this code would and did create a collapse of the divine endorsement of the mission.

3. Those Muslims who diverted from the path of the *salaf* were to be considered as infidels or apostates. Being Muslim and abiding by the five pillars of religion, in the eyes of Ibn Taymiya, was not enough to please Allah and promote the state. Muslims had to be comprehensive in their affiliation and adherence to the literal word of Allah and his messenger. And to do so, they had to follow the injunctions of the clerics, the "scientists of Islam" or *Ulama' al Islam.* Only they could determine what Allah had planned for humanity and Muslims. Muslims who did not follow this precise path and abide by the code were deficient, apostates, and deviant.

4. There could be no peace with the infidels. This more radical stance with *dar el harb* was no doubt influenced by the events of the Crusades and the Mongol invasions. Ibn Taymiya and his school radicalized the perception of the infidels. Understandably, the caliphate did not acknowledge the fact that the *fatah* was an invasion of other nations and lands. It perceived them as "blessed" movements to liberate the "others" from ignorance and bring them into the fold of the true path. But the commanders of the believers were also architects of a balance of power. They knew when they could or could not achieve the higher goal of subjugating the *kuffar.* With the counteroffensives coming from *dar el harb* with the Crusades and the Mongols, the jihad scholars established more ideological grounds for the confrontation with the infidels: They made a matter of state into a matter of ideology.

TAKFIR

To equip this Inquisition-like movement with a tool of punishment and sanctions against apostates and infidels, the new radicals developed the doctrine of *takfir.* The term, derived from the word *kafir* (infidel), means the action of defining someone as an infidel. According to this doctrine, the right ruler (the caliph or his appointee) or the legitimate scholars (clerics) can designate someone or a group as *kafir* and put this label on the enemies of the state or the opponents to jihad. The designation as infidel allows the ruler(s) to declare jihad and mobilize the *umma* (nation). But in contrast with designations from past centuries, which were general, the action of *takfir* as structured by the radical schools of thought aims at concentrating on specific groups including Christians and Jews, but also Shiites and Druze, considered offshoots from Sunni Islam. The *takfir* doctrine extended "demonization" to use on

Muslim Sunni themselves if they did not abide by the strict rules as adopted from the *salaf.* In simple terms, the *takfir* doctrine was a weapon of incrimination against the enemies of the Islamic state. It was an invention by the most radical group within the empire to block the evolution of ideas, reforms, and interpretations. In the logic of these radicals, "progressive ideas" are a diversion from the code. Only the return "back" to the latter would provide victory and advancement

JURISPRUDENCE: *IJTIHAD*

The instrument of legal development known in the West as jurisprudence had an equivalent in Arab Muslim culture: *ijtihad.* It had a comparable meaning—the power to reexplain texts in light of the general evolution of thought and history—and gave Islam a powerful tool to advance in various fields for centuries until about the Middle Ages. Many schools of thinking, with heavy Greek, Aramaic, Hebrew, and Persian influences, and departing from Arab Muslim tenets, were allowed to evolve in parallel to western and Oriental counterparts. In view of the divine nature of the Qu'ran, only jurisprudence was able to move political culture and scientific discoveries forward. Baghdad under the Abbasids—and despite their ruthlessness—was making progress within the world of postantiquity, and often led the West in a multitude of fields, such as medicine, mathematics, architecture, and urban structure. But the introduction of doctrinal jihadism and early salafism by Ibn Taymiya and others, when combined with the collapse of the Arab caliphate, put an abrupt end to the developing jurisprudence and replaced it with a discretionary power at the level of the caliph—in addition to the growing influence of the state clerics.

FROZEN IN THE MIDDLE AGES

Ibn Taymiya's thinking expressed the vision of those more fundamentalist elements among the dominant establishment in the empire. In fact, they had their disapproving eye on a number of schools that promoted rationalist thinking within Islam, such as the *Mu'tazelits,* or those who developed a more spiritual interpretation of Islam, such as the Sufis. Many attempts to rationalize, reform, or change Islam had taken place between the seventh and the fourteenth centuries, but the crisis of the Middle Ages froze the power of the Islamic state to move freely toward the future and plant the seeds of reform. In essence, the rise of the Salafi doctrines of the fourteenth century later impeded the capacity of the caliphate to catch up with the European renaissance, revolutions, and modernity. This equation may be debated by many scholars and historians, but the Salafi stream, at least, ended up producing the modern-day terror ideologies. The literature of the modern jihadists, their speeches, their texts, and their Web sites lead directly back to Ibn Taymiya's thought. All modern Sunni fundamentalists draw their intellectual and theological inspiration from the body of work left by this "elemental force" of the Arab Middle Ages. He and many other similar thinkers produced the roots of universal jihad, inserted it into the religious framework, paralyzed interpretations that could have produced jurisprudence, and unleashed an eight-hundred-year-long jihad movement.

TIME TRAVEL

When Osama bin Laden traveled to Afghanistan eight centuries later, he was executing the orders of Ibn Taymiya: fighting the infidels, reestablishing the pure Islamic state, and laying the groundwork for the return of the caliphate. When the Taliban took over, they applied the eight-hundred-year-old code of jihad and *takfir:* destruction of non-Muslim religious symbols and Muslim non-Salafi symbols, elimination of infidel arts, implementation of medieval traditions of punishments against women, and separation of genders. It may be hard to accept (outside novels and Hollywood) that the modern jihadists of al Qaeda and its sister organizations embody thirteenth-century jihad in the framework of twenty-first-century global politics. But this reality explains most of the irrational behavior of modern-day jihadists, including suicide bombers, and the litany of extreme, violent acts and statements for which they have been responsible—which to reasonable people seem to belong to another age.

MAMELUK

The doctrine of Ibn Taymiya and the *takfir* and jihad currents never disappeared. The Dark Ages stretching from the burning of Baghdad in the thirteenth century until the end of the Mameluk dynasty in the sixteenth saw the growth of intolerance and spread of raw jihadism. The central Islamic state was in pieces. The Abbasid dynasty was eliminated, and multiple local monarchies, emirates, and khanates emerged. Surging from the rubble of the caliphate, a harsh and extremely radical dynasty—the Mameluk—extended its power from Egypt to Syria, controlling access to Arabia and its holy sites. Looking like the modern-day Taliban, they defeated the infidels from the east (the Mongols) in the famous battle of Ain Jalut in Palestine. They followed them through the deserts of Syria and Mesopotamia and fought a war against the western infidels on a second front in the Holy Land and Syria. Succeeding the Ayubids of Saladin in their warfare against the crusaders, the Mameluk defeated the last remnant of the European Christians on the east coast of the Mediterranean.

Drawing heavily from the hard line of jihad and *takfir,* this Sunni dynasty turned against all non-Sunni minorities—Shiite, Druse, Christians, and others—in the region of its influence. In 1305, the Mameluk sent an army to Mount Lebanon, an enclave where Christian Maronites and Druse took refuge, and massacred tens of thousands of them. The new order of the Middle East in the Dark Ages bears a sinister resemblance to the Afghan, Sudanese, and (albeit Shiite) Iranian regimes of the twentieth century. What bin Laden and Zarqawi are killing for in the early twenty-first century, regular armies and states had applied as policies from the fourteenth to the sixteenth centuries.

THE OTTOMANS

Jihadism as spread by the Mameluk was influenced by Ibn Taymiya's ideas, but it remained nevertheless a state business. Unlike the modern jihadist cells, holy war was not yet privatized. Today's Islamist terror networks refer to the Dark Ages as examples of powerful jihad and go back to the founding era of the *salaf* as a ground for their ideology. But all these jihadic activities were conducted by the central authorities of the *umma* (nation), not by gangs and networks. In a sense they were part of state warfare. Under the Mameluk, the authority of the Abbasids collapsed but the moral authority of a theoretical caliphate survived. It became much more than just theoretical when a new dynasty arose in the Middle East: the Ottoman Turks.

In the first century of their ascension to power, the Ottomans waged not only jihad, but also conquests *(fatah)*—the ultimate expression of jihad. But historians realize that the Turkish invasions, although branded as falling under jihadic doctrine, were mere colonialist enterprises, like those of many other powers throughout history. However, the similarities between the Arab and Ottoman jihads are striking. Both groups started originally as nomadic tribes from remote and marginal regions. Both converted to Islam before they undertook their expansion and hence acted under the leadership of spiritual and military leaders simultaneously. Both invaded areas on three continents tenfold the size of their birthplace and populations. Hence the followers of Ibn Taymiya's thought acclaimed the Ottoman thrust into infidel lands, especially into the Balkans and central Europe. As long as the Turkish sultans were marching into the *dar el harb,* conquering lands, subduing monarchs, and stretching *Sharia* laws deep into the *kufr* (infidel) zone, the jihadic currents relied on the state to push forward the agenda of the founding fathers. In many ways the Ottomans fostered the Arab acceptance of their rule by showing a willingness to expand the borders of the caliphate into remote frontiers.

The Arab *fatah* stopped at the edges of Asia Minor, unable to conquer Constantinople for centuries. Often in twenty-first-century chat rooms modern-day jihadists discuss the matter as if it were of great current importance. "Why did the Arab Caliphate stop the *fatah* in northern Syria and not defeat the Rum (Byzantines) all the way to their capital?" asked one. (This debate over ancient history seemed as urgent as the contemporary one of striking American forces in the Sunni triangle of Iraq.) In a sense, the reading of history by today's jihadists has no historical framework. A cleric answered: "Because the Umeyad and Abbasid dynasties were victorious till they built those castles and practiced lavish lives. Allah stopped his blessing and cursed the Umma. But when the Ottoman Sultans took the sword of jihad and resumed the conquest into the land of Kufr, Allah the merciful sent his angels again to slaughter the enemy."[8] When the Ottomans marched forward under the banner of the *Sharia* and jihad, the more fundamentalist quarters of the empire praised the sultans. But as the rulers of Istanbul (the renamed Constantinople) commenced to look toward significant reforms of their institutions, the reforms were regarded as a diversion from the true path. This was the history of struggle within the Ottoman Empire between the reformists and the radicals. But as long as the Turkish sultanate held the power of the Islamic caliphate, the radical school had to accept the rules coming from the Sublime Porte. The emperors were either inclined to modernize and reform or to return to the old narrow conditions of the past, but one fact superceded everything: There was a high authority in the Muslim world that decided all global matters of war and peace and ruled over all subjects of the Islamic state. Even if fundamentalist factions started to emerge in the beginning of the eighteenth century and criticized the Porte, the sultan remained, until the last hour of the caliphate, the supreme guide of the believers. Under the Ottoman Empire and even outside the sultanate, jihadism attempted to push the agenda of conquests and regression into strict religious behavior. But Istanbul, as the only heir to Baghdad and Damascus, stayed the final course of world Islamic policies until a secular power dismissed the last successor of the Prophet in 1924.

THE POST-OTTOMAN JIHAD

With the end of World War I and the collapse of the Ottoman Empire, jihadism and its followers were freed from an ultimate Islamic authority for the first time since the seventh century. As a result of the shattering of the succession, and since no major theological reform by mainstream clerics was operating within the Muslim world, the genie was out of the bottle. From the moment the secular and nationalist government of Ataturk caused the Sultanate to disintegrate in 1923, Salafi currents around the Muslim world felt their time had come. The caliphate is dead, long live the future caliphate! Eighty years later, a bearded man declared on an Arab TV network that "Muslims had lost the initiative at that moment." He said, "since then jihadists have been struggling to bring back the rule of Allah on Earth." The man's name was Osama bin Laden, and the videotaped remarks were played on al Jazeera TV. The connection between the Salafi movement that rose after the collapse of the caliphate and movements such as al Qaeda is organic. Not all groups chose the same path, procedures, and timing; many shade under one umbrella. In their minds, what unites them is a common ideological ground, one vision of history, and similar global objectives.

THE JIHADIST IDEOLOGY

The complex ideology of the Salafi jihadist movement could be defined in simplest terms in this way: It is a movement that wants to return the Muslim world to the times of its early conquests and move forward from there. This movement wants to bring back Muslim society to a strict application of *Sharia* laws, despite all the intervening evolution accomplished by Muslims through history. Finally, it is a movement that wants to resume *fatah* and conquests despite all norms of international relations and laws. The Salafi current rejects any laws higher than its own, any institution above the caliphate, and any authority beyond the one of the clerics. The Salafi ideology, called *al Aqida al Islamiya al salafiya* (the Islamic Salafi doctrine), is grounded in the works of many clerics, chronicles, imams, and a panoply of leaders.

THE THREE MAIN OBJECTIVES OF THE JIHADISTS

The jihadists as a whole have outlined three major objectives since the collapse of the Ottoman caliphate. These objectives include *tahrir, tawheed,* and *khilafa.*

TAHRIR: LIBERATION

Jihadists want to liberate all Muslim lands from non-Muslim powers. The question is: How does one determine what a "Muslim land" is? Many theories exist, but one is prevalent: Muslim lands consist of all lands that were conquered by the legitimate caliphate or surrendered to it, or whose population had at some time submitted to the caliphate. The jihadist logic is pretty cohesive. Whatever land that came formally under the Islamic state is Islamic. Whatever population that is in a position to rule itself that came to join the Islamic state brings its lands with it. For modern-day jihadists, Israel, Kashmir, Spain, and Chechnya are Muslim lands that will have to be "liberated" at some point in time. It is the historic and religious duty of all able Muslims to offer and sacrifice for the battles of liberation. In the absence of a high authority that could regulate war and peace within Islam or promote reforms, the demand for the "liberation of Muslim lands" by Salafi and jihadists cannot and will not stop.

TAWHEED: UNIFICATION

After the land is liberated, or while the process is taking place, all Muslim countries must be reunified within common borders. *Salafist* jihadists want to cancel the frontiers between the "fake entities" of all Muslim countries, starting with the Arabian Peninsula and the greater Middle East.

The goal is to dismantle the actual nation-states of Egypt, Libya, Syria, Iraq, Morocco, Algeria, all the way to Indonesia, Nigeria, and Turkmenistan, and reshape the civilizational borders of the Muslim world. This vision is drawn from what was the widening frontier of the *fatah* through the centuries. Later on, the Taliban, al Qaeda, Sudan's Turabi, Algeria's Salafis, and theoretically the Wahabis of Arabia would be projected into a world state. But this unification is not because of economics or other incentives; it is sought as the fulfillment of a command issued by the early founders of the religion—always, of course, according to the interpretations of the jihadists.

KHILAFA: THE CALIPHATE

Once the land is freed from the infidels and unified, the most important task is to reestablish the caliphate. The proponents of this aim emerged before and after the Ottoman collapse. Already in the nineteenth century, a movement of Salafis had depicted the Turkish institution as apostate and wanted to reestablish the older, purer, and more legitimate *khilafa* (caliphate). But with the decline and dismantling of the Istanbul sultanate, all Salafis today have one objective: to reinstate it. The calls for this are numerous and impact the behavior of modern-day jihadists. The reestablishment of the succession will signal the resumption of the external jihad (i.e., toward the *dar el harb*) and bring about the return of *fatah*.

The liberation and unification of the lands must come at the hands of pure jihadists, totally committed to the mission. It must take place under *Sharia* law and through the codes defined by recognized clerics.

Three major waves of jihadi have haunted the Middle East and beyond with this vision of the world. The first two—Sunni—developed from Ibn Taymiya's teaching, while the third one emerges from within the long-time marginalized Shiia.

FIRST WAVE: WAHABISM

The first wave of jihadism in the modern world came from what is today Saudi Arabia. Toward the end of the eighteenth century, Mohammed Abdel Wahab, a Sunni cleric from the remote Nejd desert province, launched the greatest Salafi movement of all time. Borrowing heavily from the teaching of Ibn Taymiya, he declared that Islam must be determined by the sayings and the actions of the founding fathers. He therefore developed a doctrine of Salafism with this logic: The *salaf* under the Prophet launched the Islamic state and divided the world in two, and so should the present-day Muslim countries. The *salaf* after Mohammed established a caliphate, as should present Muslim governments. But since the Ottomans had arrogated to themselves the supreme institution, Abdel Wahab accused them of diverting from the teaching of the *salaf*. He used the tool of *takfir* to cast a theological curse on them and on all those who would not see eye to eye with his views.

A federation of Arab Bedouin tribes from Nejd adopted his teaching and installed their power in Riyadh: the al Saud. By the early nineteenth century, the al Saud had become the leaders of Wahabism and waged a series of attacks against Ottoman power and their suzerain monarchs, including, in the beginning of the twentieth century, Sherif Hussein, the Hashemite of Mecca. These tensions between the legal Islamic state, embodied worldwide by Istanbul and locally in Arabia by the governor of Mecca, and the Wahabis in Nejd existed until the 1920s. The Wahabis—the Taliban of the nineteenth century—waited patiently for their moment. Note that the actual mainstream Muslim power was not necessarily Salafi or Wahabi. The Ottomans were embarking on a reform process, but were not always successful: Even the Hashemites of the Hejaz (the province centered on Mecca and Medina) resisted them.

In 1914, Turkey aligned itself with Germany and Austria in the world war. Sherif Hussein instead linked up with the British. Istanbul declared a jihad against the allies, and Hussein declared his own jihad against the Ottomans. The Wahabis stayed out of the conflict. The Ottomans were defeated and the Arabs of the Hashemite Hijaz province moved north to take over Jordan, Syria, and Iraq, leaving the peninsula an open field for al Saud. In 1924, Kemal Mustafa Ataturk declared the Republic of Turkey and abolished the caliphate, beheading an institution that had lasted more than thirteen centuries. Before the Hashemites secured their position in the Fertile Crescent, the Saudi Wahabis attacked Sherif Hussein's forces in the Hejaz and occupied Mecca and Medina. Since the mid-1920s, they have declared most of Arabia as a Saudi Wahabi monarchy. This entity became the first Salafi regime in modern history. With the emergence of the Saudi power out of the peninsula and the fall of the Ottoman Islamic legal entity, the protectors of the two shrines of Islam would project themselves as the most revered and respected moral and theological authority in the entire Muslim world. Geopolitical events helped the Saudis to survive the first half of the twentieth century before ascending to a world position; from that launch pad, they have been able to unleash waves of Wahabism, the last of which—even if not fully under their personal control—slammed into the Twin Towers and the Pentagon in 2001, before spreading from Afghanistan to the Iraqi Sunni triangle.

Wahabism installed itself with amazing ease in the mid-1920s in the birthplace of Islam, a location that many dynasties only dreamed of acquiring. Ibn Taymiya and Abdel Wahab's doctrines became the law of the land in the peninsula. Spared from the effects of the events leading to World War II, the new regime took advantage of decades of peace and left installed the foundations of one of the strictest applications of Islam in the modern world. Outside jihad against the infidels was out of the question. Until oil became a tool in international relations in the 1950s, the Saudis were mostly interested in applying Wahabism inside the kingdom. Jihad in international terms had to wait until after the domestic institutions and religious culture had been well grounded. For that purpose—and here is the heart of the equation—a historic alliance was forged between the ruling emirs and the powerful clerics. The princes would rule the land on behalf of the clerics, and the imams would manage jihad and *takfir* on behalf of Allah.[9]

During World War II, Wahabism did not lean toward one side or the other. It cleverly stayed on good terms with British power, which was embodied by multiple military bases around the peninsula in Yemen, Iraq, Jordan, and the Red Sea. Strategically, Wahabi thinking knew that unless the British infidels were totally defeated by the Nazis, there was no realistic chance that they would evacuate the region. They were right. While a number of nationalist Arab leaders in Iraq, Palestine, and Egypt threw their lot in with Germany, the Saudi dynasty was wise. The Wahabi vision was much more global than that of the other Islamic opponents of the West. The Salafi movement is not a local group with limited objectives, national or ethnic; the Wahabi agenda is universal. It analyzes the global balance of power in terms of the situation, interest, and relative strength of the *umma* (nation). Hence it does not let itself be dragged into sideshow battles, limited arenas, and short-term confrontation.

As oil started to provide strategic revenues and power to the Saudi institution, with an excess of influence since the 1950s, the dynamics of state Wahabism mutated. For the next twenty years the religious kingdom developed two policies: an internal one that focused on Islamic puritanism and an external one that developed a new international agenda. Pressing always forward to spread the Wahabist doctrine worldwide, the clerics intensified their activities in several Muslim countries using all the revenues and resources of a suddenly rich country. Mosques, religious centers, libraries, hospitals, and other projects were developed in many Muslim countries. The other side of the coin was Wahabi (read Salafi) education. With each socioeconomic initiative overseas, an Islamic fundamentalist investment was made. Year after year, the Wahabi influence penetrated deeper and deeper into Muslim societies in various areas and under various regimes. Saudi clerics were able to influence their colleagues as far as Indonesia, India, Pakistan, Nigeria, Sudan, and even the Soviet Union. The supreme privilege of being the administrators of Mecca and Medina and thus of the *hajj* (pilgrimage) process gave the kingdom's clerics even greater influence.[10] Imagine the twentieth-century Vatican in the hands of Christian fundamentalists preaching crusades and reaching out to a worldwide network of bishops and priests. That alone would produce an enormous network of religious structures under the control of a militant ideology.

With the oil crisis of 1973, the Wahabi network leapt ahead internationally. Backed by the endlessly growing power of the Saudi state, the Salafi militants and preachers targeted the West (with full-fledged support by the public treasury). Western Europe and the United States became prime destinations for the advocates of Wahabism and its derivatives. By the end of the cold war, projihadist organizations had filled up universities and other institutions or built their own and had created a vast infrastructure within the émigré communities. Wahabism produced the religious schools; the religious schools produced the jihadists. Among them was Osama bin Laden and the nineteen perpetrators of September 11.

SECOND WAVE: MUSLIM BROTHERHOOD

The second wave of Salafi jihadists came out of Egypt: *al Ikhwan al Muslimeen* (the Muslim Brotherhood). In the early 1920s, urban Egypt produced groups of Islamic fundamentalists who believed in using radical means to reestablish the Islamic state. One of the main articulators of that trend was Hassan al Banna, who founded the Muslim Brotherhood (a better translation would be the "Muslim Brothers"), an organization that would impact the future of political Islam in the region. If Wahabi jihadism started within the tribal society, the Brotherhood rose out of urban areas, and its evolution was marked by the traits and complexities of cities. The Brotherhood was loaded with heavy ideological literature, dense teachings, and complex organizational structures. Because it was born under political suppression, its entire political life developed in the shadows of the underground, even when it was allowed to operate freely. This characteristic of covertness shaped its strategies and modes of action. Most Brotherhood leadership structures are secret, and its tactics always extremely careful.

Because the organization was not always in the good graces of the Muslim rulers, the *Ikhwan* devised a dual track: a short-term tactic that allowed them to survive regimes and permitted them maneuvering room, hiding their long-term goals; and a long-term strategic track, which aimed at a final takeover of the government. Unlike the Wahabi Salafists who were state-sponsored, the Brotherhood was for most of its career within the opposition. But along with their Wahabi colleagues across the Red Sea, they have adopted the three major objectives of Salafism and jihadism.[11]

Although the Brotherhood flourished in Egypt, branches were established in most Arab countries and beyond. Among the most powerful extensions are those in Syria, Iraq, Lebanon, Palestine, Sudan, Algeria, and Jordan. At times, when suppressed by Gamal Abdel Nasser of Egypt, for example, they took refuge in Saudi Arabia—but of course the Saudi-protected Wahabi network did not allow them to lead the world Salafi movement. At times they ran for office and got members elected to parliament in Egypt, Jordan, and Kuwait. Elsewhere they took up weapons against the "ruler" under the *takfir* mechanism, as in Syria under Hafez Assad and Egypt under Anwar Sadat. For many analysts, the Brotherhood, as a second wave of Salafism, is the most sophisticated web of jihadism. Members are fine tacticians and long-term strategists, known for their high-level education and patience. Their practical thinking impacted many leading figures of jihad terrorism in the twentieth century. Among the names highly influenced by their doctrines are Sayid Kutb, the Trotsky of Islamism,[12] and Abdallah Azzam, the Che Guevara of jihadism.[13] But the most important legacy of the Brotherhood remains its offshoots.

At times during the struggle, many *ikhwan* or their students decided that the mother organization was unable to carry on the struggle properly. They thought that the Brotherhood was a first stage in modern jihad, but had stagnated. Many jihadists felt that the Brotherhood courted regimes instead of fighting them. Most important, especially during the cold war, the jihadi critics of the Brotherhood concluded that it did not do enough in fighting the infidels. The group was criticized from the inside for abandoning the direct war against Israel, for not confronting the communists and the Soviet Union, and for playing party politics in the Arab world. Dissent led to the formation of offshoots. These groups, choosing the path of "jihad now," have become notorious on the regional and international scene: Hamas and Islamic Jihad emerged among the Palestinians; the National Islamic Front of Hassan Turabi in Sudan; the Front de Salut Islamique in Algeria; the Gamaat Islamiya and Islamic Jihad in Egypt; as well as many similar groups in the region and around the world, including south Asia's Jamaat Islami and Abu Sayyaf.

These second generation Brotherhood offshoots were the main jihad terror groups in the 1980s. They waged local jihads in multiple battlefields around the globe, at times joined "national" struggles against foreign "infidel" forces, such as the Soviets in Afghanistan or the Israelis in the West Bank and Gaza, and took part in civil wars against *kafir* enclaves in southern Sudan and Lebanon. As they grew stronger, an elite from within all these groups decided to assemble an international army of jihad and fight the greatest powers of the infidels. Their analysis, structuring, and strategies are reminiscent of the communist international network, and their logic paralleled Trotsky's global war against the enemies of the proletariat. But the international jihadi waged their holy war against the infidels, starting mainly with the communists themselves.

The Soviet invasion of Afghanistan in 1979 gave the impetus to those elite jihadists to gather in one battlefield against one major enemy, the atheist Soviets. They poured into Afghanistan from a variety of countries, including Saudi Arabia and the rest of the Arab world, to "assist their brothers in religion." Among them was a man who would take world jihad to its ultimate form: terrorism. It was Osama bin Laden.

THIRD WAVE: KHUMAINI

The initial and widest waves of jihadism were Sunni and Salafi. But almost unexpectedly, another wave of jihadism came from formerly less active quarters:

the Shiite community. Since the Muslim civil war in the seventh century, the followers of Ali had been defeated and marginalized within Islamic world politics.
The Sunnis, who claimed direct theological and historical lineage to the
Prophet and the early companions, seized the caliphate. The Shiites were left
out for centuries. The world Muslim community living under the "just and legitimate" caliphs did not perceive them to be carriers of jihad. In reality,
throughout history, many Shiite leaders and communities took part in jihads
led by the Sunnis. In some cases, local Shiia dynasties, such as the Fatimids in
Egypt, waged their own forms of jihad.[14] But the Shiia call for holy war did not
carry enough doctrinal weight. Besides, it was considered "illegitimate" by the
Sunnis. And as the Ottoman Empire inherited the Sunni Arab caliphate, the
Shiite jihad was marginalized for centuries. In 1979, things changed.

After overthrowing the westernized secular Shah of Iran, a network of Shiite clerics led by Imam Ruhollah Khumeini grabbed power and declared the Islamic Republic of Iran. To the surprise of the masses in the region—already
radicalized by Arab nationalists and Islamic fundamentalists—the Shiia Islamists elevated the level of antiwestern feelings and declared a direct war
against the United States. Arab nationalists and Sunni Islamists were both anti-
American, and most Pan-Arab forces were allies of the Soviet Union, but most
Sunni Islamists were allies of the Saudis. The Wahabi regime in Saudi Arabia
was in the midst of a strategic alliance with Washington against communism.
Hence, the breakthrough by Shiite fundamentalists in the late 1970s attracted
significant support not only from Shiia in Iran, Lebanon, and Arabia, but also
political sympathy from Sunni Arabs such as the Palestine Liberation Organization and secular nationalists such as the Baath of Syria.

The Khumeini revolution opened a space for Shiia radical politics to rise.
It equipped the group with a new Islamist ideology, relying not on the legitimacy of the Sunni caliphate but on the historic legacy of Ali.[15] For the first time
in thirteen centuries, a Shiia power was claiming the leadership of all Muslims
against the infidels. Departing from the "quietist" tradition of spiritual leaders
such as Ayatollah Sistani of Iraq and his predecessors, Khumeini and his
imams created a new creed. Instead of a caliphate, they installed a *vilayet el
faqih* regime. Translated as "mandate of the religious scholar," it meant that
Shiites and Muslims in general would have to follow the wisest imam while
awaiting the return of an absent religious messiah, the last survivor of the followers of Ali. Some may conclude that the radical Shiites were taking advantage
of the absence of the defunct Sunni caliphate. Putting the theological complexity aside, Ayatollah Khumeini created a novelty: an Islamic republic. Unacceptable by Sunni Salafi standards, the "republic" took very radical stances

toward fighting the "common enemy"—the *kuffar*. The Wahabi of Arabia did not buy the new Shiia jihad, nor did the Brotherhood—particularly in view of the fact that, on the face of it, it was a new competitor in the war against the enemy. In a sense, it seemed that whichever party succeeded in jihad could claim the Islamic leadership. Even worse, it was exposing some of the strategic alliances formed by the Wahabi with some of the infidels.

The Shiia Khumeini jihad bypassed and embarrassed the Sunni Salafi machine.[16] Clashing simultaneously against the two infidel powers of the Soviet Union and the United States, the Iranian regime appeared more politically and ideologically correct in the eyes of the radicalized Muslim masses of the 1980s. It opposed *all* infidels. Tehran engaged American power head-on in many ways and battlefields, especially in Lebanon with the U.S. Marines barracks bombing in 1983. Furthermore, Iranian Jihad created a regional tool for local battlefields against Israel: Hezbollah. Directly supported by Iran and protected by Syria (which was ruled by a Shiia offshoot, the Alawites), Hezbollah became the main Shiia competitor to the Salafi jihadist forces in the region. However, with time, the two international networks of jihadism—Sunni and Shiite— would converge on one path: relentless war against the United States.

Chapter Three

AFTER THE CALIPHATE

MODERN-DAY JIHADISTS, AND THOSE WHO WOULD BECOME al Qaeda and its nebulous offshoots and imitators in the 1990s, trace their legitimacy to what they call a "low moment in Muslim history." Osama bin Laden and several other leaders of the networks have clearly indicated that they have "assumed the responsibility of Jihad after the fall of the authority that was entitled to wage it for centuries: the caliphate." This statement is crucial for the understanding of current and future jihads. The terrorists the international community is facing do not consider themselves "illegal terrorists"; it is not only because they believe they have a cause, as most terrorists around the world do, but because they see themselves as the highest authority on Earth and heirs of the caliph—himself successor to the Prophet. This and only this explains their tenacious adherence to the jihad struggle in all its forms, including all types of violent behavior. To put it bluntly, in their minds, they represent the will of Allah on Earth. They consider themselves legitimate.[1]

The utter conviction of divine sanction, as unacceptable to the international community and even to Muslim mainstream governments and associations as it is, nevertheless remains the essence of the jihadi raison d'être. The historic melodrama that created a political body living in the present but with a consciousness from hundreds of years past started—as bin Laden and his associates have said—with developments in the first two decades of the twentieth century.

THE STATE OF JIHAD

From the first successors of the Prophet in the seventh century until the last Ottoman sultan in the twentieth, jihad was a state business. Under the caliphs, no call for jihad could be made outside of their authority; nor could any supersede

it. Even though, in the Middle Ages and after, many monarchs and local governors declared their own "holy wars" on neighboring enemies, the highest order
of the land remained that of the caliph. The rationale of the hierarchy was simple: The decision for war and peace rested in the hands of the successor of the
Prophet and the founding fathers, the *salaf.* The mission *(al rissala)* could not
be reinterpreted and could not change its drive. Jihad as a means for achieving
policies could be adapted to circumstances, both technological and local, but it
was not to be used for any mission other than the original one. Or at least that
is how it was accepted by the followers of the Ibn Taymiya doctrine and the
partisans of Abdel Wahab and Hassan al Banna. The Shiite brand of Islamism
developed a similar interpretation to that of the caliphate, that only the Islamic
state can wage jihad, but of course, intended a Shiite state.

Before and after the fall of the caliphate, debate raged on about such questions as: How does the state launch jihad? Are there conditions? Does it need
specific religious edicts, known as *fatwas,* or is it at the discretion of the
supreme commander of the faithful? What happens if the caliph does not con-
sult with religious clerics? All of these issues have caused tensions for a thousand years, and continue to do so among the followers of modern jihad. One
of these questions may be particularly relevant as we analyze the question of
future jihads.

As mentioned, when World War I exploded, there were Muslims on both
sides. The German-Austrian axis had the Ottomans, the bearers of official
Islam, with the sultanate as a caliphate. The Franco-British allies had millions
of Muslims who resided in their colonies—but more important, they struck a
deal with the Arab governor of Mecca, Sherif Hussein the Hashemite, a Sunni
descendant of Prophet Mohammed's tribe. With the encouragement of Berlin
and Vienna, the Sultan declared a jihad against the infidel allies. And at the
suggestion of London and Paris, Sherif Hussein declared his own holy jihad
against the Central Powers of Germany, Austria, and Turkey. As events showed
during that war, one jihad against another jihad equals no jihad. Deciding how
to solve two opposing jihads could have been the highest priority on state
agenda, had universal Muslim states survived the century. But by the mid-
1920s, the Muslim states had vanished; the Ottoman sultanate collapsed, and
the power to authorize world jihad was shattered.

COLLAPSE OF THE UNIVERSAL STATE OF JIHAD

A nationalist military leader and radical secularist terminated abruptly the thirteen centuries of the universal caliphate. In 1923, Kemal Mustafa (known also

as Ataturk, the father of Turks) took over power in the Ottoman Empire, abolished the institution of the caliphate, and declared the republic. By all the old standards of the seventh century, he had performed a putsch. Had a military officer canceled the caliphate in earlier centuries, he would have been branded as an apostate and put to death. But in the beginning of the twentieth century, the age of modern nationalism was rising and religion was somewhat marginalized, even among many revolutionary elites in the Arab world. The state institution of the caliphate was dismantled, and no other Muslim or Arab government has since reestablished it. The matter is extremely serious because, if reenergized, the caliphate could become a new superstate above the sovereignties of all Arab or Muslim governments. The question was and remains: Who would dare to declare himself the new caliph? As a corollary of the caliphate dilemma is the question of state jihad. If only the caliph has ultimate control over war and peace and the resumption of *fatah,* no one else could claim the authority to launch worldwide jihad except a caliph—or whoever claims to be one.

But here the situation becomes very complicated. If no government immediately claims the religious and political "inheritance" of world legitimacy of the caliphate, then ideological movements are tempted to step in and fill the gap. This is just what happened in the 1920s, and it goes to the heart of the entire question of legitimacy of jihad. Here lie the historical and ideological roots of today's terrorism and the war on terror. The taking up of jihad by the Salafis and their multiple jihadi forms and mutations has led to the universal "mission of jihad" that has emerged since the vanishing of the succession with the end of the Ottoman caliphate. The 1920s was a crucial time in this regard: The sultanate was dismantled, but the Wahabis took over in Arabia in the same period. From their marginal desert bases around Riyadh and Nejd they invaded the province of the Hejaz, seizing the immense prizes of Mecca and Medina. The holiest shrines of Islam fell into the hands of one of the most fundamentalist regimes in the history of modern Islam—the Saudis. Also during the 1920s, another fundamentalist network came out of Egypt, a more urban one that spread throughout the region: the Muslim Brotherhood. Had the caliphate still been in existence, both movements would have been under its purview and subordinate to it. But with no universal Islamic state holding ultimate authority, movements of individuals or sects controlling a single state apparatus could launch new kinds of factional jihad. Even by Salafi logic, no one really knows how a legitimate authority of jihad—a caliphate—would act and react to the modern world of international relations. Many Muslim states entered the world stage fully adhering to international law. The Islamic fundamentalists, however, though not comprising a state, decided to pursue jihad anyway, in their belief that they were the heirs of the Islamic state.[2]

THE JIHAD DIVIDE: WITHIN OR OUTSIDE INTERNATIONAL RELATIONS?

Perhaps the most challenging debate that grew out of the caliphate's disintegration dealt with the direction of jihad. At issue was not only who had the authority to wage it, but also at what level. Would the new jihadists—Wahabi, Salafi, and other fundamentalist Sunnis—accept international law as binding on their wars? Would they accept international institutions such as the League of Nations and eventually the United Nations? Would they accept norms higher than holy war and *dar el harb?* The debate is not over, and the jihadists seem to have split on the issue. But to be correct, the divide is about the means, not the principle. In the absence of a caliphate, all Salafi and jihadists postulate that no laws are higher than their own interpretation of *Sharia* and no obligation can supersede their jihad. Starting in the 1920s, in the absence of an ultimate authority that could command the believers, the militants—both regimes and organizations—spread out and propagated their different schools and doctrines.

THE WAHABI SAUDIS: TOP-DOWN JIHAD

When they established the basis of their government before World War II, the Saudis were a marginal but puritanical federation of tribes controlling the vast deserts of Arabia and the holy sites. The outside world was alien to them, especially as the greatest "infidel" powers were colliding in an apocalyptic fashion. The Saudi emirs, the Bedouin princes of the house of Saud, always acted pragmatically and shrewdly. Although faithful to the Wahabi doctrine, they knew how to align ideology with reality. Hence, with the end of the war, the Saudis made two historic choices. First, they adhered to international law as a tool of international relations. Yes, *dar el harb* was there ideologically, but their primary interest was *dar el Islam:* its revival, liberation, unification, and empowerment. Second, they chose the lesser of two evils among the infidels and allied themselves with the United States and the capitalists against the atheist communists (see chapter four). Their jihad was protected by the state, it did not undermine the state.

In the long run, the Wahabi Saudis, endowed by nature with some of the world's greatest oil resources (known since the 1950s), opted for a top-down approach. Their regime would organize the various stages that would make jihad viable over half a century. Not all emirs subscribed to it, but the general trend was to precede ultimate jihad with the development of an acceptable international environment. For jihad to be successful, it needed societies that believed in it; it also needed modern technologies and influence within the other camp (the *dar el harb*). The Wahabi state logic was perhaps the most perfect one: Float with the world, release the teachings without violence, let the teachings plant the seeds, wait for their growth, irrigate them with money, and make sure to mollify any abrupt reaction from the other side. The rich oil state maximized its advantages to the highest: oil and religious proselytzing.

This smooth strategy of "selling" the doctrine within the Muslim world, school after school and country after country, needed internal backing from within the kingdom. A historic deal was cut between the emirs on the one hand and the radical clerics on the other. The monarchy would manage the finances and political power, including diplomacy, while the scholars would be in charge of the souls, especially the young ones. The other component of the equation, the Salafi clerics, roamed the world preaching Wahabism with state funding and encouragement. The Saudi model of jihadism was endorsed by the rulers and funded by oil. The spread of Islamic fundamentalism was backed by the economic superpower of the Wahabi Saudis. In this environment, many future jihadists would choose the path of war against the infidels. The Saudi state generated an immense pool of Islamic fundamentalists inside the kingdom and worldwide, but ultimately it was not able to keep all these "students" under the check of the "teacher." One of those students, a model to others, was Osama bin Laden.

THE MUSLIM BROTHERHOOD: BOTTOM-UP JIHAD

With almost the same ideology, the Muslim Brotherhood of Egypt chose a different approach to spread its ideas and political influence: from the bottom up. Not trusting the rulers but willing to work with them, the Ikhwan strategy is as patient as the Wahabi but articulated differently. The Brotherhood of Hassan al Banna, one of the scions of modern-day jihadists, aimed to spread at the grassroots level outside the control of the government. When weak, the network lies low and expands slowly. When strong, or when events favor it, the group accelerates its activity and pursues its goals mercilessly. The "brothers" are keen to inculcate deep ideological teaching before engaging in the political struggle—but when they do, they are ruthless. They are neither intimidated by oppression nor swayed by causes greater than theirs. They wait for their moment in history, unimpressed by what the dominant political culture wants or calls for.

During World War II, the Brotherhood hoped the Nazis would win. After Israel was established, the Brotherhood, unlike most Arab regimes, preferred to gain support within the Arab world rather than to support what it perceived as a coalition of failing Arab regimes. To the Brotherhood, the war against the Jews and Israel cannot be won with un-Islamic (or not sufficiently Islamic) governments. During the cold war, their priority—like the Wahabis'—was to fight and defeat communism first before facing off with the capitalists. The *Ikhwan* opened chapters in most Arab and Middle Eastern countries as well as within émigré communities in the West. Competing with the Wahabis, they would become the backbone of most Islamist and jihadist organizations of the future. Behind the dominant and most extremist organizations of the 1980s and the 1990s lies the shadow, if not the umbilical link, of the Brotherhood. This rock-solid network generated waves of militants, one decade after another. Over generations they came to penetrate and influence the complex educational system in the region, as well as its religious and media apparatuses. Above all, they would eventually provide masterminds of terrorism to jihadist movements, including al Qaeda's number two man, Ayman Thawahiri.

The Wahabis and the Brotherhood are the pillars of Sunni Salafism. They intertwined, merging at times but competing fiercely at other times. They both produced offshoots, including leading jihad groups from Algeria to the Philippines. But the shattering of the caliphate not only released subcurrents among the Sunni radicals; it also allowed non-Sunni Muslims to emerge for the first time in history as a jihadi power.

KHUMEINIST JIHAD: SHIITE SUPERPOWER

The Shiites had been marginalized by the Sunni caliphate for centuries. With the decline of the Ottoman Sunni sultanate, Shiite political power rose again out of Persia. Modern Iran was already in existence when the caliphate was abolished in Istanbul. However, it would be several decades before fundamentalism among the Shiia community would surface into world politics. The Pahlevi dynasty ruled Iran throughout much of the twentieth century, focusing on developing national rather than religious power. With Iran blessed with oil, like Saudi Arabia, the modernizing but authoritarian regime of Reza Shah Pahlevi survived multiple crises until the end came in the late 1970s. The shah was able to muster the support of the clerical hierarchy by allowing them to share in his power. But the rise of Sunni fundamentalism was putting pressure on the Muslim world—and particularly on the Shiia, whom the Salafis often accused of being apostates.[3]

Iran's Shiia clerics could not allow further westernization by their monarch without attracting the criticism of their Sunni Wahabi competitors. But a series of power crises with the shah gave them the opportunity to rise up and remove him. An Islamic republic was established in the country in 1979, just in time to parallel the beginning of Sunni Wahabi uprisings against the Soviets in Afghanistan. Shiia fundamentalism produced a Shiia brand of jihadism. With a different dogma but with similar anti-infidel objectives, the Shiite jihadists aimed at the same enemies as did their Wahabi and Brotherhood counterparts.

But Iran's jihadist strategies were determined by the demography of the Shiites. While the Salafis could struggle and recruit wherever Sunni communities existed, the Shiia Islamists were limited to Iran and a few other countries in the Middle East where this minority branch of Islam flourished. As soon as Imam Khumeini took power in Tehran, the global drive of his regime was to build a superpower within the frontiers of Iran and assist the small Shiite communities in developing their own militant networks. Hence, the two arms of the Khumeinist jihad, as of 1979, were the arming of Iran as a greater power in the region and the spawning of terror networks, as in the case of Hezbollah in Lebanon.[4]

In the final analysis, after the collapse of the Sultanate in the 1920s, an unparalleled void was created in Islamic world politics. To most political establishments in the Muslim world, joining the emerging international relations was the right choice. However, to the fundamentalists, the future of Islam depends on its return to its past. Hence, as it was clarified by Ayman Al Qadiri, spokesman of the Hizb al Tahrir (Jihadist Islamist Movement founded in the 1950s in the Middle East), "the ultimate goal of our Islamist struggle is to rebuild the Caliphate, as a greater power and rebuild its armies. Only with state power we can achieve the goals of establishing Muslim power in the region and facing the West . . . only then we can resume the Fatah."[5]

Chapter Four

THE NAZI ALLIANCE

W E CAN SEE HINTS OF POSSIBLE FUTURE ALLIANCES forming among the ji-hadists by looking at the complex alliances of the past. After most of the Arab Middle East fell under European rule as a result of the Ottoman collapse, the Islamic fundamentalist movement began to look worldwide to find poten-tial allies against the Franco-British occupation. The Muslim Brotherhood, the Wahabis, and even the Pan Arab nationalists viewed the rise of radical nation-alism in Europe as a historic opportunity. The convergence between the two currents across the Mediterranean, although ultimately fruitless, had grounds in pure geopolitics. From various quarters of the region, including Cairo, Jerusalem, and Baghdad, leading figures of the transnational Salafi movement opted for a rapprochement with the emerging Nazi and fascist regimes in Berlin and Rome. The jihadi movement operated through the ancient geopolitical logic that the enemy of one's enemy could be a potential ally. Thus arose the Ji-hadic-Nazi-fascist axis.

Ideologically, the equation had no philosophical pillars. The National So-cialists of Germany promoted German racial superiority. Arabs and other Mideastern Semites were at the bottom of the ladder, lower even than the Slavs and Turks. The racist ideology of nazism was thus inherently incompatible and could not be adopted by the Islamic fundamentalists because of their own eth-nicities. In a global society ruled by the Third Reich, by "Aryan standards" Arab Muslims would be one level above the Jews. In Nazi thinking, a universal Germanic empire would not be coruled with southern Mediterranean "races" who were considered inferior, and a long-term joint venture between Hitler and potential allies in the Arab world was impossible.

For the Italian fascists, with their idea of the Roman "Mare nostra," the Mediterranean could accommodate neither Arab nationalism nor Islamic fundamentalism. On the Arab Islamic end, cooperation also was not possible, for the simple reason that the agenda of the jihadic forces called for the removal of *all* infidel presence from Arab and Muslim lands. Mussolini had been engaged in the opposite activity, having invaded Ethiopia and dreamed of a new Italian empire. Italians would have had to evacuate Libya and the Germans (if successful) would have to surrender British and French colonies and mandates back to a caliphate. Further down the doctrinal and geopolitical road, the supporters of the Islamic conquest—or *el Fatah*—were dedicated to resuming it beyond the borders of the old Ottoman empire. Thus, after the Axis victory over the Allies, another round of jihad would take place against the German Nazis and the Italian fascists. An ultimate confrontation along the lines of the clash of civilizations, regardless of who was on the other side, was ineluctable. The logic of jihad is not flexible, but can absorb a time factor. In sum, Salafi political thought throughout the late 1930s and at the onset of World War II sought an alliance with the German-Italian *kuffar* against the Franco-British *kuffar*, even though, on doctrinal grounds, a universal project with Nazis and facsists was not possible. But the calculation was rational, even within the Islamic fundamentalist ideology, insofar as the ultimate goal for the jihadists was to reemerge as a force capable of restoring the caliphate. What superseded in the jihadist agenda was the return of the global institution inside the Muslim lands. Reestablishing the caliphate was equated with satisfying Allah, and therefore benefited from divine support. Striking deals with some *kuffar* against other *kuffar* was in line with Salafi thinking; they often referred to examples from the preceding founders and even from previous caliphs. According to these references, in the early days of Islam, Prophet Mohammed had concluded agreements with non-Muslims as a way to concentrate on other enemies (also non-Muslims). Also, Abbasid Caliph Harun el Rashid signed treaties with the "infidel" emperor Charlemagne to balance power with the other "infidel" emperors of Constantinople. Islamic history abounds with these examples, and the twentieth-century Salafis used all of them to show theological legitimacy for their strategic choices.

But in view of the situation prevailing in the Middle East since the 1920s, the jihadic rationale in the 1930s was first and foremost geopolitical. Hitler's and Mussolini's armies were the rivals of French and British powers. Most Muslim lands were occupied by the latter colonial powers. The resources of industrial Germany and agricultural Italy were being massed against the interests of the Allies, and therefore were beneficial for jihad and *fatah*. The Ottoman Empire adopted a similar strategy at the beginning of the century. Istanbul perceived Britain, France, and Russia as its greater threats; hence the Turks sided with Berlin and Vienna against London and Paris, forming the Central Powers alliance. Although the move was clearly based on geopolitical equations, it was perceived by the post-Ottoman Islamic fundamentalists as a deliberate choice by the ruler of Islam—the sultan—to use the forces of two *kuffar* powers against even more threatening infidel powers. But after the abolition of the caliphate and the sultanate in 1923 at the hands of Kemal Mustafa Ataturk, the central decision-making authority in the Muslim world vanished. The Wahabis and Muslim Brotherhood took it upon themselves to embody the international decisions of the caliphate. They felt, like all Salafis, that the jihadic strategic decisions were to be decided and developed by them until the return of the *khilafa* (succession). Hence, as the collision between the Berlin-Rome axis with the London-Paris axis was projected, Islamists (but also many Pan Arabists) saw the strategic convergence of interest *(Taqatuh al Masalih)*. Germany had developed enough military power to confront France and England in Europe, potentially weakening them in the Middle East and North Africa. At the same time, fascist Italy would disrupt British and French maritime power in the Mediterranean. Although all these considerations favored siding with the Axis against the Allies, perhaps the most inflammatory argument in favor of an alliance with the Nazis was the Jewish question.[1]

The Jewish question in the Salafi doctrine is threefold: theological, historical, and geopolitical. It is obviously a major feature of the current jihadist-Jewish conflict (to be discussed in due course), but already in the 1930s both Arab nationalists and Islamic fundamentalists had perceived the growth of Jewish settlement in British-mandated Palestine as a "dagger planted in the midst of the *umma* (nation)." Arabs in Palestine had launched an insurrection against British rule and aimed at uprooting the developing *Yishuv* (the term for the local Jewish community prior to 1947). The Salafi-jihadic movement intended to reverse the process of infidel settlement on that very strategic area of Muslim land known to the West as the Holy Land. Their vision of events in Palestine was as follows: The British invaded the Arab Middle East, including Palestine, in 1919. The Jews had concluded a treaty with the British in 1917, embodied in the Balfour declaration. British infidels had since allowed Jewish infidels to immigrate onto the Muslim land of Palestine. Hence, by the same logic, the growth of the Jewish community in that area was not the result of natural demography under Muslim sovereignty but a consequence of a strategy designed jointly by two *kuffar* powers: the British and the Jews. The conclusion to this jihadic logic was simple: The Islamic fundamentalists had to shop for an ally with an ideology that sought to destroy the Jewish community universally and that had enough military strength and intent to clash with the other infidel power protecting the Jewish entity in Palestine. In the 1930s, such an ally was not difficult to identify: Nazi Germany. Thus, the jihadist solution to the mounting threat of Zionism in Palestine was to develop an alliance across the Mediterranean with Hitler's regime. A Nazi higher technology that would confront Jewish technological superiority and its British protection in Palestine, coupled with the Nazi's intention to destroy Jewish communities wherever they encountered them and their imminent confrontation with and likely defeat of the British empire, made the Nazi option too attractive in realistic political terms to be analyzed in strictly theological terms (under which, of course, it would have to be rejected). While Nazi infidels were ultimately anathema to jihadists, the alliance answered all their practical needs at the moment.

By the end of the 1930s, Islamic fundamentalist networks, often under the auspices of traditional leadership and sometimes within the wider context of radical Arab nationalists, sought rapprochement and alliance with Berlin. In Egypt, the Muslim Brotherhood hoped a war with the Axis would bring in the German-Italian forces from Libya across the border to seize the Suez Canal, ejecting the British from the region. In Syria and Lebanon, fundamentalist leaders envisioned that a defeat at the hands of the Germans would evacuate the French from the area. In Palestine and Iraq, revolts were brewing, waiting to be triggered by the advance of Nazi forces across Europe.

JIHADISTS AND WORLD WAR II

As the Wehrmacht marched into Czechoslovakia and Poland, and as the Luftwaffe bombarded the British Isles after the invasion of France, the Islamic fundamentalist and Pan Arabist movements of the Middle East rose up at different times, in different areas, and in different circumstances. In Cairo, according to Anwar Sadat's memoirs, the Muslim Brotherhood and a number of officers in the military were preparing to revolt had Bernard Montgomery's 8th Army not been able to stop Erwin Rommel's Afrika Korps. The plan was to inflame Egypt from the inside and explode an intifada along the valley of the Nile all the way to Ethiopia. In Palestine, the clearest pro-Nazi move was embodied by the mufti of Jerusalem, al Husseini.

Descending from a prominent *Qudsi* (Jerusalemite) family, which claimed its own descent from the Prophet, the Husseini were the most visible leaders of the city and of the Arab population. But the religious cleric Hajj Ali al Amin al Husseini jumped from anti-British colonialism to radical anti-Semitism, becoming Hitler's closest ally in the Arab-Muslim world. Traveling to Berlin, Mufti Husseini met with the Fuhrer, established an alliance, and projected himself not only as the Arab leader of Palestine but as the Third Reich's leading Muslim ally. The Nazi strategists wanted to see him play a role beyond Palestine; with a special program in Arabic broadcasting on Radio Berlin, the pro-German cleric mobilized Muslims in the Balkans against the Serbs and called on Muslim soldiers serving with the Allies to desert or rise up. Husseini was the highest hope Berlin had for an offensive south and east of the Mediterranean behind enemy lines.

In Iraq, Mohammed Rashid al Kailani led a military uprising against British rule in 1941 centered in what is today the Sunni triangle. In Syria and the Muslim areas of Lebanon, similar groups readied themselves for an eventual German landing as Nazi forces reached the Greek island of Rhodes. Had the Axis forces been successful at El Alamein, jihadic insurgencies would have met up with them in Egypt, Palestine, Syria, and Iraq. But the British were fast on all fronts: They eliminated Kailani's militias in Iraq and invaded Lebanon and Syria with de Gaulle's French forces to remove the Vichy France representatives. More important, they destroyed Rommel's Panzers in the Egyptian desert and in 1942 went on the offensive in Libya, rolling back the Axis and severing the strategic bridge between Nazism and jihadism. The attempt to defeat the infidel allies using the fascist infidels was over by 1943; with the fall of Berlin two years later, a new era started and the forces of jihad had to consider new strategies.

World War II was a major subject of contemplation for the Sunni Wahabi and Muslim Brotherhood and, later, for the Shi'a Khumeinists. Throughout the decades, jihadi intellectuals would rethink their strategies based on what their contemporaries had witnessed and the accounts by historians. In the years after September 11, 2001, bold extrapolations would be made public by Islamist thinkers. On al Jazeera TV, leading Ikhwan scholar Sheikh Yussef al Qardawi often cited World War II as a "war to learn from" and repetitively went over its *imthula,* or lessons. Similar conclusions were found on the web, particularly on al Muhajirun, al Khilafa, and al Ansar.

Al Qardawi spoke of the huge military machinery that "consumed millions of humans and an incredible amount of material within the world of *kuffar.*" He drew the viewers' attention to the fact that the infidels had destroyed each other's powers in an incredible way in the twentieth century, particularly during World War II. Asked about the wisdom of his predecessors—meaning the jihadic forces of the 1930s and 1940s—having sided with the Axis, he argued that Muslims should perform their *wajib* (duty) and Allah would decide the case. The Islamists focused on the fact that the West may well possess huge military power and resources, but Allah has his own way to destroy it. Some Salafi analysts reminded their audience of the mere size of the infidel global force at the eve of the war. "Just imagine," said a cleric in a chat room:

how gigantic was the combination of all kufr powers in 1939. Just add the military strength of Great Britain, France, Germany, Italy, Russia, America, let alone Japan. By our *aqida* [doctrine] they are all Kuffar. Had they united against Muslims in the 1940s, we wouldn't have had any chance. We were occupied, divided, weak, uneducated, and deprived of military power. But Allah subhanahu [religious praise] unleashed them against each other. They destroyed their military machines against each other in Europe, Russia, and the Pacific. Every battle they fought was a battle where the infidels were being destroyed, whatever was the winning side. That war [World War II] was preparing the path for Jihad. It helped us weaken them, then remove many of their armies from our midst.[2]

The philosophical conclusion is that jihadism does not have to fight all wars to defeat all enemies. The injunction to the mujahidin is to sacrifice all they can, including themselves when needed. Their contribution is part of a greater plan. A Salafi commentator reminded his audience of the early stages of the *fatah:* "Remember when our ancestors left Arabia in the first century [seventh A.D./C.E.]. The two superpowers of the time were the Persians and the Byzantines. They have been at each other's throats for hundreds of years."[3] When the Muslim armies moved forward, he said the *kuffars* were weak and exhausted.

Islamists have explained World War II in Europe as a sign by Allah, signaling the impending decline of the infidels after centuries of military and economic rise. Before the war, most of the Muslim world was under colonial infidel occupation. In the years after the war, one land after another was freed from the British, French, Italians, Dutch, and Portuguese. Hundreds of millions of Muslims obtained independence from foreign occupiers. This was seen as stage one of a Muslim "reconquista"—first of the traditional Muslim lands of the caliphate and later of the *dar el harb.*

By attempting to ally themselves with the Nazis and fascists in midcentury, modern Islamists sent this message: Their strategies for jihad and *fatah* supercede human rights, democracy, and peace. They were able to hold their noses and countenance an alliance with the Nazis. To them, jihad and ultimately *fatah* are all there is in international relations. Their alliances with the antidemocratic forces were not a "balancing act"; there simply was not anything else on the other side of the scale. Many westerners still believe that there is some sort of restraint on what the jihadists will do and what their ambitions are. But theoretically there is no limit to the *fatah* until the *dar el harb* ceases to exist, and there are no limits on the tactics to be used against the infidels.

Chapter Five

THE COMMUNIST DILEMMA

THE IDEOLOGICAL CONFRONTATION BETWEEN ISLAMIC fundamentalism and Marxism is universal and irreversible. It draws its endless enmity from the total opposition between Islam and atheism. Islamic theology projects itself as an heir to Judaism and Christianity (even though throughout history wars have been common between Muslim and Judeo-Christian civilizations) and sees itself as the last monotheist message from Allah. But between Islam and communism there is zero tolerance and no space for coexistence. Nonbelievers in Islam are perceived to fall into one of three categories. First, there are the faithful of the Abrahamic religions, revealed by Allah's prophets from Adam to Issa (Jesus). Theologically, Jews and Christians are admissible in the *dawla al Islamiya* (Islamic state) under the *dhimmi* status, until conversion occurs, as discussed earlier. The second category encompasses the religions that are either monotheistic, but not "of the Book," or polytheistic. These faiths have no place in an Islamic state, but arrangements can be made so that conversion takes place promptly. The third category is the worst by the norms of the faith. Believing in another monotheistic *risala* (mission), but believing in God (Allah), as is the case for Jews and Christians, is something that can be understood and absorbed. Believing in another religion or deistic belief system (i.e., another god altogether) is unacceptable and should be combated. But believing neither in Allah nor in any other god is completely outside the Islamic space. Hence al ilhad (atheism) is the total antithesis of Mohammed's religion. This total negation is the root cause of the Islamists' struggle against communism in all its forms. Since the inception of Marxism-Leninism until the collapse of the Soviet Union, the Salafis and the other brands of jihadists perceived and dealt with communism as the ultimate enemy of Islam, to be destroyed first. All religions, not just Islam, are philosophically opposed to atheist materialism and therefore to communism. But the Islamists, who are militantly opposed to all other ideologies, particularly the atheist ones, are on a direct path of war with Marxism-Leninism.[1]

Little was written by Muslim scholars in response to the surge of Marxist and socialist ideas at the end of the nineteenth century. The caliphate and its jurists were busy contending with the continuous weakness of the sultanate in Istanbul and with the growing non-Turkish Muslim discontent with the Ottoman Empire. Sunni Islamic scholars were worried about the Turkish Muslim state, and their Shiia counterparts were busy reemerging within the Persian monarchy. The Wahabis did not spend significant time on international political thinking, so they did not yet engage a threat that was perceived as the fruition of infidel political culture. In the eyes of Arabian Salafis, whose priority was to grab power in Muslim lands first, the Marxist-socialist thinking was a remote poison, which had not yet gained control of *kuffar* military power. Up until World War I, communism and Islamism were radical and antithetical ideologies, but were still brewing inside the areas of their genesis. Two sudden developments, however, would bring the radically opposed movements face to face.

In 1917 the Bolshevik revolution brought communist rule to Moscow—the single largest land empire of the infidel world. In 1919 the central Muslim empire, the Turkish caliphate, disappeared from world politics. The ascension of international communism and the collapse of the world Islamic state, coming virtually at the same time, could not have more starkly set the stage for an upcoming war of ideas and of militants. By the mid-1920s, Lenin and Stalin had launched the Soviet Union—perceived by the Islamists as the "eastern atheist power." In the Arab Muslim world, Salafi clerics and activists rendered their verdict: The Soviet Union was one of the most dangerous forms of *kufr*. Ideologically, Marxism-Leninism was out-and-out state atheism. Not only secular, as the French Revolution and the American political culture had been, it was actively antireligious, anticlerical, and the total enemy of Allah. On these grounds alone, and regardless of geopolitics, the Islamic fundamentalist movement was in total conflict with communism and with its state, the Soviet Union. Following the appearance of both state communism and radical Islamists in the 1920s, there would be no truce, no joint programs between the two, even though their geopolitical interests would converge at some points.

The history of the conflict between Islamism and communism grew as politics forced the two movements to clash and to intertwine. Ironically, in the mind of Salafis, the Soviets were another form of Russian power, extending past Slavic Orthodox ambitions into modern times. The Russian-dominated Soviet

Communist Party was perceived as the heir of Imperial Christian Russia—itself considered a historical extension of the defunct Byzantine Empire. Islamists are firm believers in the "civilizational" lineage. In the same way they see the United States as a modern transatlantic European power, regardless of the founding fathers' separation from the old continent, so they consider the Soviet Union as basically an old foe—the same Orthodox Russia, dressed in red with communist symbols.

The mere declaration of the Soviet Union as a new country, replacing the tsarist empire, brought under it large territories with Muslim populations. The Islamists in the Middle East considered Chechnya, Dagestan, Kazakhstan, Turkmenistan, and the other central Asian Republics as occupied Muslim territories. The Wahabis and the Muslim Brotherhood had the same logic in international relations: If a non-Muslim power controlled Muslim lands, it was an infidel power that fell under the shadow of jihad. The Soviets, as both communists and occupiers of Muslim lands, were therefore in a double sense infidels who had to be fought against urgently. They were perhaps the most dangerous part of the *dar el harb*.

Two more reasons put Islamic fundamentalists and communists on a collision course: The Soviet government adopted a policy of universal repression of all religions, including Islam. Stalin's harsh suppression of minorities and religious groups covered vast Muslim areas in central Asia and the Caucasus. Moscow's antireligious campaign did not single out one particular religious group, as it suppressed Catholics, Jews, Orthodox Christians, and Muslims alike. But ironically fundamentalists viewed the actions by the Soviet power against religions not only as atheist suppression but also as a Russian Orthodox war against Islam.

Another tactical reason behind the Salafi resentment of the communists was the increasing attraction of the latter to Muslims around the world. Marxism-Leninism and its socialist brand made tantalizing promises to the poor in all countries. Not only in the West (including America), but also in the Arab and Muslim worlds, intellectuals were naturally drawn to its logic and promise of social justice. This posed a significant problem to the rising Islamists. Many Muslim intellectuals, cadres, and academics adopted the Marxist-Leninist ideals, and many of them adhered to the communist parties. Furthermore, even some who did not integrate the Soviet doctrine formed nationalist secular parties with socialist ideologies, such as Baathism in Iraq.

The Islamists' no-tolerance attitude toward communism in the 1920s would shape their future conflicts and choices. For example, it would reinforce their sympathies with Nazi Germany, the enemy of their enemy. The Muslim

Brotherhood was actively seeking a victory of the Axis against the allies, including the Soviets. Berlin fantasized about an all-out jihad in Soviet central Asia, inasmuch as World War II Germany hoped Muslim colonies would rise up against British and French. In terms of future jihads, one can draw a few lessons. For example, the theological position explains why the Salafists chose to fight the communists and the Soviets first after the end of World War II. It reveals the rationale for an alliance between the United States and the jihadists—although they were the same Islamists who would attack America and who are in fact planning on doing so for the coming decades. In short, the Islamists, as an ideological group, have a doctrinal logic and a rationale of their own, one that can be understood and projected ahead of time.

In the 1930s and the 1940s Islamists stood by the Nazis and the fascists against the Allies, including Americans and the British. Then they converged with the Americans and became their allies against the communists during the cold war. After the collapse of the Soviet Union, they gradually moved to become the allies of the socialists and the left wing against the United States and its coalition. The jihadists have a strategy of their own and final horizons they aim to reach by playing one power against the other, until no power can stop them.

Chapter Six

ISRAEL'S FATE

THE DECLARATION OF THE STATE OF ISRAEL IN 1947 and the ensuing war was a massive event for the Islamic fundamentalists, Wahabis, and Muslim Brotherhood alike. The Zionist movement in Europe, the immigration into Palestine, and the ethnic conflict between Jews and Arabs in the Holy Land were not issues relevant only to the Salafists. Arabs of all backgrounds in the region (and Palestinian Arabs in particular) were in a state of war with Zionists around the world and with the Jewish community in Palestine in particular. Arab nationalists, monarchists, communists, secularists, and Islamists all adopted a common view of the emergence of a Jewish state, but Islamists adopted the most historicist and theological attitude toward the movement that would give rise to the state of Israel in 1948. Along with others, Islamists would join in the struggle against the Zionist state, but they would go beyond the other political currents insofar as they developed a unique doctrine on the concept of Jewish return to Israel. They would also build a theologically grounded analysis of the conflict and of the American relationship with Israel. First, we turn to the most salient issues in the jihadist perception of the Jewish state.

ISLAMISTS AND THE JEWS

Islamists of all schools see the Jews from a dogmatic perspective *(aqida)*. Moderate Muslims focus on the concept of "people of the Book," or *ahl al kitab,* an interpretation based on a number of verses of the Qur'an. Jews and Christians, according to the moderate view, are monotheist communities with a common bond to Islam. Without delving into the theological debate among the three religions, it is enough to note that the orthodox view in Islam postulates that Allah sent his prophets to humanity starting with Adam and sealed the message with the last Prophet, who is of course Mohammad. In between, Ibrahim (Abraham), Mussa (Moses), and Issa (Jesus) were all in fact Muslim prophets. The explanation of faith developed by Muslim theologians is that the peoples of the Book (the Bible and New Testament) were given the message, but did not apply it properly. Hence, according to mainstream teaching, the people of the Book are special communities related to but not in conformity with Islam. Some may make an analogy of the people of the Book to Muslims as being similar to what the Jews represented to early Christians, but many Christians reject this comparison.

Whatever the theological debates about the perception and relationships between Islam and the previous Abrahamic religions, it remains in the domain of religious philosophy. As was analyzed in chapter one, the Islamists, as an ideological movement, draw heavily from Islamic texts to define their political and legal relationship with others. In the case of the Jews, the Islamic fundamentalists undertook a "politicization" of both theological texts and past history. Their enmity to the Jewish phenomena, preceding the question of Palestine and also going beyond it, has important roots.

HISTORICAL ROOTS

Islamists admit that Jews are from *ahl al kitab*—but as portrayed by the jihadi literature, they are "bad" people of the book. The Salafi interpretation of the Qur'an and Hadith is tight, restrictive to the letter, and selects just those verses and paragraphs that depict the Jews as infidels *(kuffar)*. The theological dialogue among religions can use strategies to diffuse definitions and to moderate written descriptions. But the Wahabi-Salafi current wants just the opposite: to define Jews as "infidels" and as negatively as possible. Building on a rigid definition that is frozen in time, they consolidate it with examples from Islam's early history in the Arabian Peninsula. The main "story" presented by the fundamentalist reading is the episode of Khaibar, a town north of Mecca. The entire literature of Sunni and Shiite jihadists reminds its audience of the military confrontation between the Muslim army of Mohammed and the Jewish tribes in the oasis of Khaibar in the seventh century. According to historical accounts, the Arabian Jewish tribes refused to convert to the new religion. The Islamists' version accuses the tribes of betraying agreements made with the Prophet. Regardless of the historical uncertainty, bloody encounters certainly did take place and the Jews were defeated; many converted, many were killed, and others emigrated. But instead of seeing it as an episode of ancient history, the Salafi doctrinaires apply that episode to the rest of history. When Israel was formed in modern times, jihadis chanted, *"Khaibar, Khaibar ya yahood, jaish Mohammed sawfa ayud"* (Remember Khaibar, O Jews, the army of Mohammed is coming back). As mentioned in the early chapters, the main characteristic of the jihadist movement is its synchronic view of history. Today's battles are a direct continuation of millennia of confrontation, regardless of later developments.[1]

The bottom line to jihadists is that Jews are infidels who betrayed the Prophet, and were defeated by him, and later became *dhimmi* people who were governed by the Islamic state. In no case can the Salafi paradigm provide a space to the Jews outside this equation. Throughout history the Jews have been viewed as second-class citizens under a discretionary caliphate. But in contrast with other *dhimmis* and people of the Book, or with other dominated infidels, the Jews were perceived as weak, isolated, and irrelevant. Under the vast Umayyad and Abbasid empires, Jewish communities seldom resisted or received support from an outside power. Moreover, in the eyes of Salafi historians, Christian persecution of the Jews in medieval Europe further discredited them as a potential threat. For twelve centuries, Jews (unlike Christian *dhimmis*) were equated by the most extreme factions under the caliphate with evil, but seen as a *powerless* evil.

HISTORICAL EXCEPTIONS

There are two exceptional stages in the history of Jews under Islamic empires. The most noteworthy in the West was in Arab-conquered Spain. In general, Jewish life was relatively better in Muslim Andalusia than in the rest of the empire. Western scholars have attributed this fact to the theoretical concept of the people of the Book and its benevolent results when thoroughly applied by the Islamic rulers. Many Jewish and Israeli intellectuals have even hoped the Andalusian model could be borrowed to solidify twenty-first-century peace processes between Arabs and Israel. If Jews lived in peace under Arab Islamic power in Spain, they argued, they can also live in peace with Arab Muslim governments in the Middle East. Although the debate is wider and more complex, it remains the captive of political and historical realities. If we compare the situation in Arab-conquered Spain with today, the central issue is precisely the difference between "under" and "with." The theoretical possibility for Jews to live "under" Islamic rule existed in Spain and under the Ottoman Empire, as will be described shortly. Both experiments indicate that the option is possible—but only as long as Jews operate "under" Islamic rule, not alongside. An Islamist view of history, which draws from the precedent *(salaf)* and not from any vision of the future, may accept a *dhimmi* status for the Jews, as long as they live as a community adhering to Caliph Umar's conditions (*shurut Umariya;* see chapter one). But this acceptance is limited to the status as designed by the caliph. It does not extend to the concept of self-determination. In other words, Jews may be *dhimmi,* but they cannot develop a nationalism of their own that would claim an independent state—Israel. Jews have no more right to a separate political existence under the strict Islamist interpretation than any other group of infidels.[2]

The same perception applied to the second exception in history: Jews living in the Ottoman Empire. As many of the communities fleeing persecution in Spain at the hands of the Christian "reconquistadores" ended up in Istanbul, the sultanate devised a tolerant policy toward those who would become the Anatolian ladino.[3] The practical need of the Muslim central power to absorb Jewish skills into the Ottoman Empire was almost identical to the same "need" recognized by the rulers of Andalusia. The reasons for strategic tolerance in Spain and the Turkish sultanate can be debated by historians, but Salafi reinterpretation of these two exceptions is enlightening. Marginalizing that debate, the jihadi party line sees these two eras as in contradiction with what *should* have been and should be: little tolerance to empowering the Jews within the Islamic state. Wahabis, the Muslim Brotherhood, and other Sunni radicals—and even Shiite Khomeinists—draw their anti-Jewish ideology from their interpretation of theology and history. They do not see a free space for Jewish political culture within the state they intend to rebuild. They definitely reject what is even worse than an independent internal status for Jews within a caliphate: a full-fledged nationalist movement leading to the establishment of a sovereign state for the Jews.

Indeed, the rejection of Zionism was and remains at the base of all Islamist attitudes toward the Arab-Israeli conflict. When the Zionist movement spread throughout Europe, its impact was not recognized in the debates taking place in the Arab-Muslim world, especially under Ottoman rule, or even among Wahabi Arabian tribes. Arab and Muslim intellectuals from Cairo to Baghdad were busy finding answers to the dilemma of the caliphate, modernity, colonialism, and Pan Arabism. In reality, as long as Zionism was an idealist doctrine circulating in the European ghettos, it did not challenge the "think tanks" of the region. Many other minorities had many dreams and visions, but none transmuted into geopolitical realities. By the time early Jewish settlement took roots in the upper Galilee, along the coast, and in Jerusalem, the Islamic fundamentalist paradigm was in place. The logic of the Salafists—at some point overlapping with that of Arab nationalists—was simple. If Zionism means that the Jews are a people, this is fine, even if we have a negative impression of them. If they wish to live as a nation on a specific land, they can do that if they have the resources. But it cannot be an Arab land, and particularly not Palestine.

WHY NOT PALESTINE?

Why can Jews not resettle a land they see as ancestral, as far as the Islamic fundamentalists are concerned? The answer of the Salafi paradigm is enigmatic by historical standards, but can be explained in terms of geopolitics. To Islamists, every land that was conquered—or technically, opened—during the *fatah* under a legitimate Islamic authority *cannot* revert back to the infidels. This is the case of other nations and countries invaded by Muslim armies, including Spain, most of France, and parts of India and Russia. Zionism is attempting to take back a land that had been duly Islamized (by jihadic standards). On that ground alone, Islamic fundamentalists reject the very premise of Zionism. It is not about the size of the land or the regime established or the type of economy, or even the demographic changes it causes. Stretched to the limit, the Islamist approach would accept the relocation of Arab Muslim populations back and forth, if it was in the interest of the *umma,* but would not tolerate the relocation of an infidel population on a Muslim land if it was not authorized by the caliphate—and more important, if it were to develop into a sovereign infidel entity in the heart of Muslim territory.

The Salafi movement, encompassing the Muslim Brotherhood, the Wahabis, and other pro-*takfir* movements, saw the growth of the Jewish population of Palestine with the same anger as did Pan Arabists and local Arab populations. But the transnational Islamists calculated differently. While it was an issue of daily struggle for local Arabs in Palestine, the Salafists looked at the whole region. The tragedy was greater: France and Great Britain occupied the whole region. A mostly Christian nation was emerging in Lebanon. A Coptic prime minister was appointed in Egypt.[4] The Shiites were empowering themselves in Iran, and there were other issues as well. The Islamic fundamentalists had a variety of "global matters" to deal with, such as the reestablishment of the supreme world authority for Islam, the role of the Wahabi state, and internal issues in each Arab country. Hence, some Arab nationalists went so far as to accuse the Islamists, particularly the Muslim Brotherhood, of not putting Palestine at the forefront of their struggle before 1948. In reality, until about 1947, not everyone in the movement assumed that a Jewish state was imminent, especially during World War II. But events unfolded quickly at the end of the war.

JEWISH VICTORIES INTERPRETED

The first real victory of the Jewish state in the eyes of the jihadists was its recognition by the United Nations. This fact added an additional ingredient to their ideological refusal to recognize any international authority higher than the caliphate. The various Islamic fundamentalists in the region perceived the newly established international organization as a "product of the *kuffar*." The international legitimacy granted to the young Jewish state in 1947 was seen as a world conspiracy—instigated by the Jews themselves—to dominate a part of Muslim land and transform it into infidel land. From 1948 on, both secular Arabs and fundamentalists pressed for the dismantling of Israel, but from two different ideological angles. In future decades, the Palestine Liberation Organization, a secular movement, would begin to negotiate "pieces" of Palestine, a move rejected by the Islamists.

The Suez campaign of 1956 added more fuel to the Islamist theory of what we might call kuffarism. When Britain and France attacked Gamal Abdel Nasser's forces in Egypt, Israel's army was simultaneously invading the Sinai. The mere sight of this coalition operating jointly against an Arab Muslim country further convinced the Salafi movement that Jews and Christians were in full alliance against Islam. However, the Islamists were not positioned in the front row of the struggle against their Zionist enemy. In Egypt, Nasser had adopted a nationalist and socialist line, and had established a dictatorship intolerant of all political parties except his own. The Muslim Brotherhood went underground. It did not engage fully in the war against Israel, since the Arab regimes took the lead: Egypt, Syria, Iraq, and Jordan—most of them socialists and the Jordanian Hashemites pro-western. Only Wahabi Saudi Arabia was considered an Islamist regime, but it had no direct borders with the Jewish state.

A SIGN FROM ALLAH

The Islamists saw the third massive victory of Israel against the Arabs as a sign from Allah. In June 1967, Israel invaded the remaining Palestinian lands, as a result of Nasser's military mobilization. The Islamists hated Nasser almost as much as they hated Israel. In their view, Nasser had launched a losing war against a powerful and dangerous enemy, while oppressing the real warriors—the jihadists. Besides, the Salafists—and Arab nationalists—realized that Arab regimes had lost all of Palestine, which was now totally occupied by Israel. The June 5 war was a major wakeup call to all militant forces in the region: It elevated the Palestine Liberation Organization, a secular umbrella organization, to the top as a national liberation movement. The PLO under Yasir Arafat moved ahead of the Arab regimes in the resistance against Israel. The Islamists of the Muslim Brotherhood and the Wahabis remained in the back seat of the revolution. To the Arab in the street, the real choice was between the "regimes" on one hand and the "left-wing and nationalist" movements on the other. With the exception of Saudi Arabia, Arab countries and national societies such as the Palestinians did not yet see in the Islamists an ascending force. Perhaps one reason was the fact that both militant regimes and progressive forces made significant references to Islamic history, and their discourse was highly radical. The Islamists did not impress the masses with their actions, and their discourse was not radical enough to beat that of the regimes.

But with the Yom Kippur War of 1973, the Islamists had their first shot at a war against the infidel Jews. At first, the Egyptian armies of Sadat and Hafez Assad threatened to overrun Israel's front lines in the Sinai and the Golan. But with significant U.S. supply support to Israel and a counteroffensive on the southern front, the Egyptian third army was surrounded and later the Syrian forces were pushed back toward Damascus. Never in history were two Arab capitals so threatened by a Jewish army. The Islamic fundamentalists in both countries, and in the entire region, no longer believed that socialist Arab regimes had any hope of victory against Israel. In their historical reading of the war, they saw two messages in Israel's overwhelming victory: Only a "true Islamist" state can defeat Jewish power, and for such a victory, a strategy of assembling forces around the *umma* was needed. Hence, waging jihad all over the world was also a global fight against Zionism. Direct engagement with the Jewish state can succeed only when a greater Islamic power arises and when the fight against Israel is done on totally "Islamic" grounds, that is, according to their own code.

As the Jewish state became a reality and prospered, Islamists viewed the entire existence of Israel as an aggression. The initial settlement was illegitimate to start with; Jews had no rights to "return" or come back to an Islamic land. The problem was not the number of Arabs who were displaced, often the putative justification for Arab and Palestinian claims. It was not the size of Israel before and after 1948, or the nature of any agreement or settlement. It was about the principle of a non-Muslim state reemerging on a Muslim land. Following the logic of the *fatah* and of jihad, any territory that was at some time "opened" by a legitimate Islamic authority cannot revert to a non-Islamic authority. The matter in Islamist ideology is in the first place doctrinal, not geopolitical. The jihadist solution does not offer any kind of borders, neither the pre-1967 nor even the Jewish enclaves prior to 1947. It only strives for the "removal" of the organized and autonomous Jewish presence from Palestine, period. Moreover, it is not only about Palestine but also about any other territory that was conquered and absorbed by the caliphate (technically, until 1923). In one of his speeches in the fall of 2001, weeks after September 11, Osama bin Laden said the "tragedy which Muslims are experiencing is eighty-seven years old." Of course, he was referring to the year the sultanate collapsed. To Islamists, all world Islamic order is to be recaptured, reorganized, and reintegrated. The question of Palestine is therefore not one of national resistance. Palestine is a part of the Muslim world that was "taken away by the settler Jews," not just a homeland that the Palestinian population has lost.

JIHADISM IS WIDER THAN PALESTINIANISM

The Islamist jihad logic may overlap pragmatically with the Arab nationalist ideology, Palestinian patriotism, and related ethnic claims, but jihadism is wider and more global and answers higher challenges. Palestinian Islamists may be fighting alongside Palestinian nationalists, but their project is about the whole empire, not just one of its "provinces." From that perspective, the Islamists see the connection between the infidel state of Israel and the American infidel power as organic. The Jewish state is an outpost to a global infidel empire that is America. By ideological standards, the United States is a *kuffar* power. But its actions make it a highly dangerous one. As will be analyzed later, American policies of support to other "infidel" powers increased its deeply negative image in the eyes of the Salafis. Because it supports Israel, it has become implicated in the battlefield of the Middle East—and against the fundamentalists.

But the capacity of Salafi thinking to be global and strategic has produced complex choices understood only by those who plan and manage the Islamists' "world governance." Here is the most contradictory position the jihadists have adopted toward the United States in modern history: After the invasion of Afghanistan by the Soviets in 1979, the Islamic fundamentalists had to make a difficult choice. In the Middle East, they had adopted the concept of an all-out refusal of the Jewish state since its inception. They were not successful at first in leading the fight against the "Jewish entity" because of the dominance of the secular Arab "regimes" and the ascendance of the secular PLO. But nevertheless they continued to consider America one of the major infidel powers. But despite this ideological attitude, the Muslim Brotherhood, Wahabis, and all other Salafi were in agreement that they should conclude an alliance with the United States against Soviet occupation of the "Muslim land" of Afghanistan. This strategic equation is typically jihadist. It explains how the Islamic fundamentalists view their world map. Striking a deal with the United States on Afghanistan while still considering the United States their chief enemy ideologically (and the main supporter of Israel) is the greatest example of their strategic flexibility and malleability. It demonstrates, as in many other cases we will review, that a universal doctrine on *taqiya* (dissimulation) has been used and will continue to be used in future jihads. One enemy can be used against a more immediate enemy; with their eyes on a prize that was theirs in the remote past and for which they are willing to work for decades, Islamists can afford to exploit and cooperate even with the United States.

From 1948 until the mid-1980s, the global Islamists maintained their doctrinal attitude of total rejection toward Israel but participated in the military efforts only when their organizations were the leading forces on the ground or when they distinguished themselves as the "brightest" and the most legitimate. Their goal was more to destroy Israel than to establish a Palestinian state. Some of their jihadi cadres traveled thousands of miles to fight the *kuffar* in the remote lands of Afghanistan even though "Zionist infidels" were deploying their military power on Palestinian lands. It was only when the global equation of jihad saw a strategic opportunity to unleash a prime Islamist struggle on Palestinian lands that the movement materialized on the battlefield of Gaza, the West Bank, and eventually inside pre-1967 Israel. The Muslim Brotherhood, which continued to build its own infrastructure for decades within the Palestinian communities, became more sophisticated after 1973, when the Wahabi regime of Saudi Arabia used the weapon of oil against the West. The Salafi movement among the Palestinians maneuvered cleverly within the Fatah organization,[5] the networks of religious clerics, socioeconomic entities, schools, and other less visible institutions until their moment came. As soon as the PLO was ejected from Lebanon in 1982 and went into exile in Tunis, Islamist groups emerged inside the occupied territories. By the mid-1980s, to many Palestinians, the "Islamist movement of Palestine" had partially replaced the exclusive legitimacy of the PLO.

HAMAS AND ISLAMIC JIHAD

When the first intifada exploded in 1987, a new offshoot of the *Ikhwan* spread throughout the Palestinian communities: Hamas. The group, whose full name is Harakat al Muqawama al Islamiya (the Movement of the Islamic Resistance), was a mixture between a more aggressive Muslim Brotherhood and battlefield Wahabism. It drew its ideology from the first generation of Islamic fundamentalists but presented a platform for a local Palestinian arena for jihad. The

Palestinian Islamic Jihad (PIJ) erupted after Hamas as a more reduced and less populist organization. Hamas's institutions have received the financial support of the Saudi government and charities since the early 1980s. But the new jihadist forces developed their own funding from their networks of donors, including some in the United States.

As of the late 1980s and particularly since the early 1990s, Hamas and PIJ opted for a relativist doctrine regarding Israel and the United States. In what is most likely a strategic choice made by their own leadership, and possibly following the advice of the central jihad mother ship in Saudi Arabia and beyond, the jihadists of Palestine went into a full-fledged war against Israel, sinking all attempts for a peace process. But these two groups were extremely careful not to engage U.S. targets worldwide or within the U.S. mainland. There are two reasons for this Palestine-centered battlefield strategy. One was that both Hamas and Islamic Jihad had decided to build a network of fundraisers within the West in general and the United States in particular. It would have been difficult and counterproductive to attack American targets under a "Palestine Jihad" label while sitting comfortably on U.S. campuses and in American neighborhoods, collecting money almost openly for the war against Zionism and America. Many in the United States and the West could not understand why Hamas and PIJ would not conduct attacks or suicide killings in American cities and towns. The main reason is that they have chosen to fight one infidel at a time and to concentrate their resources on America's main ally in the region, Israel, hence ultimately weakening the United States. The second reason, emerging after September 11, is the distribution of roles. The main vehicle of jihad—at the moment, al Qaeda—fights America head-on and everywhere. It will decide when and how to handle jihad against the greatest infidel power. Meanwhile, Hamas and PIJ are "regional" jihad forces whose battlefield is restricted to Palestine. This is another example of the complexity of the international holy war against the infidels in general and the United States in particular.[6]

ISRAEL AS A LOCAL BATTLEFIELD

The Islamist Salafis of Palestine are engaged in their local battlefield in Israel and will continue to focus there until another equation presents itself. Individual jihadists among the Palestinians are engaged against the United States either overseas or inside America, and also against European targets. The "organized" entities, such as Hamas and PIJ, have developed networks in the continental U.S. mainland and internationally but have not attempted to engage directly in the war against America. But, as they are connected to the international mother ship on a multitude of levels, they provide information, technical assistance, and financial contributions, and would send militants to battlefields if the international command so decided. But the most dangerous war effort provided by Hamas and PIJ membership and supporters within the United States, and around the world, to al Qaeda and future global jihadists is related to political and national intelligence. PIJ members have built or integrated political organizations under American and European laws. These lobbies, operating within the system, can and have been able to serve the interests of global jihad inside the American institutional establishment—legally. This activity ranges from building networks on campuses all the way up to lobbies that have been received at the highest echelons of government, including the White House. Although al Qaeda would find it very difficult to penetrate the U.S. system directly, its allies who operate through American-based organizations can provide assistance. Hence, the structure of Palestinian Salafis' jihad against the United States is complex and multidimensional.

In Palestine, Hamas and Islamic Jihad wage their most relentless war against their direct enemy, the state and the people of Israel. In the United States, these networks are (or were, at least until September 11) protected by or hidden inside American-based pro-jihad organizations. The latter join forces with other jihadi political networks in the United States to provide al Qaeda and the international jihadist web with a valuable assessment of American national security. Such networks exist in Europe and other regions, to varying degrees. The Hamas and PIJ networks in America and Europe are "reserve forces" for the next wave of global jihad attacks against the West. This distribution of roles allows the "reserve" to grow, while supplying the mother ship with assistance. The next greatest danger to America's security, in the context of the war between Palestinian jihadists and Israel, is when the "global jihadists" unleash all their forces and allies—including Hamas and PIJ—simultaneously within the United States and against worldwide targets in a planetary assault.

The jihadists see Israel and the United States as one bloc, but have designed a complex strategy to confront them. This strategy can be found at all levels of international jihad. It has been applied to all other enemies of the fundamentalists—across the Atlantic and around the world.

Chapter Seven

WHAT THE COLD WAR
MEANT FOR THE FUTURE

OFTEN SALAFI COMMENTATORS PRESENT A REVISIONIST VIEW of the monumental clash of World War II. In their writings, and recently on their Web sites and on al Jazeera panels, jihadi ideologues describe the encounter between the military machines of infidel powers in the 1940s as a punishment from Allah. They perceive it as the divine will to break down the arrogant empires that had insulted Allah for too long. I have been amazed how jihadi minds link together historical events separated by thousands of years, and I have wondered at times if they were actually right in some ways. The Salafi analysis compares the latest world wars, particularly insofar as they bear on the European powers, as a reminder of the wars of antiquity that raged around the Arabian Peninsula. Modern fundamentalists compare what Arabs know commonly as the *Jahiliya* (prehistoric times of ignorance) with the twentieth century.[1] The fall of the caliphate has brought *Jahiliya* back and its attendant wars between the various infidel nations. In 2003 Sheikh Yussef al Qardawi, the principal thinker behind the Muslim Brotherhood, described on al Jazeera TV the perception of that war: "Terrible machines destroying each other, exactly in the manner the Kuffar kingdoms destroyed each other before the Fatah." But in 1945 the world was radically different from the earlier *Jahiliya* period he referred to; instead of being multipolar, the bipolar world of the cold war had emerged, and would dominate for another forty-five years. How the Salafis saw the cold war period, and how they decided to deal with it, clarifies many issues that led to contemporary and future jihads.

THE TWO INFIDEL EMPIRES: BACK TO THE FUTURE

With the United States and the Soviet Union forming their respective blocs and alliances after World War II, the world split into two zones. Instead of *dar el harb* and *dar el Islam,* the planet was divided mainly between the North Atlantic Treaty Organization (NATO) and the Warsaw Pact. But in the eyes of the jihadis, both alliances were ideologically part of the *dar el harb.* By their standards, it was a balance of terror inside the enemy zone. Both Americans and Soviets were seen as heirs of the Judeo-Christian civilization, regardless of the Marxist identity of Moscow's regime and the capitalist culture of Washington. Both superpowers were infidels; both were a threat to the reemergence of the caliphate. Even if reincarnated, the caliphate would be faced with having to combat both these infidel empires. It was Byzantium and Persia all over again. Not surprising, then, that the post–World War II period brought the resurrection of jihad.

With a powerful synchronic comparison with the seventh century A.D./C.E. context, modern-age jihadists drew a similar painting: The Americans are the Byzantines to the west; the Soviets are the Persians to the east. In the middle, the Muslim world is divided and weak, and within it are the holy fighters of Allah, armed with faith and determination. In such a predicament, how should the forces of jihad organize and strategize to achieve their goals? The answers to this question explain their policies during the second half of the twentieth century and allow us to project their thought patterns into the next half-century.

The United States is a remote power, a nation of immigrants, with little experience in the Arab and Muslim world. Its identity is still in formation and its foreign policy priorities are simple. If U.S. national security is not threatened directly, then the nation's most important pillar is economic. It is a society living off and dedicated to an open market economy; it has no other hard ideology or mission worldwide. Hence, as long as you do not wage a direct war against the U.S. mainland or threaten it with strategic weapons, you can escape its power. Even better, if you find common enemies with the United States and also provide it with essential resources (oil), you are shielded from its retaliatory power. Ironically, you can criticize it, incite your masses against it, and even call for its destruction, and it will not turn its power against you. In strategic terms, the Islamic fundamentalists understand very well that the United States is an ultimate cultural enemy—but a very sizable and attractive one. So, even without the oil weapon, Wahabis and Salafis chose to manage the western powers led by Washington and to concentrate on the red "devil" instead. The global jihad strategy was to "contain" the new Byzantium while "rolling back" the new Persia.

The Soviet Union was seen as a greater danger to the return of the caliphate than the capitalist West. I have already mentioned how, because the communists were atheists, they had no place under Islam, according to the fundamentalists. They had no link to the Abrahamic story. Chat rooms on the Web provide "educational sessions" on the subject, and I have heard lectures in which it was stated: "Communists and socialists cannot be part of the Islamic state; they are the antithesis of it. Christians and Jews can be *dhimmis,* because they are people of the Book. Communists aren't in any book. Marxist Leninists didn't exist in the seventh century, and jihad [theological jurisprudence] has been declared closed; hence, any new doctrine that came after is unacceptable and unfit to exist within Islamic society." The first wall is unbreachable: There is simply no status possible for all non-Abrahamic communities.

But there were other more practical considerations as well. As mentioned earlier, the Soviets were not only dominating large areas of the Muslim world in Asia, but they were de-Islamizing them by force. In contrast with the ailing British and French colonial powers, the rising Soviet empire was uprooting mosques, suppressing religion, and, in the eyes of the fundamentalists, imposing socialism—ironically perceived as a Judeo-Christian product. All this in addition to the fact that it fell within the worst of all theological categories, atheism.[2]

But ultimately, politics talks: The communist parties were making progress in the Arab and Muslim world. They were well organized, equipped with a solid ideology, attractive to the lower classes, and fighting the other "infidels": the West. The public in the Middle East saw the communist parties as anti-imperialists, helping the weak nations against European occupiers. The "culture of the Kalashnikov" and the portraits of Che Guevara were sexier than the long treatises of Hassan al Banna or the stiff appearances of the Saudi regime. Nasser was supported by Moscow; so were the Baath rulers of Damascus and Baghdad. The eastern bloc essentially sustained the war effort against the Zionists. Algeria's revolution was socialist, and the only support that came from inside western societies was from the left. So how could the obscure Islamists gain respect and admiration among Arabs and Muslims? The Soviet sun was too bright to be eclipsed by the "reactionary" Islamists' invitation to return to the Dark Ages. The Soviet-backed struggle was more efficient than the promise of religious jihad. Decolonization was moving fast in the Arab world, thanks to the eastern bloc; communist Vietnam was ultimately defeating the United States. Clearly, the worldwide left was dislodging western imperialism. It became strategically crucial for the Wahabi regime, the Salafi clerics, and the Muslim Brotherhood to engage the communists. Defeat the more dangerous enemy first, then turn to the less dangerous one. One enemy at a time.[3]

THE "ISLAMIC CAUSES" BETWEEN JIHAD AND NATIONALISM

The Islamists had to address one major challenge under the cold war: How to prioritize the jihad. They had to conciliate "national struggles" of the Muslim peoples within the "Islamist cause." In other words, they had to decide whether all national causes in Muslim lands are really "Islamic." In many regions, from South Asia to North Africa, local resistance movements were active against "foreign occupation" or other ethnic nationalities: in Kashmir in India, Algeria, Sudan, northern Cyprus, Iraq, and so on, including, of course, the most central struggle in the region—the Arab-Israeli conflict. Whenever one side was at least nominally Muslim, the Salafis sided with that side in all causes. The adage "rescue your brother if he is an oppressor or an oppressed" *(Ansur akhaka, Thaliman kana aw Mathluma)* applies firmly. Brotherhood in religion is justice, in the eyes of the Islamic fundamentalists. For example, they supported the northern Turks over the southern Greeks in Cyprus regardless of the chronology of events.[4] They endorsed the Muslim separatists in the southern Philippines but not the Catholic Ibarra secession in Nigeria. They supported Muslim Kashmir's self-determination but not southern (and Christian) Sudan's. The cause was not the issue; it was the priority of the supreme issue, religion, over all others.

In a very complex analysis, the Islamic fundamentalists chose jihad over national secular resistance and opted for strengthening the higher cause of the caliphate over the lower nationalist causes. They obviously stood against Israel—not to build a Palestinian secular state, however, but to reestablish an "Islamic" Palestine. This worldview of jihad was not well understood during the cold war, or even now, by most western academics and politicians. For example, after September 11, 2001, many rushed to conclude that bin Laden was attacking because he wanted a Palestinian state. In fact, the leader of al Qaeda never uttered the word "state" in connection with the Palestinians. He wanted Israel eliminated, but never pledged a state for the Palestinians, for in his mind "Palestine" was to become simply a province within the caliphate, not a country in itself. In sum, the jihadists were swimming with the third world crowd but had their own ideological agenda. Only after 2001 did the West begin to grasp this sophisticated and Machiavellian tactic of the jihadists.[5]

WAHABI STRATEGY: USING THE INFIDELS' POWERS

During the cold war, the Wahabis adopted a peculiar strategy from their fortress in Saudi Arabia. Although the doctrine was not expressed in any particular public policy agenda, its traces can be detected all over world politics. Inside the kingdom and throughout the clerical networks, an ongoing debate examined the concept of using the resources of the infidels to achieve the goals of jihad. The more isolationist and narrow-minded religious zealots opposed any contact with the *kuffar,* period. They considered them as "impure" and untrustworthy. They argued that all righteous Muslims should strictly apply the *Sharia* law (Islamic legal code). By doing so thoroughly, Allah would be pleased and would grant victory to the *umma.* This could be called the "maximalist" position among the Salafis. But then there were the "realists," who believed firmly in Allah's ultimate role in defeating the infidels, but argued that people of faith should carry the torch and offer sacrifices to please Allah, so that he could assist them. The Wahabi state had the resources capable of promoting global jihad, which the Wahabi clerics legitimized. They converged on the strategy of using the services of one major infidel superpower, the United States, to weaken and defeat the other superpower. The Saudi regime argued that its state institution needed arms, protection, technology, diplomatic recognition, intelligence backing, and allies to face the most imminent threat, the communist influence. It also kept alive the recognition that the Americans are infidels.

The Wahabi strategy ran as follows. Inside the kingdom, the *Sharia* law would be applied in the most restrictive way. Pure Wahabism would start at home. Saudi Arabia became the most Salafi-run country in the world: no political parties, no separation of powers, few rights for women, and the application of the religious code at its most draconian—beheadings, chopping off of hands, and so on. And, of course, there was to be no religious freedom. And as the "true Islamist state" was being rebuilt in Arabia, a jihad-shaped foreign policy was put in place.

It followed two tracks. The long-term one was a sustained policy of financial and diplomatic support to Islamist networks around the world, within the framework of charities, mosques, hospitals, orphanages, and of course religious schools. During the four decades of the cold war, several waves of Wahabi sympathizers and adherents traveled around the world. Tens of thousands of believers in jihad became the pool from which jihadists would be recruited by radical organizations in the future. The Wahabi graduates of the Saudi-funded institutions, both inside and outside the kingdom, are the result of a systematic policy of indoctrination lasting almost half a century. No wonder that al Qaeda and its sister organizations around the world have enjoyed an endless strategic depth and source of manpower. They recruit not just from their own schools of cadres, but also from what oil resources have allowed the Wahabi realm to foster worldwide for many years.

A second track of Wahabi international strategy was to use its own natural and financial resources to influence the West, build alliances and diplomatic support for its regime, and shield Islamic fundamentalism under the protection of the "infidels." This incredibly astute (not to mention ironic) strategy was at the origin of the jihadists' success in the late 1980s and 1990s against the West and the United States. In short, the Wahabi international policy aimed at growing and protecting the Salafi groups by using oil-based influence. In turn, the rising networks took advantage of the Arab-led Saudi lobby worldwide to escape scrutiny and in some cases even to be hailed as allies by their future victims, including the United States.

The very first achievement of Wahabi policies during the cold war and in the decade after its end was to situate itself as mainstream and respectable in world politics, particularly within the industrialized and liberal West. Ironically, a regime that was grounded in extreme religious radicalism was revered by liberal elites calling for democracy everywhere—except within the kingdom and its protégés. Using its privileged position as protector of the holiest shrine of Islam, Saudi Arabia attracted significant diplomatic recognition and support from the United States and the western bloc. As it was staunchly anticommunist, the regime was welcomed into the global anticommunist effort. It was able to apply antiwestern rules inside the country, spread radical anti-infidel teaching worldwide (even within the countries of its own allies), and yet was backed by Washington and its partners in Europe and elsewhere.[6]

The Wahabi strategy during the East-West conflict was unparalleled in modern history: It was fighting the Soviets with the power of the United States even while it was spreading the very ideology that was to target the security of America in the future, after the Soviet Union had fallen. There could hardly be a better illustration of the long-range thinking of jihadists, who are always already working toward the long-term defeat of their current allies. Furthermore, as the diplomatic shield was growing worldwide, Wahabi activities within the West and the United States grew even bolder and took roots inside the political establishment. For example, there was a massive effort by the Saudis to get the documentary *Death of a Princess* pulled from PBS. Around the same time, they ran a series of ads promoting how "progressive" the Saudi state was. Saudi grants to schools, pro-Wahabi lobbies, and friendly businesses spread even inside the lands of the "infidels." A culture of "camouflage" rapidly spread within the western political establishment: Wahabism was sanitized to such an extent that it could even weigh in on the American perception of jihadism. As I will detail later, Wahabi influence penetrated the political culture of America and the West so deeply that the latter lost the ability to see Wahabism for what it was. No wonder the jihadi literature found its paths to campuses and public forums and was able to form support networks in the open. Consider the example of the female Federal Bureau of Investigation officer who in 2001 rushed to warn her superiors after learning that a number of Saudi flight students were learning how to fly but not to land aircraft. Washington's response was typical of the times: There was no answer.

The political economy of oil added huge power to the Wahabi thrust worldwide. The "economic partners" of the Saudis in the West—the multinational energy corporations—became the first extensions of its influence on all levels. If the Saudi regime planned on weapon acquisitions, its friends would cut the deals. If the Saudis wished to introduce their views—or to impose them on—the U.S. educational system, their "American" partners did the groundwork. The greatest achievements of the Wahabi lobby were its "American" tentacles. But with the 1973 boycott crisis by the Organization of Petroleum Exporting Countries (OPEC), a new factor added itself to the "respect" created by the Saudis' anticommunism and the oil partnership: the looming threat of an interruption in the supply of oil. With a global show of force, Riyadh's establishment and its Arab partners sent one striking message to the West: You will do as we say in international politics, you will not undermine our Wahabi doctrine, and you will abide by our policies within the Arab Muslim world—otherwise, you will find yourselves biking to work like the Dutch! (As a result of the 1973 oil boycott, many European countries, such as the Netherlands, had to face draconian measures, including gas rationing. The response in the Lowlands was to use their bicycles for months.)

In the midst of a raging cold war, with the Vietnam crisis lurching toward its torturous end and a boiling Arab-Israeli conflict, the West submitted to the god of oil and opened its gates even wider to the flow of Wahabi influence. But were the Saudis using this influence to feed terrorism directly, as some have concluded after September 11? The situation was never that simple. The long-term objectives of the Wahabi strategic planners were to achieve gradual technological superiority, use the power of the West to reach foreign policy goals such as facilitating Wahabi influence in the region, and ultimately spread the ideology worldwide, all at an acceptable pace. This worked well, but what the Wahabis did not predict was the speed of growth in its own product: the neo-Wahabi. This issue will be explored later on.

MUSLIM BROTHERHOOD STRATEGY: USING THE POWER OF MUSLIMS

For their part, during the cold war the Muslim Brotherhood followed the general guidelines of the Wahabis, but since it was not in control of a government and was in most cases suppressed by other regimes in the region, it developed a different strategy. While the Saudis had the luxury to use the powers of others, mainly the United States, the Ikhwan preferred to use the powers of the community they wanted to mobilize. The group's dense and complex writings over half a century focused on infiltrating the group's home countries, starting with the Arab and Muslim societies, so that they could be in full control of their destinies. The Brotherhood was extremely careful so as not to engage the regimes before reaching full capability. Their military and subversive doctrine was amazingly fluid and adaptable to circumstances. Their ideal shortcut was to infiltrate the ranks of the military and proceed with a coup d'etat against the government. Their next choice was to "advise" the ruler and influence him instead. This approach would start from the bottom-up and then reverse into a top-down mechanism. Hence, the Brotherhood would be interested in spreading through the elites, converting them patiently into the Salafi doctrine, and only then enlisting them in the organization. The Muslim Brotherhood often created front groups, both inside the Arab world and within emigre communities. Known to be very patient, the members distinguished themselves in smart deception.

In contrast to recent more radical organizations such as al Qaeda and its allies, the Brotherhood has made sure to camouflage its literature.[7] As I noted in many of the documents I reviewed for U.S. and European courts dealing with terrorism cases, a significant segment of the "intellectual material" was marked by Ikhwan's influence: The group seldom called for a direct confrontation with the ruler *(al haakem),* which was a recourse of last resort if he stopped abiding by the rule of *Sharia* or if he became obstructionist. The Brotherhood wanted full legitimacy on its side and projected an image of being the "aggressed," not the aggressors. Members acted as hardworking militants transforming the society in which they live into a *gruyère* (a French cheese, full of holes). Their ideal plan is to make ideological reversal impossible. Educational and media institutions are the ideal tools for their campaigns. Their impact will be felt across the school system and in many cases within the media web. This trait was omnipresent in the audiotapes I examined as the government's expert in one particular terror case. The speaker, a Salafi cleric from Egypt whose words reached as far as Detroit, said clearly: "We need to preach jihad in schools; the culture of jihad must become the first nature of our youth."[8]

Indeed, the Brotherhood's ideology is clear and self-explanatory. The path to power resembles a pyramid, from the community up to the governing bodies. The Ikhwan's jihad is more flexible politically than that of the Wahabis, although they are equivalent ideologically. The Brotherhood has accepted, for example, the need to participate in the political process, including legislative elections. Although inconsistent with their Islamic fundamentalist vision, which does not accept the concepts of republic, democracy, secularism, nonreligious courts, and so on, the Brotherhood and related organizations practiced the "political path." In Jordan, the group has an official presence in parliament. It has accommodated to the political structure in the hope of achieving further inroads. Will elections eliminate the struggle for the caliphate? Many westerners thought they would, but they have not understood the very long-term strategy of the Muslim Brotherhood. In 1991 the Front de Salut Islamique (FSI), an offshoot of the Ikhwan, ran for election in Algeria and won more than 51 percent of the seats. Many citizens frustrated with the previous totalitarian government voted for the FSI, despite the fact that it signaled openly that it would transform the republic into an "Islamist state" with all that entails: elimination of political parties that disagree with a new constitution and ultimately elimination of pluralism and the basic institutions of the republic.[9] The Muslim Brotherhood invented "political jihad," which means using democracy to come to power so that one can destroy democracy. Most western analyses, particularly academic research, overlooked this dimension of jihadism. American and European scholars imagined that any step toward some democratic practices was a slow concession toward liberalization. The western apologists could not comprehend the overarching global goals of the modern jihadists; and they made the same analytical mistake with regard to jihadi violence.

In 1991 I attended a series of panels at the Middle East Studies Association of America (MESA), the national elite in the field. In one panel, a veteran of research in the region said the North African Salafis have produced what he called NVIs (nonviolent Islamists). He made a distinction between the violent and the nonviolent Salafis.[10] But the next ten years in Algeria were a hell waged by the Salafis against seculars; more than 150,000 were killed. Many scholars in the United States and western Europe seriously misunderstood the jihadists and tried to classify them into categories. In fact there were and are distinctions, but these are drawn by the fundamentalists themselves. They can chose to be violent or nonviolent at their discretion—not at the discretion of western experts. During the cold war era, the Muslim Brotherhood got bigger and more complex and gave birth to offshoots, as noted earlier. But the third wave of jihadism, as we saw in chapter five, was not Sunni but Shi'a. It developed its own cold war strategy.

KHUMEINIST STRATEGY: BECOMING A SUPERPOWER

The mullahs of Iran chose a third path: no alliance with the infidels against other infidels, no dependence on the superpower's power, and direct jihad when circumstances allow. The Iranian Islamic Revolution opted for the concept of "superpower now." From the beginning the Khumeinist revolution described the United States as the "big devil" *(al shaytan al akbar)*, the Soviets as the "red devils," and Israel as the "little devil." It projected itself as the leader of the Muslim world, brushing aside the Sunni-Shiia divide and going so far as to attempt to assign itself the mission of defense of all underdogs in the world. The Khumeinist revolution wanted to emulate the communists by declaring itself the leader of the "weak" *(mustadafeen)* and struggling against what it called the "condescending" *(al isti'laa')*. Unlike Saudi Arabia, Iran was large and technologically advanced enough to claim grandeur. And unlike the Muslim Brotherhood, it was backed by the resources of a powerful state. But unlike both, the Iranian jihadists were fewer in numbers. There are ten times more Sunnis than Shiia worldwide, and thus Salafis are ten times greater in numbers internationally. This matter may have convinced the Iranian Khumeinists to follow a state-jihadism line instead of the patient Muslim Brotherhood long-term strategy.[11]

Tehran's mullahs developed a form of Shiia Wahabism. Departing from the historical "quietist" line of the Shiia community, today embodied by Grand Ayatollah Sistani of Iraq, the new "spiritual capital" of Shiism was moved to Qum in Iran. Ayatollah Khumeini's circles argued that as long as Iraq was under the Baathist secular apostate regime, the world center of Shiism must be under the protection of Iranian power. The "revolution" developed an old-new institution called "the mandate of the wise" *(vilayet e fakih)*, the highest institution of militant Shiism. It was the parallel of the Sunni caliphate. In short, it proclaimed the institution as the heir of Ali, in the same way as the Salafis viewed the caliphate as a continuation of past caliphs. But on geopolitical grounds, the Khumeinist strategy was twofold: Develop a high military power in Iran, and organize a regional-international terror network outside the country. Using Iranian oil resources, Tehran's regime aimed at developing strategic arms, including a vast conventional military and weapons of mass destruction. Obtaining chemical and biological systems was a first stage before developing nuclear weapons. The logic behind such a trend was to create an umbrella under which the regime could conduct its activities and "protect" its regional allies, such as the Hafez Assad regime in Syria.[12] By obtaining the doomsday device, Tehran would gain a status similar to that of all other owners of atomic military capability. It wanted to become a sort of Islamist Soviet Union with weapons of mass destruction to balance U.S. power, while creating international networks to use in low-intensity conflicts.[13]

State jihad was the choice of Iran in its challenge to the *kufr* powers (the United States, the Soviet Union, and Israel). But it also challenged the Sunni countries in the neighborhood: Arab Gulf, Saudi Arabia, and Iraq. By adopting radical policies in all directions, the Islamic republic thought it would reduce the criticism by the Sunni Salafis against its Shiite identity. Furthermore, and through its followers in Lebanon's Shiite community, Tehran was able to help create a long tentacle of jihadism: Hezbollah. During the cold war, Iran's jihadism was centered on the growth of its own power as a state and on the development of its terror network. And in order to aggrandize itself in competition with the Sunni jihadists, the Iranian Khumeinists clashed with the United States head on. With the U.S. embassy hostage crisis, Iran's jihadists showed no fear to take on the "greatest devil." And after blowing up the Marine barracks and the U.S. embassy in Beirut and taking hostages and executing them in Lebanon during the 1980s, Hezbollah's jihadists were viewed by Islamists as ahead of the Salafi jihadists in the region.[14]

The race to escalate jihad against the infidels was on between the Sunni Salafis and the Shiite Khumeinists, particularly in the 1980s. The cold war continued between the two great "infidel" superpowers, but the jihadists were fighting both empires on different battlefields.[15]

AFGHANISTAN: THE PROMISED LAND OF JIHAD

Up until 1979, Salafi jihadists from both Wahabi and Muslim Brotherhood backgrounds had involved themselves in wars around the region, but these were not their "holy" wars. Rather, the jihadists were holy warriors fighting in conflicts led by secular forces. One of their earliest military engagements was in West Beirut and Tripoli during the Lebanese war of 1975. They formed small militias, such as the Gamat Islamiya and Harakat al Tawheed. I remember reading their pamphlets and seeing their graffiti. They were not catching the attention of the street yet. The masses and the elites did not yet take seriously the Islamic fundamentalists, although they were clear on their world vision of *dar el harb.* Most "battlefields" were controlled by nationalists, progressives, or socialists; Israel was faced by either non-Islamist Arab regimes or by the secular PLO. All other fault lines where jihadists could have played a leading role were under the control of regimes or organizations not affiliated with Islamism, for example, Sudan, Lebanon, the Philippines, Nigeria, and so on. There was no "ideological" room for the Salafis to bring in their jihad—yet. The Islamists made the point that unless the purists stepped in and ran a *halal* (Islamic equivalent of kosher) fight, the fake jihad would not be successful. They argued that

Arabs and Muslims had been losing all confrontations with Israel because Allah was not satisfied with the doctrinal performances of Nasser of Egypt, the Baath in Damascus and Baghdad, or the Hashemites with their western inclinations.[16]

The Wahabis hinted that Saudi Arabia was not a contiguous country with Israel and hence was not given a chance to prove its credentials. Moreover, the Saudi strategy in the confrontation with Israel followed a Wahabi global plan: Use the influence of one infidel power, the United States, to curb the influence of another infidel power, Israel. Hence, and in contrast with other Arab regimes such as Syria's Baath, the Saudi jihad against Israel was indirect and mostly financial and diplomatic. It became clear as of 1973, with the oil boycott, that Wahabi influence would impact Washington first, before coming back at Israel through its own ally, the United States. But the Sunni Salafis worldwide had a strategic need to fight the infidels face to face, somewhere, under the jihadist rules of engagement. Suddenly their archenemy, the communists, gave them a historic opportunity.

In 1979 Soviet forces invaded Afghanistan, a Muslim country that has been marginal to world politics for decades. The establishment of a communist regime triggered a worldwide Wahabi Salafi call for jihad and mobilization. It was the perfect war and a huge opportunity for the jihadists worldwide. The major effort came from the Saudi government, which viewed supporting the Islamic resistance to the atheist Soviet occupation of Afghanistan as a single stone that could kill two birds: One, it mobilized the international Salafi movement behind the Wahabi regime in their new jihad in central Asia. This war would give Riyadh the opportunity to fight a jihad for the first time outside its borders (which pleased its clerics) and free from coordination with other "apostate" Arab regimes in control of the efforts against Israel. Two, the Afghan jihad would also provide the Saudis an opportunity to show the West that they were fighting Soviet influence on the ground, recruiting thousands of Arabs and Muslims to engage in an international crusade against the West's common foe. Incidentally, it also provided an arena in which Sunni radicals could compete with the surge of Shiia radicals out of Iran.

But perhaps the most important yet hidden dividend of the war in Afghanistan was to drag the United States not just into the war efforts—which were a natural part of the global containment policy against the Soviet Union—but into a strategic alliance with the jihadists. Wahabi skills during the cold war were endless. They used the Afghan conflict to recruit and train men for the worldwide jihad. They basically transformed a national resistance movement, the true Afghan mujahidin, into a hub for radical Islamists—those who would become the Taliban and later on al Qaeda. But the greatest achievement perhaps was to have the United States bless the movement and support it. In 2001 CNN aired a documentary showing then U.S. National Security Advisor Zbigniew Brzezinski delivering a speech to the fighters at the Pakistan–Afghanistan borders. He told them to fight for their land, which was fine, but then asked them to fight for their religion, for Allah. That was the line that should not have been crossed. To have the infidels not only support the fundamentalist character of a resistance movement over a nationalist one, but to endorse it, was an indicator of a U.S. failure to absorb the underlying reality. It was also, of course, a huge Wahabi success to have enlisted America's own help and blessing in growing the jihadi influence.

The Afghani "battlefield" drew "fighters" from various countries. It was the long-awaited breakthrough. The Muslim Brotherhood, other factions, and Salafis of all backgrounds headed to the new Promised Land of Jihad.[17] It became the basis out of which "the mother of all modern Jihads" would spring again (interestingly enough, "base" in Arabic is *al-Qaida)*. Hence, the last decade of the cold war was the launching pad for what probably will be the longest war of the twenty-first century.

THE WORLD MAP OF JIHAD IN THE COLD WAR

From 1947 until about the early 1970s, the Islamists were involved in activities worldwide but had not yet had an opportunity to implant their organized networks into real battlefields. The bulk of their action concentrated on preparing for the ultimate war against the infidels. Jihad was omnipresent in many world conflicts, such as the struggle for Algerian independence (1954–1962), the Arab-Israeli war (1948–1973), the India-Pakistan wars, and the Sudan conflict (1954–1972), to name a few. But these calls for holy efforts were contained within state-run policies and were under international law. Even when radical organizations such as the PLO or other underground groups used the reference to jihad, it was not under a specific jihadist ideology yet.

After 1973, and as the Saudis flourished the oil weapon to solidify their position worldwide and to further penetrate the West, the jihadists mobilized globally. Coincidentally, both Sunni Salafists and Shiia Khumeinists leaped into *dar el harb* in the same year: 1979. The Salafists moved against the Soviet Union and the Khumeinists against the United States. With the end of the cold war, the international Salafists redirected their efforts against America, while the Khumeinists concentrated on Israel. The geopolitics of jihad were set to clash with the infidels, one at a time.

And while conducting their holy wars against the other side, meaning the *dar el harb,* another jihad was ongoing against Muslim moderates within what the jihadists perceived as *dar el Islam.* This other more lethal jihad was directed against youth, women, democracy movements, artists, minorities, and other forces of Muslim civil societies around the world. Toward the end of the Soviet era, the years of networking during the cold war suddenly bore fruit in jihads against both infidels without and nonradical Muslims within.

Chapter Eight

THE NEW JIHAD

A S LONG AS THE COLD WAR WAS ON, jihad terror was a secondary priority in the West. In many cases, the latter was perceived as an "objective ally" against the Soviet Union. There was little awareness that jihad was separate from both superpowers and that once it defeated one, it would turn against the other. In fact, in the West's major centers of learning, the actual notion of a "threatening jihad" was being dissolved. Even if by instinct decision-makers knew that the holy warriors were not followers of democratic ideals, their first priority was naturally to contain the intercontinental ballistic missiles on the other side. But the United States and its allies won the cold war and a new era dawned. They were then left with the problem of how to deal with their supposed jihadist "allies." Ideas abounded, but events moved faster than the evolution of western understanding; the former jihadi "allies" in the struggle against the Soviet Union did not wait long before they launched their new jihad—against their American "friends."

THE AFGHAN CROSSROAD, 1989:
WHO DEFEATED THE SOVIETS?

"*Ihna asqatna al soviet!*" This short sentence expresses the jihadists' main challenge in the 1980s. It translates to "we brought the Soviets down." It was used in a discussion between Salafi militants online in the late 1990s. Then came another short sentence in response: "*la' mish ihna, Allah asqat al Suviet.*" (No, not us. Allah brought the Soviets down.) And with this simple answer, one could have figured out what was to be the jihadi challenge in the 1990s and beyond. This fragment of chat room indoctrination is perhaps too simple to uncover a complex doctrine, but is very revealing to students of jihadist political thinking. The jihadi debate that ensued after the victory achieved by the mujahidin over the Soviets was crucial in the strategic decisions made by many jihadists, particularly those who would later form al Qaeda. The essential question is historical: Who defeated the Soviets in Afghanistan? The answer in the minds of the Salafi analysts is simple: The jihadists did. Another, more adventurous question was contemplated: Didn't the Soviet Union collapse immediately after it was defeated in Afghanistan? By Islamist assessment, yes. If you were a mujahid in 1989 and you witnessed the Soviet army retreating from the country, an event followed shortly by the collapse of the whole eastern bloc and the Soviet Union itself, the conclusion would be crystal clear. Jihadi forces had crushed the infidel Red Army in Afghanistan and brought about the end of the Soviet empire. One push, well administered in Afghanistan, destroyed the most dangerous and lethal enemy of Islam. Further conclusions will then ensue. If a war against a historical enemy is led by the right people (the Salafi jihadi) at the right time (when ordered by the clerics), and under the guidance of Islamism (a movement that subscribes to the rules), the enemy cannot but be defeated, regardless of its power and size. This doctrinal and indeed almost metaphysical reasoning was the basis on which the next decade would be perceived by the terrorists who would attack America in 2001: It suffices to "please" Allah.

The logic is understandably mechanical, if entirely ideological. The jihadist theorists do not factor in structural economic factors or geopolitics when they design their explanation of victory. They may refer to them as necessary but not as sufficient. Their analysis of the jihadi victory in Afghanistan missed at least three major ingredients. One fact is that it was a war of national liberation against the Soviet occupation. Even if the Soviets had been Muslims, rather than Orthodox or communists, the Afghan ethnic groups would have waged war against them on the basis of nationalism alone. Bringing in the Wahabi and Salafi components helped in the war but did not decide its outcome. A second (ignored) ingredient was the outside support obtained from the Americans, as well as the Pakistanis and Saudis. Without that backing, the Afghani resistance may have taken a longer time to weaken Soviet domination. But more important was the third ingredient of Afghan victory: the crumbling of Soviet power from the inside. As of 1985, the reforms of Mikhail Gorbachev—perestroika and glasnost—moderated Moscow's traditional repression of local resistance movements. The Soviet economy was imploding, leading to popular discontent. In sum, the Red Army was not really motivated and was morally defeated by the end of the 1980s. Stalin would have treated uprisings within his nation differently; but international relations had changed since his death in 1953.

Nevertheless, the Salafi theory of the Soviet defeat in Afghanistan overrides all rational analysis. Their explanations are ultimately theological; in the final analysis, whatever the circumstances were, it was Allah who gave the final victory to his fighters. The Soviet giant was invincible in earthly terms, according to the wise scholars of holy struggle. Therefore, it must have been a divine power that ensured the victory, which thereby proved also that no power on Earth can defeat jihad. The Islamic fundamentalists refer back to "precedents," such as the Prophet's unequal battles with the pagans, or the early *fatah* in the Middle East. Because these religious accounts remain unchallenged by reformed and modern explanations, the followers of jihad cannot but adhere to the logic—which also provides fuel for future wars.

THE ARAB AFGHANS: FATHERS OF AL QAEDA

Those thousands of mostly Arab fighters who traveled to Afghanistan beginning in 1979, and increasingly after the mid-1980s, gradually formed the first international brigade of modern Islamists. They came from Egypt, Saudi Arabia, Jordan, Palestine, Syria, Iraq, Algeria, and elsewhere. As Salafists and products of either Wahabi *madrassas*[1] or Muslim Brotherhood schools, they had one goal in mind: Fight the infidels face to face, as real jihadists, not soldiers of Arab apostate regimes. Since the collapse of the sultanate in 1923, their ultimate goal has always been to reinstate it. Many among them were even more ambitious. They felt they were bringing history around again to the "purest times" of the Rashidun caliphs, the first wise rulers of the empire thirteen centuries ago. As with the gathering of Mordor-sympathizing and Gondor-hating forces in *The Lord of the Rings*, the fighters gathering from the four corners of the *umma* met in Afghanistan to re-create a golden age. They vicariously experienced the good old days of the *salaf*, like the early companions of the Prophet, and simply bypassed or reversed a millennia of Muslim history, civilization, and world developments. Their ultimate victory in the war seemed to confirm that such a grand strategy and the wiping away of centuries of history was possible; more than that, it was sanctioned, approved, and rewarded by Allah. It was not just possible to return to great days of the *salaf*; it was happening.[2]

Inspired by an obscure mujahid from Palestine, Abdallah Azzam, and educated by a vast Wahabi literature, the men from the "prestigious past" looked forward to martyrdom or victory. The concept of *istishaad* (martyrdom) began to be applied at this time to the suicide attack, although (as I will detail later) it entails different meanings, including military ones. Those men, known in the region as the Arab Afghans, later became the core of the fighting machine of al

Qaeda, and potentially the post–al Qaeda jihadists. During my Beirut years, after I published my first book dealing with pluralism, I was engaged in an exchange with Salafi thinkers and clerics in the media. It was between 1979 and 1982, just when foreign mujahidin were beginning to travel to Afghanistan. The "Salafi intellectuals" out of Beirut and Tripoli focused on my writing about the *fatah* and caliphate only. As the argument went back and forth through newspaper articles, I realized that their main interest was the global jihad, not the actual nationalist struggle in Lebanon. In the midst of the Lebanon conflict, both Muslims and Christians were arguing about sovereignty, government, and foreign intervention, but the Islamic fundamentalists, many of whom were parts of Muslim or Arab nationalist militias, were not really and exclusively focusing on Lebanon's crisis yet. They were looking elsewhere: Afghanistan. Other Islamists in other countries were also looking toward the promised land of pure jihad.[3]

During the cold war, most Arab regimes, particularly those who had an alliance with the Soviet Union, such as Syria, Iraq, Sudan, and to some extent Algeria and southern Yemen, mistrusted the "Arab Afghans." They were also problematic for the pro-American governments such as those of Jordan, Egypt, Tunisia, Morocco, and Kuwait. But one government had a sustained policy of support to the mujahidin in Afghanistan and the "international brigades" coming to fight with them: the government of the United States. Washington's foreign policy establishment, helped by the Wahabi lobby, saw the mujahidin as international freedom fighters. To many within the intellectual elites, they were heroes leaving their homes to join the poor tribes of Afghanistan against mighty Ivan.[4] The Wahabi media machine blurred the distinction between the genuine resistance movement of Massud Shah and the Wahabi "volunteers." In popular culture, you could not see the difference between the insider nationalists and the outsider terrorists-to-be. Sylvester Stallone's thriller in Afghanistan, *Rambo III,* embodies this American 1980s state of mind: The Soviets are the enemy; those fighting them are friends. But the strategic equation goes beyond this simple formula. To Washington, whoever helps the enemy of our enemies is a friend. As "international brigades," the Arab Afghans were perceived as the friends of the Afghani resistance, and were therefore not only tolerated but sometimes trained, equipped, and financed. And to make sure there was a moral and political rationale for their behavior, the Saudis and their allies in the Pakistani intelligence services assured the United States of the justness of the "Arab Afghan" ideals and their jihads! Like a Trojan horse, the men who would form al Qaeda were smuggled into the American camp during the struggle against the Soviets, aided and protected by the Wahabis of Saudi Arabia.[5]

The most infamous result of this alliance with America was to empower Osama bin Laden.

OSAMA BIN LADEN

A lot has been written about bin Laden in the West, and just as much has been said in the Arabic media. But most of what has been said and written has skipped the essence of Osama's mind. Far more important than his biography, his private life, his wealth, his trail, and his hideout since Tora Bora, are his vision and his strategies, which constitute the road map for future jihads against America and the West. Certainly, the investigation of his leadership abilities and his organization are of vital interest to governments and agencies, particularly since September 11, but his impact on the jihadist movement was earth-shattering for more than one generation. His personal story is now part of the history of terrorism. Whatever his fate and the future of al Qaeda, one matter is sure: Osama bin Laden's role in shaping the new jihad and his strategic legacy will impact future wars to come.

As strange as it may be, I first learned of bin Laden before I knew who he was. It was in Beirut in the early 1980s. An acquaintance told me that some Saudis who used to visit the country before and during the early part of the Lebanon war of 1975 came here to entertain themselves but hated everything this culture stood for, including pluralism, democracy, modernism, free education, and equality for women. One of them, he said, was the son of a very rich entrepreneur from the kingdom, the well-known bin Laden. He told me that he met bin Laden in a popular outdoor coffee shop with other Saudis and some Lebanese. They were watching people and particularly women. Suddenly Osama bin Laden said: "This is a small America, with its *kufr*, filth, and whores, but soon things will change."

Beirut indeed was an enclave of freedom compared to other Arab capitals. Most opposition figures in the region had taken refuge in the city. With five universities, a growing middle class, and multiple languages spoken, it was the antithesis of what the Salafis wanted. No wonder that Osama hated the place in the 1970s. Decades passed before I heard of him again. He was mentioned in the jihadist circles of the early 1990s, but he had not yet distinguished himself as a central figure of the movement. All that I heard, other than through the media, was coming from businesspeople in Saudi Arabia about "that one son of the bin Laden's who was fighting jihad in Afghanistan and was in trouble with the Saudi authorities." There was nothing significantly unusual in that. But back in 1996, in one of my classrooms, I had invited a Salafi cleric to give a presentation on Islam. At the very end of the lecture, I asked him which country he considered the truest Muslim state. He said it was not Iran; it was not even Saudi Arabia. He added, "it is just emerging now, it is in Afghanistan; it's called the Taliban!" The students weren't sure what he meant. I was. So I asked if he thought there was a caliph-in-the-making. He said with a smile: "Yes, there is one who will be declared in the future. He is from Saudi Arabia, but he is in Afghanistan now."

That sentence made an impression on my mind. The analytical consequences were immediate. I realized from that one encounter with a Salafi preacher what Salafism has produced: a new era. The second stage of modern jihadism had started. I have since seen its evidence and have read its literature from the early 1990s on, but sometimes one defining moment is needed to bring it all into focus.

THE LORD OF THE RINGS

It was not difficult for me to read the mind of the leader of al Qaeda. I had read the same history books he read. We have looked at the same pictures, heard the same legends over and over. I listened to the same type of Friday preaching *(khutba)*, read the same Qu'ran and Hadith, and devoured the same Salafi accounts that he did; so did millions of others around the Middle East. All of what an Islamic fundamentalist, including Osama bin Laden, has learned about Islamic and Arabic history and politics I have learned about. But other experts and students of Islamic politics have read the same material and studied the same history; what accounts for the difference in the conclusions drawn? That is a long story, but one answer depends on when and at what time of his or her life someone read, learned, and listened to these histories and interpretations. If you absorb the material as a student of Middle East studies or as an adult, you are already conscious of it as being detached from you. But if you learn it at a young age, as part of your childhood curriculum and political sociology, then you receive the material as a jihadist receives it, even if you are not yet one. Compare it with the concept of being absorbed by it but not being digested by it. Many authors who lived in the same cultural context as bin Laden were able to receive the same education but were immune to its indoctrination.

Osama bin Laden is not what Marx or Lenin were to communism. He did not create jihadism—just the opposite, he was *created by it.* His story is very typical in the Arab world. From his early years he was immersed in Salafi teachings, as were millions of others from Arabia to Morocco. However, his family's prominence in Saudi Arabia and its closeness to the hard-core clerics in the kingdom played a singular role in firming up not just his acquired beliefs but also his conviction that he had a key role to play in the advancement of these ideas and that vision, which revived the self-conception and worldview of the Arab Middle Ages.[6] I often compare this story to *The Lord of the Rings'* legend. In reality, the lord is very important in the legend, but not as important as the rings. That is a critical point of the entire analysis of jihadism; without an understanding of the jihadist equation, no war on terrorism can be won, nor can any war of ideas be successful. It must be understood that the "jihad genes" have been passed down for centuries—at least since Ibn Taymiya's thirteenth-century doctrine of *takfir* and jihad were propagated in the region. At times, self-proclaimed figures, such as Osama bin Laden, rise, wear those "jihad-rings," and become the leaders of the movement. They drive on the fighters for Allah, but they themselves are controlled by the "teachings." They can innovate in warfare, but not in the ideas behind it. They can adapt to technology but cannot reform the philosophy. They are mentally trapped in previous centuries although living physically in the present.

But the post-Ottoman jihadists do have one truly "innovative" quality that had not existed during the previous thirteen centuries: They are out of control. Without a caliph, the clerics ruling over the *fatwa* (religious edicts) that feed the organization's actions have a free hand in legal rulings and sentencing. Twentieth-century clerics from Saudi Arabia and others from Egypt and Syria have developed a Salafi-jihadi constellation of laws, regulations, and edicts outside the oversight of any caliphatic authority. To put it in Tolkienian terms, the Lord has died but a surviving sect (the Wahabi clerics) has stolen the rings since the death of the caliphate in the mid-1920s. They now wield those powers and use them to control the dynasty ruling in Arabia.[7] With the wealth of "dark gold" (oil), the sect propagates the message around the world, brainwashing millions of minds and inducing them back into the "dark ages" of jihad and *fatah*. With no caliph to take back the "rings," and with no reformers to open the eyes of the follower, and no international campaign to help break the cycle, jihadism spins out of control. A bin Ladin had to exist, even if he as a person was not born. An "Osama" had to be produced by the post-1923 hothouse of unfettered jihadism.

BIN LADEN'S MUTANT JIHAD

The Arab Afghans assembled in unusual historic circumstances. They were incited by clerics who were free from higher authority; they were supported by rich powers, including the Saudis and, at times, the United States; and they witnessed the collapse of a nuclear superpower, the Soviet Union. And they were mentally hostage to an ideology from the Middle Ages, jihadism, and unable to escape it. If you process these ingredients, you get modern-day apocalyptic jihadists. If the jihadists are convinced that Allah is on their side and that they are executing his orders, there is not any force on Earth that can free them from this state of mind. If their clerics have boxed them into a Salafi space and laid down the path to take, there will simply be no other path than jihad—and then *fatah,* when the greater offensive is set to resume. Wave after wave, they will head toward the objectives indicated by their emirs (princes) and by the commander of these princes, the "Emir of the faithful." The quasi-legend is real, very real; yet this one has not caught the attention or imagination of Hollywood—nor will it, given that the intellectual elite in the West has been incapable of understanding what these waves of jihadists are and the source of their beliefs. And how can the elite comprehend them, if their teachers have failed them in the classroom? We will come back later to revisit the blindness of the West. Meanwhile, let us continue to explore the blind march of jihad.[8]

Bin Laden, as a phenomenon, is the ultimate ideological development of the "dark minds" who have been self-appointed keepers of the flame of jihad for almost a century now. A new "lord of terror" had to arise to lead the armies of jihad worldwide. It was Osama, and the land of the launching was the promised land of Afghanistan, at the edges of the Middle East and oppressed by Islam's public enemy number one, the atheist Soviet Union. It provided a perfect *qaeda,* or base of operations, for these jihadists. Protected by local lords of jihad, the Taliban, the war and Osama bin Laden himself attracted Wahabis, Brotherhood members, Salafists of all tendencies, Takfiris, new converts, and old militants.[9] Growing inside the Taliban web (itself protected by the fundamentalists' sympathizers within the Pakistani intelligence services) and backed by the clerically influenced Saudi regime, the group that became al Qaeda was set to face the new realities of the post-Soviet world.

Meanwhile, the older clerics whose works had influenced al Qaeda's founders, and who lived mostly in the Wahabi kingdom, had passed away, but the "ring" was passed on to a network of new clerics, whose juridical judgments no longer had masters to come back to. The new world and its precarious balances of power was now theirs to explain and "conquer." The Wahabi clerical network produced a neo-Wahabi organization that was now freed from the Saudi regime and shaped its vision of the future solely on what it perceived as direct signs from Allah. This even more dangerous development was also completely lost on the academics and policymakers of the West. After 1923, there was no caliph to direct and if necessary restrain jihadism, but at least there was the Saudi state, which directed the worldwide spread of Wahabism. After the older generation of clerics died and the Saudis' grip had loosened, it could truly be said that only Allah could stop the will to jihad.

At this point, even the most purist Saudi government was not able to exercise direct control over the jihadists. From the plateau of Afghanistan, the international army of jihad and its local allies, the Taliban, felt that a great moment in history had come. If they could defeat a superpower as grandiose as the Soviet Union, there was no reason they could not defeat America, "the greedy, materialistic, dominant and arrogant infidel power." As of the downfall of Soviet communism in 1990, a new vision of anti-Americanism developed in the minds of the jihadists around the region.

Assaulting America was not a matter of sheer hatred only, but of strategic mutation. The weapons used by the jihadists against the Soviets were provided by the U.S. Central Intelligence Agency (CIA) and other United States allies. The doctrine of jihadism had to build a case for why they should turn the guns against their former ally. The case was duly built, piece by piece, by the scholars of jihad and *takfir* from within the Saudi kingdom.[10]

THE IRAQ WAR DILEMMA, 1990 TO 1991

On August 2, 1990, my assistant told me he had heard on the radio incredible news: Saddam had invaded Kuwait. In a few hours, his forces reached the Saudi borders on the other side. At that time I was in Beirut, which was encircled by Syrian tanks. In two months Assad would order the invasion of the free enclave. These were my last weeks in Lebanon before I relocated to the United States. The news astounded me. I could not understand Saddam's logic (there was none), but there was one other logic I feared: the jihadists'. There was no doubt in my mind that the United States and its allies would intervene. Oil was too big a commodity not to trigger the mother of all interventions. But the Iraq war in Kuwait was predictable: Saddam invades, the international community responds, and his forces are beaten back. What made that assessment clear was the fall of the Soviet Union. Without Moscow at his side, the madman of Baghdad was facing a crushing defeat. That is another story; what I was concerned about was the reaction of the jihadists.

Before the Iraqi invasion of its neighbor, the United States had almost no presence in the region. The last military expedition of the United States was to Beirut in 1982. It ended in a bloodbath at the hands of Hezbollah's Shiite jihadists in 1983. My question was simple but warranted: What would the

(Sunni) Islamic fundamentalists do at the sight of U.S. and other "infidel" divisions deploying in these Arabian deserts? True, the "infidel" CIA had helped them during the cold war against their first enemies, the communists; but now the Salafi militants had gone into the twilight zone. They had finished with one great enemy, the Soviets, but had not started with the other. Here was the perfect opportunity. Unfortunately, I was right; the Iraq invasion of Kuwait and the subsequent liberation unleashed the long-awaited reaction by the Salafists. It gave them the opportunity to move from the eastern front to the western front. Now that Persia had been taken, it was time to move against Byzantium.

But the Islamic fundamentalists, united against the communists, were divided on the policy toward America.

Evidently, the Saudi government was not going to wage a jihad against the United States after American-led forces saved the dynasty and the country from an impending Iraqi invasion. Riyadh's long-term policy, well implemented for decades, was to acquire influence in Washington and make inroads from the inside. Get the best arms and technologies, and protect the spread of Wahabism inside the United States until it becomes a second nature to the country of George Washington (meaning until average Americans will accept it as a cultural tradition among one of its communities). The Wahabi strategy toward the United States and the West was a very long-term one. But the jihadists of Abdallah Azzam, Osama bin Laden, and Ayman al Thawahiri (the leader of the Muslim Brotherhood's offshoot, Islamic Jihad) did not see eye to eye with the "masters" in the kingdom. The clerics were split as well. The official religious spokesmen of the regime tried to argue with the hot-headed Afghan veterans. The officials said America helped liberate Muslims from the Soviets and now they would help defeat Baghdad's socialists, who after all were Moscow's former allies. The Saudis used arguments from the cold war. But in the eyes of the Salafi jihadists, that war was over, and they felt they were the ones who won it on the ground.

The men of the "international brigades" had a different plan in mind. In audiences with the monarchy's top leaders, Osama bin Laden pleaded with them to organize the Islamic resistance against the Baathist occupation of Kuwait. He begged them not to allow the infidels to deploy on Muslim lands, especially in Arabia, the land of the Prophet, which had been purged of Jews and Christians thirteen centuries ago. He asked the regime to authorize him to lead the Islamist jihad against the Baathists. In reality, he wanted to kill two birds with one stone. By pounding Saddam's forces in Kuwait and possibly inside Iraq, he wanted to return as a leader in the Wahabi country. His real strategic aim was to be received as a commander of the jihadists and eventually, in a historic fantasy, as a newly anointed caliph. By way of comparison, he would be an Islamist Trotsky who would become an Emir Stalin, and perhaps even a jihadic Hitler. His dreams shattered when his own Wahabi rulers dismissed his plans, ignored his jihadist achievements in Afghanistan, and in the worst insult of all, extended their invitation to the very archenemies he wanted to fight next: the infidel Americans.

REDEFINING THE AMERICAN INFIDELS

In this crossroads between the end of the cold war and the beginning of the Gulf War, the new jihad was redefined. From within Saudi Arabia, radical clerics were developing what would become neo-Wahabism—Wahabism beyond the state considerations of the ruling Saudis. Many joined in without stating it. The neo-Wahabis claimed they were the true Salafists—accusing the state Wahabis, the king, and the bulk of his emirs of being false Salafis who had betrayed the pure objectives of Wahabism's founding fathers. The new wave, reinforced by the returning veterans from Afghanistan, mounted an all-out political assault on the American presence on Arabian soil. As soon as the operations ended in Kuwait and the Iraqi regime signed a cease-fire agreement, the Salafists were at work to regroup and ready themselves for the new war: the march toward the rest of the world.

But the action undertaken by the United States and the coalition changed the geopolitics of the region. For one thing, unlike Vietnam and Beirut in 1983, the "strong Americans" had reemerged internationally. Winds were blowing under their wings. Eastern Europe was free, Kuwait was freed, Saddam was boxed in, Iran was unable to play the East-West contradictions, Syria had been given Lebanon and was therefore holding back Hezbollah from attacking the United States, and most Arab regimes looked forward to American protection. The United States had become the sole superpower in the region, and in the world for that matter. In the eyes of the Islamists, America's influence and the *dar el harb* became almost overlapping. The jihadists were not happy with Washington's popularity for winning the cold war and beating Saddam; they wanted the Arab world to praise them for their deeds in Afghanistan. Hence their fatwas fused at the end of the Iraq war: America is the greatest infidel power. It must be pulled out of the region, its allies defeated, and eventually its power at home challenged.

THE FIGHTERS FOR ALLAH IN KHARTOUM

In the years following the withdrawal of the Soviets from Afghanistan and in quest for new "missions," the returning jihadis were out of touch with the realities in their home countries. By 1991 Saddam was defeated, the Lebanon war had ended, the communist threat had receded, and Arabs and Israelis had been invited to the Madrid peace conference. Beyond the Mediterranean, central and eastern Europe were free and heading toward democracy again. The Middle East had changed. It was obvious, after the deployment of U.S. forces in the region and the example made out of Saddam Hussein, that no radical regimes would be allowed to threaten regional peace with their regular armies or with weapons of mass destruction. As a corollary, it was understood that classical destructive wars between Israel and the Arabs were also forbidden, or at least frozen. The Salafi jihadists also understood that the presence of the United States in the region would have devastating effects on their plans: no more global jihads conducted by regimes.

In this new context, the returning jihadis found themselves facing off with regimes not willing to support them as they wished. Most of the moderate governments allowed Islamic fundamentalists, Muslim Brotherhood, Wahabis, Salafis, and others to form parties and run for office, as in Jordan, Tunisia, Morocco, Algeria, Kuwait, Yemen, and even Egypt. Other socialist regimes, such as Syria and Libya, still forbade them from open activities because they would be competitors to the one-party system. Iraq, although from the same category of regimes that had opened channels with the jihadists, did not allow them to conduct open activities. However, two regimes opened their doors to the jihadists: Saudi Arabia and Sudan. The Saudi kingdom was Wahabi to start with, and its clerics were direct supporters of the Salafi fighters. But relations with the United States did not allow open support to the Arab Afghans and their veterans. Osama bin Laden's relations with Riyadh were bad already. More important, state Wahabism had a different outlook on how to run international jihad. Its strategic choice to spread its ideology was via government funding of religious and sociocultural institutions around the world. It viewed a direct confrontation with the West and America as suicide. Bin Laden's "legion" saw it otherwise, however, so they turned to the only regime ready to host them: Sudan.

In 1989 a coup d'etat brought to power a group of Islamists, both military and militants, in Khartoum. Sudan became the second Sunni Islamist state in the region, after Saudi Arabia. Drawing mostly from the ideological influence of the Muslim Brotherhood, the new regime was under the control of Islamist officers led by Umar al Bashir and by the National Islamist Front (NIF), headed by a shrewd intellectual, Dr. Hassan Turabi. The Khartoum regime, inspired by the western-educated Turabi, was waging a jihad against the black African people in the south. A Taliban-like militia was formed under the name of Popular

Defense Forces (al Difaa al Shaabi) to invade the tribal south and eliminate resistance. By the early 1990s, the NIF had perpetrated genocide in the south,
erasing towns and villages and massacring hundreds of thousands. Hassan
Turabi, the chief architect of this jihad, developed a doctrine for it. He argued
that his regime was in charge of a new *fatah* in Africa. A new "Afghanistan"
was in the works on the continent. But the enemy was not a sophisticated nuclear power, as was the Soviet Union, just poor and weak African tribes.
Turabi linked the black south to the Soviet enemy by indicating that the southern resistance movement was led by John Garang, a Marxist and a former ally
of Ethiopia, once an ally of the Soviets at the end of the cold war. That was the
ideological cover. Turabi's jihadists wanted an "Islamist legitimacy" against
the mostly animist and Christian south to enlarge *dar el Islam* further into the
African *dar el harb*. In the following years, Sudan's NIF jihads bore a more
race-based sense: They were not directed only at black Christians, but also
later against black Muslims in West Sudan, particularly in the Darfour area.
The Salafi-Arab regime in Khartoum was Islamist but also anti-African. It constantly forced the "Arab identity" on the black tribes, whether Muslim or
Christian.

But in Sudan, the jihadists developed yet another weapon of mass ethnic
cleansing against the black populations: slavery. By the tens of thousands, tribal
populations were transformed into twentieth-century slaves and sold in the
Khartoum markets and around the Arab world. This ultimate mass abuse of
human rights indicated the kind of governments the jihadists wanted to establish in the region and beyond. With ethnic cleansing, religious persecution,
slavery, oppression, and terrorism, the new jihad of the 1990s had no limitation
to its vision of the return of the caliphate; if ever restored by the current jihadists it will be used to further the power of terror in international relations.

Ironically, I learned personally about Hassan Turabi while on an academic
visit to the University of South Florida in 1991. I found flyers put out by WISE,
a think tank associated with the university, and promoting an "exchange of
ideas and academic projects with the Muslim world." One summarized a visit
by Turabi, who was described as a "prominent Muslim thinker," to the university. The "prominent" Turabi had indeed toured U.S. campuses for years, talking about "dialogue and coexistence and the negative effects of colonialism."
Smooth and polished, Turabi was at the same time "prominent" in engineering
the largest ethnic cleansing and genocide in Africa's modern history: 1.5 million black Africans were exterminated by a regime whose central figure was
called a "man of intellectual renaissance" by the Middle East studies elite in the
United States and western countries. Years later, we learned that WISE, the

Tampa "think tank," was a front used by terrorists to fund-raise, sponsor terror figures, and spread the doctrines of jihad in the United States.

Well grounded in the country and still intellectually insulated in the West, the NIF regime called on the international cadre of jihadists to come find peace, comfort, and support in Khartoum. Hassan Turabi, wishing to play a grandiose role in the world of jihad, extended an invitation to Osama bin Laden, his companions, and other Islamist groups to find refuge in Sudan. The world terror network was about to be launched, and America would become its target.

"THE JIHADISTS INTERNATIONAL"

During the summer of 2004, the 9/11 Commission was holding hearings to investigate the root causes of the attacks on the United States. Both the commissioners and the witnesses, including former top officials in two administrations, were struggling over the timetable of the war declared against America. Commissioner Bob Kerry, holding onto the ace, said al Qaeda declared war officially in 1998 when bin Laden branded his fatwas. The Secretaries of State and Defense and the counterterrorism czar were perplexed and could not agree just when the Salafi war started against the country. "When did the jihadists start their new war against the United States?" asked many members of the Commission. Yet the $40 million spent to investigate September 11 and the roots of jihad terrorism were not able to provide the answer.

That gigantic figure (and failure to find the answer) deserves the following comparison. Back in 1992, I bought an Arabic newspaper in Miami. Starting on page one, a long report detailed a superconference taking place in Khartoum that week. Hassan Turabi, whose pictures were published along with dozens of other "prominent" radicals from the region, had assembled the mother of all jihadist conferences in modern history. They were all there: the NIF of Sudan, the FIS of Algeria, Gamaat Islamiya of Egypt, Islamic Jihad, the Jordanian Islamists, Hamas and Islamic Jihad of Palestine, Lebanon's Salafists, the South Asian jihadists, the graduates of madrassas who became the Taliban, the Arab Afghan precursors to al Qaeda, and so on. Some special guests showed up as well: representatives from the "secular" PLO; representatives of the Iraqi intelligence services, seeking contacts with the anti-American militants; and, amazingly, representatives from the Islamic Republic of Iran and of Hezbollah, both of them Shiite! For the first time ever, fundamentalists on both sides of the Sunni-Shiite divide had come together, at least to meet and discuss the common enemy. Also, Saddam's Baath was there—which indicated that Arab socialist nationalists, theoretically opposed to the Islamists, were exchanging views with the jihadists. What was bringing all of these forces together at the beginning of the last decade of the century? It seems impossible that anyone could have missed the answer: It was a gathering of the region's anti-American, antiwestern, and antidemocratic forces. But above all, the Khartoum conference was laying the groundwork for the surge of an international jihadist network, centered on the core jihadists who had fought the Afghan war. Not every participant in the conference would adhere to the jihad international, but all Salafists concurred that a new jihad had to be launched. The jihadists laid out a new international strategy to defeat the forces of *kuffar* and especially their head, the much-hated United States.

Unfortunately, on this side of the Atlantic, very few people recognized the mounting threat. Many have followed up on the activities of the several groups, others have focused on the personalities behind the new world movement, but only rarely did anyone look at the big picture and realize that jihad was on the move around the world and was headed west toward these shores. During the following years, I monitored the jihadi networks acting systematically on different levels in different spots, and at the same time observed our Middle East studies elite providing the wrong analyses and advice to our government, the media, and the public. These were among the most stressful years in my research. I saw that jihad was heading our way. I saw that the dominant establishment was camouflaging it, but my own voice was lost in the wilderness.

STRATEGIC CHOICES: COUNTRY JIHADS OR WORLD JIHAD?

Early on in my observation of the jihadist movements worldwide, I began to realize that above the "local" ethnonationalist conflicts there was a "central computer" out there directing the "international interest" of global jihad. Before the 1990s, it was very difficult to detect, but it came to the fore after the collapse of the Soviet Union. Ironically, fundamentalists who were omnipresent around the region, some among them engaged militarily in ethnic conflicts or against various Arab governments, seemed to have an eye on a regional, perhaps even a "world historic," importance in their local activities. They were acting locally but thinking globally.

The centrality of Afghanistan's jihad did not distract the local terror networks from engaging in acts of violence. One does not exclude the other. In Egypt, for example, Islamic Jihad assassinated President Anwar Sadat in 1981, while the Afghan jihad was taking place, despite the fact that Egypt's president was an ally of the United States—which was, at the time, providing support to the Islamic uprising in Afghanistan. So why did Islamists kill Sadat? If anything, this demonstrates that the "Salafi analysis" is not based on the idea of the enemy of my enemy being my friend; rather it is based on the idea that even if one of my enemies kills my other enemy, he remains my enemy.

The jihadi "central computer," which is a fluid network of clerics and intellectuals from Saudi Arabia to Egypt and Sudan, then had to face a dilemma of a historic dimension: Should all jihadists continue to fight on their traditional fronts and in their home countries against their respective enemies, to achieve specific victories in their personal battlefields?[11] Or should all jihadists from all countries assemble in one "international force" and attack one major enemy head on? To struggle on separate battlefields without a central command would be detrimental to world jihad and the efforts to reestablish the caliphate.[12] Besides, a major component of internationalism is to be able to move forces and resources from one area and engage them on the side of one particular jihadist army. But at the same time, it would be self-defeating and unrealistic to cease operations all over the world so that one central army could be formed. In short, the "central computer" figured out that two tracks would need to be continued in parallel.

Several principles flowed from that decision.

1. Every "battlefield" would be managed by the local jihadi forces: in Chechnya, Kashmir, Palestine, Sudan, the Philippines, Indonesia, and so on.
2. Jihadists in every Muslim country would have their local command and organizations.
3. Jihadists in every infidel country would have a coordinating body to help infiltrate its Muslim communities and local and national institutions, and would draw resources from both the various jihadi networks in Muslim countries and from the international network.
4. An international network would recruit from all national pools and from all levels to get the best jihadists. They would be trained as a central force capable of intervening everywhere and conducting the main striking missions on the planet.

That network, or mother ship, would be al Qaeda.

THE MOTHER SHIP: AL QAEDA

What is and who is al Qaeda? U.S. and western officials have been struggling with their intelligence services to answer these two questions. According to public information, the analysts in the United States and western

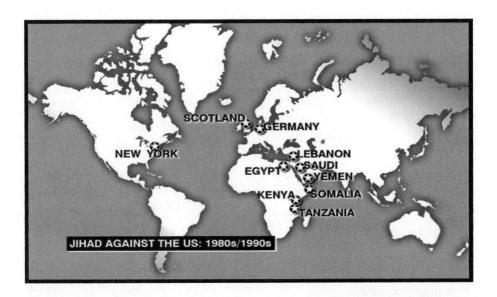

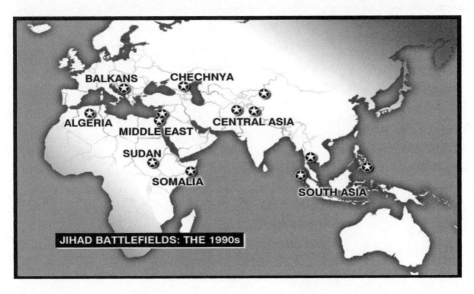

agencies have been providing the best data possible before and certainly now after September 11. The problem was not at their level. It was rather political and, even deeper, academic—which is of course also political. In other words, the problem in addressing al Qaeda's threat, and also the other jihadi challenges, was the intellectuals. While the agencies provided raw information to the political level of decision-making in the West, particularly in America, the academic establishment provided counter opinions that "explained" the same information differently. Hence, both the political leadership and the public were fooled not by the lack of information about al Qaeda, per se, but by the elite's "interpretation" of this information. A jihadist heading to the battlefield with an AK47 could be either a freedom fighter or a terrorist. The United States had plenty of pictures of jihad to look at, but it was overwhelmed by one interpretation of what they represented.

One striking example was during the ultimate investigation of al Qaeda's history during the 9/11 Commission hearings. In response to one simple question—"When was al Qaeda born?"—half a dozen witnesses gave different birthdays. The official interpretation of these variations is that their analysts may or may not have been given the same data. It also means, more dangerously, that the academic establishment dealing with these issues may have blurred the vision of its consumers: the wider policy-making establishment.

Intriguingly but informatively, Arab and Muslim government intelligence services have had more and better information about al Qaeda for a longer period of time. Salafists and other jihadists have been operating in these regions for decades. The latter's literature was widely published. Many jihadists have been arrested over the years. It is interesting to learn that although a number of intelligence services have shared information with the United States and the West for years, the latter have not gone to the level of strategic alarm. The matter remains in the hands of governments, not heads of secret services. Did Egypt, Syria, and Tunisia inform the United States and its allies of the meaning of al Qaeda? Some witnesses and historians say they did. But most experts know that the warnings were technical and tactical, not strategic and historic. Did the government of Saudi Arabia, for example, explain what is behind al Qaeda, other than its intention to strike the United States when possible? Obviously not. To do so, it would have had to reveal the Wahabi ideology that produced al Qaeda, ideology that also is a pillar of the regime itself.

In simple terms, very few leaders and regimes in the Middle East exposed the ideology of al Qaeda in addition to its terrorist character. Why not? First, to do so would have exposed their own regimes if they too were inhaling the same political culture, even though in smaller doses. Second, exposing Salafism or Wahabism in public would have opened a Pandora's box with their own clerical networks at home. In the absence of a regional reform and of a democratic debate, let alone full democracy, authoritarian governments could not expose Islamic fundamentalism without placing themselves at risk.

Al Qaeda was originally a "jinn" released by the Wahabis and the Muslim Brotherhood in the 1920s. In the late 1970s, it became a work in progress. By the 1980s it developed its own strength and experienced a huge victory. By the early 1990s it was developing its own identity. It searched for a launching pad in several countries, including in Saudi Arabia and Sudan, before it made its base in Afghanistan. It needs a piece of real estate to construct its physical presence and a central directorate, but it is omnipresent worldwide, particularly in majority Sunni countries.[13]

The founders of al Qaeda—originally Abdallah Azzam, then Osama bin Laden, joined afterward by Ayman Thawahiri—wanted a worldwide "mother ship" for the top jihadists. Since 2001 I have compared them to the "SS of jihad," not to create a sensation but simply to explain how elite, capable, indoctrinated, and frightening al Qaeda is among the constellation of jihadists. But it is also to show that the group is only the tip of the current iceberg, and many icebergs are forming behind. It is important to realize that al Qaeda is an advanced form of neo-Wahabi jihadism, but it is neither the first nor the last. It is as of September 11 the most relevant to U.S. national security and the most threatening to international security, from Iraq's Sunni triangle to Madrid and London.

Many excellent books have shown that in its design and structure, al Qaeda is a mixed organism. It has a highly centralized body, with international and also regional command centers, covering continents and vast regions. It has its own central units, deployed in many places. Before the removal of the Taliban in Afghanistan, al Qaeda enjoyed a safe haven where it was able to train, plan, fund-raise, communicate worldwide, and even produce new generations under the full protection of a jihadist regime. Bin Laden and his associates had sought these special relations with an Islamic fundamentalist regime so that they could establish themselves under the protection of a government in control of its own borders and defense and security systems. Al Qaeda's initial project, to find refuge in the central home of Wahabism—Saudi Arabia—failed in the early 1990s. Osama thought he would have a backup in Sudan. But again, by 1995, Khartoum came under tremendous pressure to evacuate the "foreign terrorists" from the country. The battles in the south against the black Africans had not been very successful, so bin Laden and his cohorts traveled back to Afghanistan, where they joined forces with an identical force, the Taliban, to take over the country in 1996. With the exception of a small northern enclave, Afghanistan fell under the Taliban, and the Taliban were under the influence of al Qaeda. Al Qaeda had become state-based and had extended its tentacles around the world. Here again, the international community saw the events but did not grasp their ultimate meaning. The Arab regimes felt the jihad boys would entertain themselves at home, now that they had a country of their own. The Europeans did not want to mess with jihadists in central Asia, fearing that doing so would enflame the Islamists deeply implanted in their midst. The Salafi war in Algeria had shown since 1992 how violent the fundamentalists were with their Muslim co-religionairies. From that could be projected how violently they would deal with infidels.

And finally, the United States was not able either to understand or to handle those holy fighters on the other side of the world. Despite the fact that strikes had already taken place against New York's twin towers in 1993 and against Saudi Arabia's Khubar Towers in 1994, and that violence was widespread from Algeria to Chechnya, throughout the decade, confusion reigned in Washington. As I will note later, the "ship" landed in Afghanistan, but the "expert elite" in the United States refused to define it as such, and made the case for a diplomatic approach—only—with the Taliban. Twice opportunities presented themselves for action against the Taliban and al Qaeda, and twice the advice was not to "complicate international relations." How ironic it is to realize that the "whisper" came from the same quarters that have refused to see a threat in Salafi jihadism. How ironic it is to conclude that by climbing the grapevine all the way up from the roots, you discover another "jihad" doing all it can to obstruct any form of awakening within the United States.

Al Qaeda's new jihad was in fact heavily relying on the Wahabi's old jihad. Al Qaeda's jihad, a younger movement, would strike in direct ways, and in indirect ways; the Wahabi jihad, older in age, would shield itself and the younger jihad from the wrath of the targeted enemy.

Chapter Nine

JIHADIST STRATEGIES AGAINST AMERICA

O NE OF THE GREATEST SUBJECTS OF INTEREST THAT HAS EVER OCCUPIED the minds and the attention of the U.S. national security apparatus since the collapse of the Soviet Union has been and remains the terrorist threat against mainland America. From the morning of the September 11, 2001, attacks, U.S. national security changed forever. Never before had any enemy been able to massacre three thousand mostly civilian Americans in less than an hour in the two most important cities of the continent, if not the world. Four and a half decades of conflict with a nuclear Soviet Union had not produced one strike on American cities, but nineteen men with no uniforms, belonging to no government, wreaked havoc on the sole remaining superpower. The damage was high in human lives and economic stability. But perhaps a greater effect was on the feeling of security and safety that Americans had enjoyed for ages, which was deeply wounded that day. Americans have suffered tremendously in previous wars, but they knew they were at war. In the terror war waged against them, the surprise was overwhelming. Hence the reaction, the rethinking, and the search for answers.

Immediately after the tragedy, the U.S. moved to lick its wounds and counterattack. The president responded to the challenge, Congress supported him, and a campaign was launched to remove the Taliban and root out al Qaeda from Afghanistan. Above all, a Homeland Security Department was created to fend off future attacks on national soil. America responded mechanically, by the book. But its response was based on what it knew, not with what it did not know. This is not a mere play on words but a geopolitical reality. If one observes the global reaction of the United States and its allies to the terrorist attacks and reviews the evolution of U.S. discourse, actions, and plans, one realizes that the current counteroffensive, both overseas and at home, is still mutating. The U.S. understanding of what happened that morning of September 11—its root causes, and the strategies to fight back—is not final or fully formed. It is moving forward, but with the learning process that accumulates as the war progresses and the nation fights its battles. The question that tops all questions—one I am attempting to address throughout the book—is this: What about future jihads or future terrorist strategies? Is the United States fighting the right war and fighting it in the right way? In other words, is the United States fighting only what it saw, what is sees, what it knew, and what it knows? And if that is the case, could the United States know the whole story and see the whole picture?

One of the unknown dimensions of the war on terror—the one that can determine the outcome or perhaps its length and the price that will be paid—remains on the other side. Questions abound: Is this an all-out war, and who is fighting it? With what means and strategies?[1] Moving forward from the historical evolution of the jihadist movement in the past chapters, let us concentrate on that missing piece of the picture. Now that we have traveled back in time to discover the deep roots of the jihadist movement, its origins, its old references, its logic, and its trajectory, the next analysis concerns how the jihadists wage their war and what their strategies are.

THE WAR AGAINST AMERICA: WHY AND HOW?

In the months after September 11, a huge debate covered the airwaves, print press, and campuses around the United States, spreading outward to the four inhabited continents. It was encapsulated in two words: Why America? Why did the jihadists strike there at that particular time? In the next chapters I discuss the variables and the multiple objectives of the war against America and the West as outlined by the Salafis in general and al Qaeda in particular. But here I provide one answer from a strictly strategic angle—one that strategists of any war throughout history have always understood as the chief reason for the conflict and one that military and political historians have not been able to escape: the jihadists decided to wage war against the United States simply because it was possible.

Throughout history the jihadist ideology aimed at taking down *dar el harb.* As long as no reforms occur in the doctrinal realm, the global objective to defeat what they perceive as the "house of war" will remain standing, for decades or even centuries. My reading of the evolution of the jihadist movement since the beginning of the twentieth century is that by the early 1990s, after the final collapse of the Soviets, the "central computer" of the international network thought that the war against the United States could be won and, more important, that Allah was on the side of the holy warriors.

A plethora of analytical evidence emerged in the last years indicating that the jihadists genuinely believed that America was ripe for defeat. And based on this belief, they designed strategies to achieve that goal. Some among us may have thought that terrorists strike just because they feel like it, or that they attack at will with no global plan. Many among us describe them as thugs and common (albeit unusual) criminals.

They can be described as such because of their deeds. But while they do indeed strike when an opportunity to hit an ideal target presents itself, I also believe they act under a strategy, which in turn operates within the confines of an ideology. To summarize and clarify, the global Salafi constellation, which draws its thinking and belief system from Ibn Taymiya, the Wahabis, the Muslim Brotherhood, and other *takfiris,* do believe in the ultimate downfall of America and the West and, in general terms, the larger *dar el harb.* But the "constellation" is complex and most of its currents are cautious, using rational thinking to analyze conflict strategies and international relations.

Regimes such as the Wahabi Saudis, the Sudanese Nationalist Islamist Front, and the Shiite Islamic Republic of Iran know all too well that a global confrontation with the United States will bring only defeat to these governments. Secular but radical, the Baathist regimes of Syria and Iraq also understand the equation. Even when he invaded Kuwait, Saddam projected a possible American reaction. But, barring apocalyptic developments and divine intervention, all of the above powers knew of the consequences of a direct war with the United States. Furthermore, they clearly assumed that with the state of world affairs and their levels of power and technology, they could not project a sustained campaign against the U.S. mainland. It was not even a possibility. Why did these regimes understand these parameters, but the international jihadists did not? What factors made the difference in thinking? Why were Turabi, Qadhafi, Assad, Saddam, Arafat, and Khumeini able to realize this simple fact, but not Osama bin Laden?

One evening during the fall of 2001, I was watching an al Jazeera panel on the "justification" of the September 11 attacks. The show, titled *Opposed Directions,* featured two vocal participants from the Arab world who were facing off loudly. Viewers who did not understand Arabic might have thought that this was a third world version of CNN's *Crossfire.* The two guests seemed to be at each other's throats, the screams bursting from the TV set. What were they arguing about? Just strategy. The show was discussing the "worthiness" of the September 11 attacks. Did bin Laden do good or bad to the Arab world by striking the U.S. mainland? Viewers might have thought that one man was for and the other against the principle of war against America. But in fact, the debate was really about *which strategy* jihadists should have used. One guest said the timing of the strikes was wrong. "They should have waited more, a few more years to perform such attacks. It was too early. There are many battlefields in the world unfinished. This is going to be very bad for Palestine." The other guest responded firmly: "Not at all, we needed to hit the head of the snake, and the snake is America. You hit there and the whole thing would collapse." He added: "Can't you see the signs? Bush has already recognized a Palestine. Had bin Laden not attacked, nobody would have spoken about Palestine."

This exchange is just one fragment of the streams of debates that took place in the Arab world, sometimes on al Jazeera, but all over the media and even more on the Internet. The discussions in the region among radicals and fundamentalists focused on the questions of "why now" and "what the strikes would accomplish." Even as recently as fall 2004, TV networks were gathering live "town meetings" and debating the rationale for a direct attack against America. The astounding thing is that almost no one among the jihadist sympathizers discussed the principle of war with America. They were concerned about the timing, the tools, and the strategy. This is amazing, because in the United States, the public debate did not even seriously discuss the actual strategies adopted by the terrorists, or by their ideological backers. America's first questions after the attacks were as simplistic as "Why do they hate us?" or even "Who are they?" The differences between the two debates are huge. As average Americans were waking up to learn about the existence of an "enemy" and of its intentions, average jihadists were already analyzing the effect of the strategies and debating which one should have been employed.

ONE STRATEGY, TWO, OR MORE?

In the not so distant future, historians and political scientists will be teaching "jihad studies," a course I was teaching even before 9/11. This course was comparable to Soviet studies or radical ideologies studies. Researching the thinking mode and the application of strategies devised by the various schools of thought of the jihadists is fascinating. But unlike the conclusions of most Middle East studies scholarship in the 1990s, a serious and thorough analysis of the plans devised by the jihadi activists, their literature, their actions, their statements, their debates, and their history makes clear the fact that strategies do exist. America's scholarly conclusion said the opposite. This statement is relevant because of the failure of the academic debate in the United States and in the West to reach a conclusion.

As I discuss ahead, one major problem that existed in U.S. and western defense systems during the 1990s was the expert elite's response to the question: Is there a jihadist strategy against America and its allies? The overwhelming answer by the academic elite, acting as a national expert body for government and media, was to say no, that there was no "threat" coming from the jihadists; it was all a "myth" created by westerners, and therefore there were no serious jihadist strategies against the United States or its homeland. At best, these "experts" described the anti-Americanism of the Islamists as a mere reaction to U.S. foreign policy.[2]

In reality, four major forces out of the Middle East—most but not all of them jihadists—have shown signs of policies aiming at undermining U.S. and western influence:

1. Salafists—neo-Wahabis such as al Qaeda and its sister organizations
2. Wahabis within the Saudi regime (not necessarily the entire monarchy)
3. The Khumeinist line of the radical Mullahs in Tehran and Hezbollah
4. And to a lesser degree of efficiency, the other radical Pan-Arabists such as the Baathists, when they operate in alliance with one of the other three currents

Against the opinion of a majority of scholars and intellectuals, I argued throughout the 1990s that there was a history and an ideology behind the jihadists, that they have strategically positioned themselves to move against the United States and the West, and that they do have strategic approaches to this task. However, I came to realize early on that instead of having just one strategy with which to confront the United States, the jihadists have two, perhaps three. Are these strategies connected? This more difficult question is addressed later. But for now, let us explore the major components of the various strategies.

Six tracks can be detected in the jihadist strategic approach:

1. Economic jihad: oil as a weapon
2. Ideological jihad: intellectual penetration
3. Political jihad: mollification of the public
4. Intelligence jihad: infiltration of the country
5. Subversive jihad: Behind enemy lines and protected by its laws
6. Diplomatic jihad: controlling foreign policy

ECONOMIC JIHAD: OIL AS A WEAPON

In 1973, as a result of the Arab-Israeli October war, the Arab oil-producing coun-tries organized through the Organization of Petroleum Exporting Countries (OPEC) a supply boycott against the West, particularly affecting western Europe and the United States. Most of us remember the pictures of Dutch people biking in droves and Americans forming lines in front of gas stations. But what memory fails to remind us are the real consequences of the 1973 oil crisis.[3] Although the direct impact was on the daily consumers, the strategic heat was felt by national economies for many years. Before the boycott, the industrialized economies of Europe and North America had been thriving in large part from the relatively cheap gas flowing from the Gulf. The shock reverberated through the various lay-ers of economic structures: communications, transportation, industry, public and private heating, electricity, and all derivatives. Oil, or rather the lack of it, was the equivalent of a weapon of mass disruption. It became clear that a sudden and strategic decision to lower or block that flow would undermine the economies of the "other camp," leading to a weakening of its defenses. The "boycott," although economic and affecting the financial realm, is by itself a prime strategic weapon.[4]

The use of natural resources as a tool in conflicts is not new. But the impact left by the 1973 OPEC move created reverberations on both sides of the oceans. In the Arab world, Salafists and other radicals became conscious of the power that energy has over the "infidel powers." They realized how powerful were the tools at their disposal in the upcoming march westward. Oil was to the West what water was to Arabs and Israelis alike. Political elites and activists popularized the myth of the "oil bomb." Ever since, political parties, media, and graffiti on city walls have glorified the weapon "sent from Allah." I remem-ber those slogans in Beirut in the 1970s, slogans such as *"silah al naft aqwa silah"* (the weapon of oil, the strongest weapon) were common. But who de-signed this strategy of using oil as a weapon, and why?

The Wahabi regime of Saudi Arabia chose to use this weapon in 1973 be-cause it felt the time had come to readjust its relationship with the West and the United States in general. Instead of being perceived as the weakest link of the relationship, the Saudis wanted to raise their position. By instigating the oil boycott, the Wahabis killed two birds with one stone: On one hand they rebal-anced their position in the equation by forcing the West and the United States to respect their influence and fear them.[5] And on the other hand, they showed immense credibility among the Wahabi clerics and their followers. The monar-chy asserted its power among its own crowd. If the Saudis could challenge the "infidels" (the United States and allies) in the midst of a cold war with the Soviets, then they could use this weapon anytime in the future, the Salafists believed. At this point, oil jihad developed on two tracks: one led by the Saudis, the other designed by the jihadists. Both tracks are fueling future jihads.

The Wahabi influence generated from the 1973 economic strike was invested inside the West, and particularly in the United States. Western governments and multinational corporations (MNCs) feared a repeat of the oil bomb. As a result, a policy of co-optation by the Saudis began to take root in Washington. It developed in two directions. Slowly but surely, the kingdom's influence solidified in the United States, as the Saudis cooperated with the West. This partnership grew stronger after the Soviet invasion of Afghanistan in 1979. Cheap oil and a joint front against Moscow opened a wide field for collaboration between "infidel America" and fundamentalist Arabia. The Wahabis saw an immense opportunity in this relationship to implant irreversible policies that would favor their plans. Oil provided them a historic long-term toehold in the western system, and they exploited it with all their resources.

First, internationally, the Wahabis of Saudi Arabia stretched their cover over all Islamic fundamentalists in the region and worldwide. The friends of the "oil allies" should be America's friends. Hence, the United States found itself linking up with Islamists in many places on many projects: with the Muslim Brotherhood against the communists; with the Salafis against the Baathists; with the Afghan mujahidin against the Soviets. The Saudi elite also hooked up with the MNCs, and for a couple decades the Islamic fundamentalists enjoyed a powerful international shield. On the one hand, Saudi oil power and MNCs, mostly American business partners, opened a space for Wahabi influence inside the United States. Through these gates, ideological penetration, political mollification, terrorist infiltration, and control of foreign policy progressed year after year, until the time al Qaeda charged in head on.

At first, the jihadists adopted the same policy as the Saudis: let the flow of influence penetrate the American system and let it take its time to reach the country in depth. Until about the early 1990s, Salafi clerics endorsed the Wahabi wisdom and enjoyed the dividends of oil influence. But with the collapse of the Soviet Union, the more daring among the Salafists and the Afghan Arab veterans felt the time was up. They thought oil had done its job. Now had come the time for military jihad.

IDEOLOGICAL JIHAD: INTELLECTUAL PENETRATION

Having spent fourteen years in American academia since the end of the cold war, I have seen firsthand how jihadist ideologies have systematically penetrated the United States, as a prelude to the more lethal terror network. This web of ideological penetration is the most dangerous long-term threat to U.S. national security, and the principal root cause of past and future jihad terror success. This type of penetration was possible because of the preceding Arabian oil influence. Historically, one led to the other. As the financial influence of the Wahabis and their American associates spread out in Washington and nationwide, the tentacles of political power started to appear. The reasoning is rational: Once you control the mind, the body will follow. For years before the terror strikes in 1993 and again in 2001 on the U.S. mainland, the Wahabis undertook a slow, methodical, and almost irreversible invasion of America's cultural system, the country's "brain," if you will. But the Wahabi ideological penetration wasn't monodimensional. It was not a brainwashing of one individual after the other, or a conversion, followed by a recruitment process, as has been the case for other ideologies. This penetration was bigger, deeper, wider, and more complex.

The United States is a huge country under a democratic constitution, with its freedoms and its way of life. It is the most powerful democracy on Earth and equipped with endless resources to maintain peace worldwide while withstanding enormous threats and defeating them one after the other, decade after decade. In the eyes of the Salafis, that was the state of affairs at the end of the twentieth century. So how would you go about defeating America if the Soviets were not able to? The answer is simple: You penetrate its mind; blind its eyes; block its ears; and open its gates to your Trojan horses. And as you are eroding its resistance to your threat, you take the control of its arms and guide them against your other enemies around the world. The jihadists and their leaders, the Salafists of the Middle East, believe that America was a giant with little experience of life—just two hundred years versus thirteen centuries of jihadism. The essence of their strategy was to avoid direct confrontation until its body was weakened, then administer the coup de grâce. This was the fundamentalists' initial master plan. And this plan was understood and endorsed by the active jihadists who benefited from it, until they got the divine inspiration that *fatah* time had come, and they leaped forward.

The ideological penetration of America developed in stages. It began with the "American associates" of the emirs building a better image for the kingdom of Saudi Arabia in the United States. So far, and as long as it was about U.S. needs to enhance relations with a friendly Arab country, the "campaign" was normal. Then a special emphasis was put on the "oil needs" provided by the Saudis to America. Even to this point, the campaign was still within the framework of international relations. But once the Saudis experienced the power of oil politics as a result of the 1973 boycott and the West's subsequent diplomatic "surrender," they moved into the cultural realm. The jihad for the minds and the hearts of the United States sprouted in all directions: government lobbying, media public relations, and more important, the influencing of academia and the intelligentsia. A distinction must be made between the promotion of the strict interests of the government of Saudi Arabia and the promotion of the ideology ruling the kingdom. At times they might overlap, but the ideological influence is wider, more persistent, and would become the long-term ingredient of Wahabi power inside America and worldwide.

As detailed in many recent books and articles, the Wahabi assault on the nation's mind targeted the academic world first. As of the early 1980s, significant amounts of petrodollars started to find their way to universities, research centers, and public libraries across the country. Some came directly, under Saudi names, and some via business "partners." All ended up as endowments, programs, grants, and other forms of educational investments. The influx of Wahabi blood in the academic body had its immediate effects. With no mechanism to regulate, counter, provide alternatives, or check the content, the scholarly tsunami thrust deep into campuses. Existing Middle East studies programs were financially supported, others were created, and programs heavily endowed. But this Wahabi generosity was not all "nonprofit," despite its legal status: By funding the very programs that were supposed to teach American students about the Middle East and its political culture, the donors were taking control of the knowledge.[6] And as many experts who have been warning about the intellectual genocide taking place on U.S. campuses have explained, the epicenter of cultural jihad is right there: in the funding imposed on the curriculum and the hiring of teachers. In order to keep and increase the stream of petrodollars into the institutions, the academic doors were opened wide to the will of the Wahabi donors. The intellectual siege on the American mind began.[7]

The Wahabi strategists were shrewd in their ideological penetration of the United States. They did not attempt to merely praise the Saudi leader. Rather they presented a sanitized version of the history of the Middle East. In the new textbooks, there was no Islamic conquest, no *fatah,* no jihad. There were no conquered peoples and no identity crises in the region. But more important, the Salafis were presented as mere "reformers" and the Wahabis as just "conservatives." Middle East studies in America were transformed: The Islamists were mutated into forces of change, but not regressive "change" toward the caliphate of the Middle Ages. Even secular dictatorships were described as "transitional regimes." Last but not least, jihad was painted as a spiritual inner experience, almost a yoga exercise. Subversion of the text was accompanied by a "cartelization" of the field. Once the first wave of takeover of Middle East studies was

digested, the ongoing process was to ensure the allegiance of the instructors.
The elites in control would co-opt the new Ph.D.s seeking jobs. At the annual meetings of the Middle East Studies Association of America, the national vehicle used by the apologists, the anointment of new generations of
Middle East studies graduates put even more teachers in the classrooms. The
travesty was not without catastrophic consequences for the largest democracy on the planet.[8]

From the classroom, the graduates were picked up to serve either as teachers for future classrooms or as public servants in agencies—State Department,
Congress, embassies, and beyond. And to amplify the "Wahabi" version of history and Middle East politics, brainwashed graduates were placed in the media,
both public and private. For more than two decades, the "Wahabi" apologists
were in a position to provide strategic advice in foreign policy, academia, and
the media. The circle was not to be broken until Mohammed Atta crashed into
the Twin Towers on September 11.

A number of authors, including María Pinto, for example, clearly defended
the jihadists by claiming that those who describe them as terrorists were dis-
traught defense planners in need of a new enemy, presumably one that would
justify their ample budgets! The blurring process is systematic: Lebanon's war,
which started in 1975, is only blamed on Israel's invasion of 1982 and not on
Syria's occupation since 1976. Osama bin Laden is described as a "Saudi busi-
nessman who served as an Islamic recruitment agent for Afghanistan and main-
tains an office in Sudan"![9]

The ideological penetration served to blur the American vision. All
sources of knowledge were blocked. All hope to understand the gathering dangers was lost. Under these dark clouds, the actual jihad terrorists moved in, in
the friendliest atmosphere possible. If the public could not see them, if the elite
did not focus on their threat, if the government was badly advised, and if the
media was misfed by experts who minimized the threat and called it a "myth,"
who could stop the terrorists?[10]

POLITICAL JIHAD: MOLLIFICATION OF THE PUBLIC

The fact that a threat is off the radar screen doesn't mean that it has vanished.
In the case of the United States and terrorists, the threat was invisible. And
when the intellectual defenses of a nation are put to sleep, its political institutions are unable to detect the threat. This was phase two in the jihadist strategy
against the United States and eventually the West. Once the government was
blocked from receiving the right advice from the research community, once it

did not receive any advice at all, or, worse, once it received the wrong advice, the country's political defenses went down.

This stage is "political mollification," which occurs when the opposing camp is successful in diverting the attention of the nation, its government, and its media from the prime enemy. The political influence of the opponent, backed with money, can blur the vision of the political establishment and paralyze its ability to become conscious of the mounting threat. The jihadist strategy aimed at anesthetizing the political establishment of the United States and the West in order to achieve its long-term objectives.[11] The Wahabi influence operated according to a recognizable strategy, as follows.

Its first objective was to deflect attention from the rise of Islamic fundamentalism in the Middle East, especially after the Soviet collapse. Since the end of the cold war, Islamist influences in the United States and the West focused on camouflaging the movement. Two lines were followed:

1. Reassure the public and leaders that the worldwide movement is not a threat.
2. Promote the idea that the movement inside the United States and western Europe is part of the political culture.

Hence, in the absence of public knowledge (due to ideological penetration), jihadism was normalized. Americans recently have been stunned to learn that for many years madrassas (religious schools) have been teaching hatred and the culture of terrorism abroad, while the United States was supporting the sponsors of those schools. The U.S. public has only recently learned that those very teachings are also being spread right here in America.[12]

A second objective of Wahabi influence was to give visibility to U.S.-based groups and lobbies that support jihadism in all of its forms overseas. Especially as of the early 1990s, more and more local organizations that firmly support jihadism and advocate its causes (some funded directly by the Wahabis) have surfaced, gaining prominence and acceptance. These groups, profiting from the intellectual space provided by the scholarly expert community, made inroads in the American system. Jihad advocacy groups built significant ties with members of the legislative branch, and some were even received at the White House. Obviously once a network of entities backed by fundamentalist regimes from the outside is able to become part of the political system, it can paralyze the capacity of institutions to identify the threat. Simply, when the U.S. government turns to the jihadists for information on jihadism, the resistance to jihad terrorism is doomed.

By the mid-1990s and despite the 1993 attack on the Twin Towers, the public domain of the United States was demobilized against the surging threat. Very few knew what jihad was, who the Wahabis were, or what Salafi doctrine was. (This applied to the Khumeinist Islamists as well.) Only isolated groups or think tanks were warning about the upcoming offensives. This and only this state of mind explains why most Americans could ask on September 11: "Why do they hate us, and by the way, who are they?" As I'll note later, this mollification caused political indecision regarding evidence of terrorism; actual terrorist acts, such as those in 1998 and 2000; and the best preparation for future terrorist attacks. Once the foe's political decision making and defenses are crippled, it becomes time for infiltration.

INTELLIGENCE JIHAD: INFILTRATION OF THE COUNTRY

The most dangerous stage for national security occurs when a wide infiltration of the system occurs—especially if this series of moves is achieved after prior demobilization and under a government that lacks decisive policies. With economic pressure to shield the ideological penetration, and that ideological penetration blinding the public and politically paralyzing the institutions, the terrain is ready for terrorist infiltration. But are we talking about a systematic cold war–like infiltration of the United States? The answer is yes and no. The jihadist infiltration of America was not only the work of state-sponsored spy agencies. Evidently, as expected during the cold war and in the 1990s, pro-Soviet regimes such as Syria, Iraq, Iran, and Libya developed intelligence networks inside the United States, taking advantage of the fact that America is a country of emigrants par excellence. It is well known that Iran, for example, has infiltrated the Iranian exile community; likewise, the Castro regime has planted spies within the Cuban exile community. So did the Baath regimes infiltrate Arab communities in North America. But in these cases, the governments were spying *against* their own immigrant communities, most of which are opposed to the regimes in their native lands. So the classic infiltration of Arab and Muslim communities by authoritarian regimes from the Middle East aims at neutralizing and combating the opposition movement in exile. However, these intelligence services are also involved in the greater task of gathering information about U.S. national security and secret diplomacy, inasmuch as it can serve the interest of their regimes. These types of spy activities are well addressed in general by U.S. or Western counter-intelligence agencies, with some exceptions. But there is a more dangerous type of infiltration that has defeated the national security apparatus for decades and constitutes the most lethal threat from future jihadist terrorism. (Note that Hezbollah had been able to exercise considerable influence in Canada until 2004, not only in the media but also within its immigration system.[13])

When the Wahabi influence spreads through financial circles, dominates the scholarly community, and establishes political credibility in the government and media, it basically asserts itself as part of the legitimate political culture, at least in the field of its interest, which is further protecting Wahabism in America and the West, promoting its activists and friends, and opening additional doors so that it dominates the debate about Middle East policies. Among the areas of increasing influence are Arab and Muslim communities, civil rights movements, the court system, the entertainment industry, and finally, the security and military apparatus. The following are a few examples of substrategies developed by the Islamists in the United States and in many western countries.[14]

As Wahabi influence increased within U.S. financial circles, government, and media, particularly since 1973 and more intensely as of the early 1990s, the political dividends were invested within the Arab Muslim communities inside the country. In less than two decades, Salafi and jihadi organizations have taken over control and/or the representation of these segments of the American society. The first *fatah* of the Islamic fundamentalists is to dominate the émigrés inside the *dar el harb*. Using petrodollar funding, the radicals sweep into community institutions and take over. Almost all mosques, educational centers, and socioeconomic institutions fall into their hands. This phenomenon has been common across the Atlantic: In addition to the United States and Canada, France, Germany, Spain, the Netherlands, Belgium, Britain, and Scandinavia have all witnessed the "invasion" of their immigrant communities by Wahabi, Salafi, and other radical currents coming from the Arab Islamic world. By the early 1990s, the Islamic fundamentalists had taken control of the communities' establishments on both sides of the Atlantic. With the political "representation" of millions of citizens in their hands, the fundamentalists have sealed the circle of their grip. Backed by the Saudis from overseas on the outside, with, ironically, the endorsement of all Arab and some Muslim governments (in deference to the Saudis and as a way to obtain influence for their own interests); supported from within the academic community by the "experts"; called upon by the mainstream media as authorities; and recognized by governments as the sole representatives, the Salafists and their allies had established a hub of power within the United States and the West by the early 1990s.

It is not difficult to guess how they will use this power. Using the communities as a shield and with the recognition provided by academia, the media, and government as a sword, the fundamentalists have moved deeper inside the national tissue. They targeted three crucial layers of society: With the power of "community representation," they established a net of connections with the Arab civil rights movements and civic associations. Amazingly enough, while their comrades oppress millions of people overseas, the jihadists within the West pose as civil rights advocates, interested solely in the "rights" of their immigrant communities. By gagging those whom they claimed to represent for years via institutional control, Wahabis and Salafists have become the sole or dominant social activists of these constituencies.[15] This layer of additional protection, very important to most Americans (or westerners in general) who are attached to the idea of civil liberties, has allowed them to strengthen their initial representation with government even further. And from this very "Americanized" launching pad, the movement was able to move inside the most sacred realm in society after religion: the justice system.

Since they had the backing of academia, which they called on when needed to testify in court, and they enjoyed the civil rights label, it was easier for the groups to penetrate the legal mind. I myself have seen the "jihad net" in action inside the courtroom. Political jihadism controls at least two of the three main players in the court: the "experts" they have already enlisted on campus, and the jury (i.e., the public), who they have prevented from learning about jihad by their control of the classroom and media. For twenty years, not one single court in America or the West has been able to indict "jihadist activities." In simple words, since the jihadists are the ones who define what jihad is in court, what can we expect these tribunals to do, if they are to judge on the substance and the historical conditions of the suspect activities? Nothing!

The fundamentalists seek the final frontier: the ultimate downfall worldwide of the U.S. military and security. Out of the jihad webs in the greater Middle East, it has been clearer and clearer that, ultimately, it is the military and security power of the United States that stands against their final project of reestablishing the caliphate by violent means. They have seen U.S. power in action during World War II, during the first Gulf War, and in the Afghanistan and Iraq campaigns. Jihadists also realize that U.S. agencies overseas and in the homeland are the major hindrances to their designs. They apply similar logic to all "infidel" armed forces around the world. But it is common wisdom that by undermining "Rome's" national and international security, the ensuing crumbling would devastate world security. Hence, a long-term objective is to penetrate the U.S. security agencies and military bodies.

The Soviet Union also recognized the need to infiltrate those U.S. agencies, but it was never able to do so strategically. Why do jihadists believe that they can?[16]

The fundamentalists have established a toehold within the United States itself, and they can focus on a slow, long-term infiltration of the military and security apparatuses. The type of infiltration is different on this side of the Atlantic from what occurs in the Middle East. In the Arab world, Muslim Brotherhood or Salafis can easily blend into a mostly Arab or Muslim army or Mukhabarat. The cultural element is already in place. The difficulty there is only "organizational." All they need is not to be caught or found to be in touch with "brotherly" ideologues outside the military. In the United States, or in any western country for that matter, the ideological affiliation does not count. You can be a full-fledged Wahabi or even jihadist, and you are still legally protected. It is only if you "act" in the interest of a foreign power that your rights are suspended. But fundamentalists and jihadists do not have a government they need to report to. They may be remotely backed by regimes to "spread the good Wahabi news" inside all U.S. institutions, but do not have a specific order to execute. The smartest part of the jihadi design in infiltrating the U.S. and western military and security bodies is to tie infiltration not to state interest, but to American domestic objectives. The objectives are to spread Wahabism in the U.S. armed forces and ultimately even into the Pentagon, and to be recruited into the Central Intelligence Agency, Federal Bureau of Investigation, and Homeland Security agencies. Militant action is not the immediate objective. The most important mission is to further recruit and grow their numbers until the "holy moment" comes. The jihadi strategy of infiltration in infidel lands is not strictly action-driven; it aims mostly to insert jihadi beliefs as deeply as possible until the global strategic signal is given to launch the final assault. As the seeds develop into a well-implanted network, the hard-core terrorists move in.

SUBVERSIVE JIHAD: BEHIND ENEMY LINES

In 1997, in the wake of South Florida University's controversy over alleged terror-related activities, I was interviewed on CNN about terrorist infiltration inside the United States. Media and the public were perplexed as to how terrorists have anything to do with U.S. campuses. I then told CNN that "in America, terrorists can build 90 percent of their network on a campus, using all facilities from desks, meeting rooms, fax machines, computers, and on top of it arrange to get a budget from the Student government."[17] It is only the last 10 percent, the final sprint toward the actual act of terrorism, that is illegal. But by the time all is in place, it may well be too late. I explained that this was the situation with the whole society, not just universities. But there are nuances.

The Wahabi ideological and political penetration and infiltration is a global movement aimed at inserting itself in the national tissue of the United States and other countries around the world. This is the strategy of the wider Wahabi-Salafi current, with long-term objectives, on domestic and foreign affairs. The objectives of mainstream Islamic fundamentalists are to control the ability of the infiltrated country to act against jihadism overseas and to increase the influence of the Islamists and their allies until a time comes when they can impact, if not disrupt, national policies. A more daring scenario would be to affect the socioethnic structure of the infidel country by provoking racial tensions, leading to a general breakdown of the targeted country. I'll expand on this long-term strategy later. But as this wider mechanism is developing, the actual terrorist networks—those jihadists who have declared war against the U.S., mainly al Qaeda in the 1990s and Hezbollah in the 1980s—have installed themselves and built their cells, communication systems, funding, and growth mechanisms. To simplify, while the main Wahabi infiltration widens its scope of influence under the laws of the land and in complete liberty, the jihad terror cells swim through this stream and land where they feel comfortable to do so. Wahabism is a current that carries jihadism, from which flows terrorism.

If the global movement has been able to protect itself, build credibility and respectability, and has inserted itself into the national culture and society, then the "special forces" of this ideological and political army can infiltrate the heartland of the United States and the West, protected from the country's attention and reaction. And where else would the terrorists choose to hide from the dragon, their ultimate enemy? In an interview with NBC in the 1990s, and with ABC and CBC after 9/11 in Florida, I said: "The safest place on Earth to hide from the dragon is inside its belly." At that time, all jihadists who were fighting on battlefields around the world, against U.S. allies, or America itself, understood that finding refuge in the United States was the most intelligent strategic achievement of the century. Hosted, granted legal status, fed, empowered, equipped with means to survive, grow, and ultimately strike[18]—that was a fantasy unparalleled worldwide. Similar possibilities were presented by Sweden, Holland, Germany, and Belgium, but the United States, the UK, and Canada surpassed them all with the support they granted the would-be terrorists—not only in logistics, but most important in political endorsement and integration. In the 1990s, you could be a jihadi, declare your enmity toward the United States, ready yourself to attack it, and even begin to do so; unless you were caught attacking, you were still under legal and political protection! And even if you were caught, the legal system had no way to indict you on what you really wanted to do, but only the lawyers' and prosecutors' ability to prove beyond doubt that you were holding that smoking gun.[19]

DIPLOMATIC JIHAD: CONTROLLING FOREIGN POLICY

Once inside the national tissue, dominating the brains and blurring the people's vision, the infiltrators can use the arms of this large body to execute their policies. The mother of all ironies is when the recipient of your national security and foreign policies becomes finally able to dictate them. The jihadi strategy is ultimately to be able to influence if not control U.S. foreign policy, and, subsequently, western policy toward the Middle East and the Arab and Muslim world. For decades, antiwestern and antidemocratic regimes and organizations in the region have been shrieking about American control of "their region, causes and destinies." They screamed it so loudly that it became the soul of what Edward Said tried to shape for half a century: The public conviction that the West in general and the United States in particular, even after the end of colonialism, are responsible for all the ills and disasters that have stricken the Middle East. In order to dodge their own responsibility for the real miseries of their masses, the conglomeration of totalitarians—including the jihadists—waged a campaign of "demonization" against Washington's foreign policy. "America is responsible for all our problems" continues to be the favorite claim of anti-American intellectuals on al Jazeera today. The stunning irony is the level of subversion reached by the jihadists in what was the widest intoxication operation in modern history. While they criticized Washington's foreign policy—easy prey as it has perpetrated significant mistakes for decades—they brought to bear all their resources and pressures so that they would be in control of that very foreign policy. And, sadly, they were successful until very recently.

Using an old Arabic saying, the Wahabis and their allies practiced the rule of *"Darabani wa baka sabaqani wa ishtaka,"* which translates as: "He hits me and cries, beats me to court and sues me." Indeed, all radical and fundamentalist critics, aided by their allies in the West, and particularly in the apologist fortresses on campuses, have put together a bible of anti-Americanism based essentially on an all-out critique of foreign policy. But the gist of it—which usually escapes the public—is not a better adjustment to human rights, democracy, and freedom in the Arab and Muslim world: just the opposite. What the pro-jihadi critics demand is a further submission of Washington to antidemocracy policies in the region. They criticized the United States for not putting pressure on totalitarian regimes in the region. But they have not explained who is

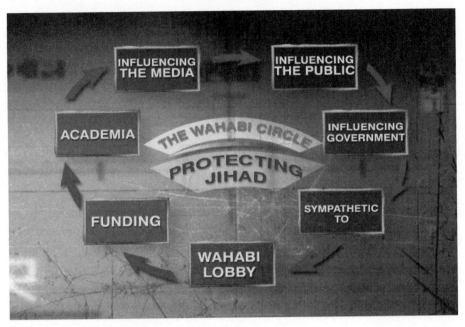

A power map of the jihadist lobby inside the United States.

asking the United States not to touch these regimes and ideologies![20] The answer is, the critics themselves. On many occasions Salafi clerics, such as Egyptian Yussef al Qardawi and Saudi al Nufeisi, openly stated on al Jazeera that "the best foreign policy the U.S. would have is not to have one." Many Salafi intellectuals and activists have screamed on the satellite networks and in chat rooms: "America, get your forces and diplomats from the world and sit inside your borders and shut up." What they did not add was what they intended to do after such a thing happened; the reader can now imagine.

The slow march for influencing and controlling U.S. foreign policy started after 1973 for reasons mentioned earlier—mainly oil. And with the coming together of all infiltrations, insertions, penetrations, mollification, and integration, the final result would merge in an unsurpassed encirclement of the foreign policy establishment and a mechanism for dictating policies. The most dramatic element in this equation was how unconscious the architects and members of the U.S. international policy establishment have been to it. In short, most of the diplomatic and policy corps dealing with the Middle East and the wider Muslim world strongly believed they were serving the best interests of the United States, and so were their colleagues elsewhere in the West. Amazingly, the Wahabi influence was so profound and subtle that it made its arms within the State Department, CIA, and information agencies think that they, not the Wahabis, were in control of policy. In fact, and as history showed until September 11, most decisions, plans, reactions, and statements dealing with subjects of interest to the Wahabis were Wahabi-inspired, through the extension of their power inside the United States and the West.

The policies designed and followed in Afghanistan, Lebanon, Yugoslavia, and the absence of policies in Sudan, Iraq, and Algeria, to give a few examples, reveal the fingerprints of Wahabism and its allies. Questions of whom the United States would ally itself with, whom it should abandon, and when, were decided by the core of Salafi clerics or authoritarian regimes; processed by their influence networks within the West and the United States; and implemented by the U.S. foreign policy establishment, which firmly but erroneously believed that it was the one generating these policies. This may sound like a harsh judgment but it is not as harsh as historians would present if they had access to all archives possible.[21] Obviously ideological forces, mostly from the left but also from the extreme right, found themselves in cahoots with the jihadi international agenda.

And as U.S. and western policies came under the control of the larger web of fundamentalist influence, the terror networks took advantage of every single case. The Taliban came to exist because the Saudis convinced the United States of their benefit; Hezbollah was allowed to take over in Lebanon because Riyadh protected the Syrian backers of the organization; al Qaeda was missed because the Wahabi influence warned Washington about "complications in the Muslim world"; a genocide took place in Sudan because Washington listened to Saudi and Egyptian advice; human rights abuses in the region were not addressed significantly because the Wahabi-funded academic establishment dismissed their reality when advising the U.S. government; the list is too long, but the common denominator is that by September 10, 2001, it was clear that Washington foreign policy had to be reformed, both because of the Islamists' arguments and because the United States was not aware of how far Islamist supporters had penetrated.

Chapter Ten

THE INEVITABILITY
OF 9/11

W HEN THE SEPTEMBER 11 COMMISSION INVITED DOZENS of officials and
experts to its hearings in 2004, it was starting from scratch in the discovery of what really happened. The commissioners, very bright and learned
personalities, were doing their homework as assigned by the U.S. Congress,
and by extension, for the American people. The commission, created in response to a call for answers by the relatives of the victims, marked the first time
that an official body of government was examining the jihad war conducted
against the United States.[1]

At the time of the attacks, and in the years that preceded the hearings, neither the relatives of the victims nor average Americans knew what kind of Pandora's box they were about to open. Most Americans, and perhaps many other
people around the world, were shocked by the strikes; it was almost as if the nation had been targeted by some evil coming from outer space. It looked like a
horror movie turned real; this was how unprepared the public was for a threat
that, as documented in previous chapters, had in fact been growing ever since
the 1920s and even before. The commission would help to reveal that there are
predictors and signs to such massive and catastrophic events.

The day after September 11, I gathered with my graduate students for our
weekly seminar and reflected on the apocalyptic images coming out of Manhattan and Washington. Most of my students were desperately searching for answers. So, I assume, were most other students and youths in the country. For in
their textbooks, lectures, and on their TV channels they were living on a different planet from the one in which the jihad was launched. This was a world
defined in the 1990s by Francis Fukuyama as "the . . . end of history."[2] They

were unprepared for this reality. And so were their elders. Their teachers were busy with tenure and grants, their families with Social Security, their political parties with Florida elections. Their weekends to some degree resembled MTV movies, and their international concerns, if any, revolved around the debate about globalization, which they knew a bit about, but not enough to understand completely. What had happened to the world they knew?

THE CREATION OF OSAMA BIN LADEN

Tens of thousands of miles away, on the plateau of Afghanistan, a man had set his sights on their country. *"Sa nudammer Amreeka,"* he told his men assembled a few days before the attacks: "We will destroy America." He lashed out against the "greatest infidel power in the history of mankind" and said: "You'll see the sign soon." That sign was the one murder he ordered in preparation for the Mohammed Atta mission, the suicide attack on Massoud Shah, the popular leader of the Northern Alliance of Afghanistan, forty-eight hours before the U.S. holocaust. When I read about the assassination during the weekend preceding September 11, I knew that there must be a very important reason for the Taliban (I assumed it was they) to send a suicide team to eliminate Massoud. The stalemate between their militia and the northerners was pretty rigid. I asked myself: Why would the Taliban kill their opponents' leader with an al Qaeda technique? The Northern Alliance would just appoint a new leader. Instincts told me that it made sense only as a preemptive strike; they killed him because they expected he would react to something they wanted to do.

In the weeks preceding September 11, all over the world there were signs that the jihadists were up to something unusual. A month before, I was observing the proceedings of the Durban conference on racism and imperialism. The speeches of the jihadists demonized the West much more than usual. In the less advanced chat rooms of the time—which now are discussed as evidence of possible terrorist attacks—the Salafists had been announcing a great strike to come. I remember reading "America, we're coming, the *Ghazwa* is ready." I realized later that al Qaeda indeed called the attack *"Ghazwa,"* a word, equivalent to *raid,* used by Arab historians to describe the *fatah.* This and other bits made me feel that something had snapped in the minds of the jihadists. Since I was swimming in jihad research at that time, I could not sleep during the last few nights before the attacks and have not slept easily on many nights since. Although it was hard to predict what might happen, at the same time it was easy to predict that something would.

THE "RINGS" FIND THE "LORD"

I have studied every video and audiotape aired on TV by bin Laden since September 11 and have been able to review his interviews since 1998 with al Jazeera. I have also reviewed other evidence, primarily in Arabic, that has enabled me to understand how al Qaeda thought. But more important by my own standards, I spent long hours before the tragedy interacting with Salafi activists and also Internet chatting with those whom I believe were linked to the organization or at least knew it extremely well. Al Qaeda's strategic thinking did not surprise me at all. Already, some twenty years ago, I had several exchanges in open media with persons I would now call intellectual precursors of al Qaeda's thinking process. From these combined sources of knowledge and all the material I have reviewed in the last few years, my assessment is simple: Osama bin Laden did not create al Qaeda. It created him.[3] By this I do not mean that bin Laden did not inspire his followers or was not charismatic: Not at all. But I believe that when historians look back and have access to a wider scope of information and testimonies, they will conclude that it was the "rings" that found the "lord," not the other way around. It may be too early to put the story together completely, but one can easily see that not only was Osama naturally inclined to lead a radical movement for jihad, but a Salafi environment in Arabia[4] readied him for the mission. A deep jihadi culture sculpted his personal wish to see the days of the caliphate return. Added to this was his life experience and drama. But first, he had to be immersed in Wahabi Salafi culture. Only in light of that does his contribution make sense.[5]

BIN LADEN'S CAUSES: BEIRUT, KABUL, BAGHDAD

Osama bin Laden, as a carrier of the Salafi ideology, resented three "infidel" onslaughts against Islam, as he saw it. According to his own accounts on TV, he was bewildered by the Israeli Air Force's pounding of the tall buildings of Beirut during the summer of 1982. I can see his reaction and understand how a jihadi would feel about "infidel" high-technology firing missiles against what he considered a Muslim city under siege (and it was). But Osama did not pay attention to the fact that the Soviet-supported Syrian troops had ravaged the other side of the city for six years before. His mind is trained to see through the lens of *dar el harb* and *dar el Islam* only. East Beirut did not belong to his *dar*—his house—hence he could not avenge its ruins, although he personally enjoyed the sight of the city from the hills of Broumana before the war. The idea of bringing down the towers of New York in retaliation to the bombed towers of Beirut may have been born there.

The second outrage that triggered bin Laden's fury was the Soviet invasion of Afghanistan in 1979. Although Moscow was a main supplier to the Arabs in their war with Israel, the communist invasion of yet another Muslim land—in addition to its invasions of the Muslim republics of the USSR—mobilized the Salafis in the region.

The third trigger of bin Laden's war against America was—as he often charged—the deployment of American forces on Muslim lands, and particularly in 1990 in Saudi Arabia, which he labeled as holy land. Interestingly enough, the actual area forbidden to non-Muslims is only the rectangle of the Hijaz area, covering Mecca and Medina. Non-Muslims, including Americans and others, in fact have been present on the peninsula for decades in great numbers. The British maintained forces in Oman for ages. But in the Salafi vision of the world, the insult is more about infidel forces crushing an Arab Muslim force: the Iraqi army. Salafi chats and websites blamed both Saddam and the Saudis for allowing the Americans to crush one of the largest and most powerful armed forces in the Arab world. This ideological vision of international relations is at the root of the Salafi anger that triggered attacks against the United States.[6] Strangely enough, the Wahabis, the state Salafists, have made the case for not engaging the Americans as long as they are (or were) supporting Muslim causes, such as defending the kingdom during the Gulf War and defeating the "Christian" Serbs in the 1990s. On both accounts the radical Salafis responded that "America is an infidel power that cannot be trusted." In the jihadi view, Americans came to help the royal family against Saddam and control oil. And in Bosnia, they allowed the Serbs to massacre the Muslims first, before they came to their rescue. There was no argument to convince Osama and his men that America was not the enemy. It was an ideological decision that transformed the ally of the past on the plateau of Afghanistan into the next target.[7]

THE FIRST WAVE, 1993 TO 1998

If we want to categorize the 1990s jihads against the United States and the West, we have to look at the global map of jihadi terrorism. Jihad warfare around the world can be divided into two prongs of attack: local terror and international terror.

LOCAL JIHAD TERROR

Beginning in 1990, Salafi violence erupted in Algeria, Kashmir, Chechnya, Israel, and elsewhere. In each of these battlefields, local conflicts were different:

political, ethnic, religious. But, in addition, they were all fueled by one international brand of ideology: Wahabism and Ikhwan doctrine. The Salafists moved inside these conflicts and made them into Islamist instead of nationalist ones. For example, Hezbollah in Lebanon asserted itself among Shiites (as opposed to Sunni Salafis) and transformed the secular struggle against Israel into a fundamentalist one. In a sense, these local jihads married the nationalist conflicts but drove them in one global direction, jihadism, connecting them to the mother ship of al Qaeda (with the exception of Shiite Hezbollah).

INTERNATIONAL JIHAD TERROR

As local fires erupted in several countries, the central force of jihad, particularly after the Khartoum gathering in 1992, targeted the United States head-on, both overseas and at home. By this point al Qaeda was in charge of the world conflict with America. The "princes" (or emirs) were assigned the various battlefields, but the "Lord" assumed the task of destroying the "greater Satan," America.

The first wave started in 1993 on two axes: One was in Somalia, where jihadists met U.S. Marines in Mogadishu in bloodshed. The United States withdrew. The same year, the blind sheikh Abdul Rahman and Ramzi Yusuf conspired to blow up the Twin Towers in New York.[8] Washington sent in the FBI and treated it as a criminal case, not as a war on terror. This was another form of withdrawal, and bin Laden and his brigades got the message. The test was clear: The United States will not fight the jihadists as a global threat. Something inside America was "paralyzing" it from even considering jihad a threat. Ironically, the first ones to understand the message were the jihad terrorists. The events of 1993 were a benchmark in the decision that led to September 11 years later. Bin Laden said later that the successful suicide attacks by Hezbollah against the Marines in 1983 convinced him that the United States would not retaliate against terror. The jihadists tested the United States twice ten years later, and twice they found the path open.[9]

In 1994, a bomb destroyed a U.S. facility of Khubar in Saudi Arabia, killing American military personnel. The "tower" was blown up by jihadists, but the investigation was not able to determine which group. The Saudis did not crack down on their radicals and the U.S. administration absorbed the strike. This was a third test, well appreciated by the jihadists. Meanwhile, three "wars" erupted worldwide with Salafists either leading or participating.[10] In Algeria, the fundamentalists have been involved in tens of thousands of murders against secular, mostly Muslim civilians. The Algerian regime was responding harshly too. But the United States and France did not focus on Salafi ideology and organizations. This was a fourth test that America and the West failed. In Chechnya, the Russians were fighting with the separatists, whom the Wahabis infiltrated. Some among them would become part of al Qaeda. Washington addressed veiled criticism to Moscow but kept silent on the jihadist infiltration of the Chechens. This was the fifth test.

By the early 1990s, the Bosnian conflict had exploded with its bloody ethnic cleansing. The United States was first to call for intervention, while the Europeans hesitated. Washington stood by the besieged Muslims against Serbs and Croats and mounted a military expedition to help them maintain their government. The jihadists formed a brigade and fought the Serbs fiercely, expending efforts to recruit elements for a local jihad—and eventually ship them to other battlefields. Not only did the United States tolerate the jihadists on the ground, but it even allowed Wahabi fundraisers in America to support their networks in the Balkans; that was the sixth test.

In 1996 the Taliban, one of the most radical Islamist militias on Earth, took over in Kabul. The old anti-Soviet Afghan allies were pushed all the way north to a precarious position. The ideology of the Taliban did not seem to impress or worry the foreign policy decision makers in Washington. The group's ruthless treatment of women, minorities, and other religious groups went unchecked. Its hosting of Osama bin Laden and al Qaeda was not dealt with. Worse, businessmen were interested in contracts under the new "stable" regime, and some American scholars were impressed with the Taliban's "achievements." This was the seventh instance of American failure to take any significant stand against the jihadists anywhere on any issue. It became almost certain that some "power" inside the United States was mollifying America's response and blurring its vision. That year, 1996, bin Laden issued his first international fatwa against the infidels.[11]

THE SECOND WAVE, 1998 TO 2001

Encouraged by the passivity of the U.S. executive branch toward the escalating jihadi assault worldwide and against American targets and interests, the "central computer" launched the second wave. This one was explicit, direct, and daring, targeting the infidel's diplomatic and military hardware.

On February 22, 1998, Osama bin Laden appeared on television for about twenty-seven minutes and issued a full-fledged declaration of war against the *kuffar*, America, the crusaders, and the Jews. The text was impeccable, with all the needed religious references to validate a legitimate jihad. The declaration was based on a fatwa signed by a number of Salafi clerics.[12] It was the most comprehensive Sunni Islamist edict of total war with the United States, and it was met with total dismissal by Washington. It evoked a few lines in the *New York Times,* no significant analysis on National Public Radio, and no debating on C-SPAN. The Middle East Studies Association had no panels on it, and the leading experts who advised the government downplayed it. During the 9/11 Commission hearings, U.S. officials said they noted it and that plans were designed to deal with it. As one commissioner asked, "This was a declaration of war. Why did not the President or anyone declare war or take it to Congress?" I asked the same question repeatedly from 1998 until September 2001, but my audience was much smaller on my campus in Florida. We must be careful not to miss these messages again.

Here was the leader of international jihad serving the United States and the infidels with a formal declaration of war grounded in ideological texts with religious references: Why did no one answer him? "Expert advice" within the Beltway ruled against it. Obviously, the Wahabis on the inside did not want to awaken the sleepy nation. If the U.S. government were to question the basis of Osama's jihad it would soon recognize the presence of an "internal jihad." For this reason, the debate about the declaration had to be suppressed and with it the warning about its upcoming threat. Al Qaeda must have been stunned. They openly declare war on the infidels, and rather than responding, the Americans are busy addressing political scandals instead. Osama must have thought: "Well, that's what the Byzantines did, when the sultan got to their walls centuries ago. They weren't mobilizing against the *fatah,* they were busy arguing about the sex of angels. This must be another sign from Allah that America is ripe. Let's hit them directly."

And indeed, in August 1998, Osama hit hard: two U.S. embassies, hundreds of victims, and massive humiliation. The retaliation? A missile was launched on a pharmaceutical plant in Sudan. Bin Laden had already left the country two years before. A wave of tomahawk missiles dug up the dirt in Afghanistan. Right place, wrong policy. Al Qaeda was indeed based in Afghanistan at the time, openly protected by the Taliban. According to counterterrorism officials and military experts, a plan was prepared to produce a regime change in Kabul. But again, the "holy whisper" in the U.S. capital advised against intervention. "It will create complications in international relations and will have a negative impact in the Muslim world."[13] Yet the following year, an all-out campaign by al Qaeda destroyed the Serbian army in Kosovo and led to a regime change in Serbia. There were no complications in international relations in that case. The nonresponse of the United States after a declaration of war and a massive attack against American diplomatic installations was not a mere signal anymore, it was an invitation to attack America.

In 1999, a plot was under way to blow up several targets worldwide. Reports circulated about an earlier plot in 1995 to down several airliners. Intense jihadi activity was going on; propaganda was spreading around the world. But in the United States, the elite dismissed any accusation against the Islamists. Worse, the "inside jihadists"[14] had initiated a defamation campaign against the very few who were trying to warn the public and government. America was driven to the slaughterhouse, politically blindfolded, and intellectually drugged. The fine-tuning between the outside ninjas and the inside cells was peaking. In 2000, al Qaeda crossed the line to test the U.S. military itself. A fishing boat blew up, damaging the USS *Cole* in Yemen. Back in Afghanistan, bin Laden analyzed the reactions. He did not have much work to do; there was no U.S. reaction. The anti-American forces worldwide escalated their propaganda campaign. One cycle led to another, as the jihadists were emboldened on all battlefields. In Lebanon, Hezbollah overran the South Lebanon Army security zone after the Israelis abandoned the area in May 2000. In September of that year, Hamas and Islamic jihad escalated their suicide attacks. And as Americans were embroiled in counting the Florida votes after the disputed 2000 election, al Qaeda was scouting the East Coast of the United States. The path to Manhattan and Washington was wide open.

Chapter Eleven

BIN LADEN'S STRATEGY AGAINST AMERICA

M ANY AMONG THOSE WHO TRIED TO ANALYZE THE PATH to the September 11 suicide strikes were not able to provide a better explanation for that attack than the general reading of al Qaeda's ideology of jihadism. Osama bin Laden hates the infidels and particularly the Americans; therefore, he ordered the strikes. Many of the analysts and commentators on jihad and terrorism have concluded this simply. But some recent good research has provided more specific assessments, such as the length of the preparatory phase, the tactical designs, the organizational skills, and the psychological impact desired from such an operation. All these works are important, albeit based on a hindsight recovery of the missing links of the 1990s. These issues deal with the structural side of the attacks: how they happened, and what it took for them to happen. A whole stream of investigation has focused on the means used by al Qaeda and why we did not prevent the attacks. The aim of that debate was to teach ourselves how to avoid future attacks: how to be better on immigration, airline security, airport security, police work, and on down the line. I agree with the measures, but I take issue with the approach. In my mind, preventing future terrorist attacks must be part of preempting future jihads. I will be clearer on this matter in the prescriptions and conclusions section, but let me underline one crucial equation at this point.

We know that bin Laden did not attack the planes, their passengers, and the Twin Towers and the Pentagon per se. He used them to attack the United States and the American people as a community of infidels obstructing his march toward *dar el harb*. Last but not least, he did not order the destruction of the Pentagon just because he wanted to bring a couple of walls down, as the

Taliban, in a symbolic act, had destroyed the Buddha statues in eastern Afghanistan a year before. He wanted to deter the *kufr* military forces from remaining deployed in what he considers "his region." These first-grade assertions are needed to stress the importance of the global picture in the understanding of past jihad as a key to the prevention of future ones. The real question, I assume, is how did Osama read the world context so that it was the right context for his 2001 attacks and for future jihadist warfare? How did he calculate victory and the defeat of his foe?[1]

THE JIHADIST PERCEPTION OF INTERNATIONAL RELATIONS

Since 2001, world leaders and international public opinion has concluded that the jihadists have no international law and relations. The Salafi ideological teachings do not recognize the United Nations, the principles of international law as we know it, other treaties, conventions, and codes, unless under their doctrinal norms. In contrast with the communists, who ideologically rejected the capitalist world but nevertheless recognized international laws and treaties (even though they often breached them), the jihadists simply do not recognize any system the international community has reached since the Peace of Westphalia; no conception of sovereignty, human rights, humanitarian rights, the Geneva Convention, or even Red Cross agreements. This may seem hard to believe, especially if you absorb the analysis of the apologists, particularly the Wahabi lobbies.[2] But the easiest way to learn about it is to read the jihadist literature, study their principles of action, and listen to their spokespersons and activists. They all confirm with clarity that the League of Nations, United Nations, Universal Declaration of Human Rights, democracy, secularism, freedom of religions, freedom of speech (when not applied in their interest) are to them all "products of the infidels." Hence, there are no boundaries to jihadist actions. Therefore, the understanding of their strategies and future plans cannot be predicted based on expectations of the international community and accepted norms. With this in mind, we can begin to understand the objectives of September 11 and the shadow of future jihads.

Of course, the jihadists, including bin Laden's al Qaeda and the myriad of other radical Islamist warriors, have a system of reference for their actions. Their clerics and "legislators" have an entire system of laws and regulations, including war codes and traditions.[3] They, the Islamic fundamentalists, claim it is the "true Islamic code"; Muslim reformers negate this claim. This debate existed in the past, continues to exist, and will be much wider in the future. But the bottom line is that the jihad terror networks abide by their own vision of international relations: It is the web of relationship between *dar el harb* and *dar el Islam.* The latter must defeat the former; the rest is details. But even in the details there are nuances, differences, and multiple subdoctrines. For example, a former member of the Muslim Brotherhood, Sayid Qutb of Egypt, developed his own vision of warfare and jihad against the infidels.[4] He centered his doctrine almost entirely on constant violence again the "enemies of religion" until they submit. He did not spare Muslims of Shiite background or Sunnis of non-Salafi background. Qutb may be one of the most radical fathers of modern jihadism, a logical inspiration to al Qaeda, Zarqawi, and future extremists.

When mounting operations in the 1990s, Osama bin Laden and his men had no limits with regard to international relations and did not take world opinion into consideration. In contrast, the state Wahabis were very concerned about al Qaeda's tactics, fearing they would destroy the credibility of Islamic fundamentalism worldwide. In the United States and to a certain degree in Europe and elsewhere in the West, the oil-financed apologists had the choice between condemning the jihadists and covering up for them. One of their major mistakes was to attack the target—the United States—instead of the jihadists. In fact, the apologists were forced by their ties to the Wahabis to cover up for the political objectives of the terrorists, and for a simple reason: in the long term, both the Wahabis and the terrorists have the same objectives. If the terrorists are exposed, so too will their ideology be exposed. If that happens, the long-term objectives of the lobbies that are working within the law internationally and in the United States will be exposed; and just as much as al Qaeda, the lobbies too believe that the *dar el Islam* is destined, and in fact, obligated to overwhelm and absorb the *dar el harb.* As mentioned in an earlier chapter, the various parties who debated the September 11 attacks on al Jazeera television were not arguing about whether the attacks were wrong or right; they were arguing about whether they'd been mounted at the right time.

It remains to explain why the American public and the international community were not informed or educated as to the jihadists' real attitude regarding world affairs. Why were the terrorists presented either positively, as "freedom fighters," or negatively, as "mere gangs," and never realistically, as an ideological network with a worldview rooted in hundreds of years of tradition and example (the caliphate), and now aiming at the destruction of the world international structure and the United States in particular? The fundamentalists realized that they were operating in an ideal context: Not only were they not on their enemies' radar, but someone on the "inside" was blurring the enemy's understanding of the networks.

THE JIHADIST ANALYSIS OF AMERICAN POWER

Ayman Thawahiri, al Qaeda's number two man, traveled to the United States several times, as did many cadres of the organization. Sayid Qutb, the ideologue of extreme violence, stayed in America for a while. Hassan Turabi made lecture tours on U.S. campuses. Abdallah al Shallah, the head of Palestinian Islamic Jihad, was a professor in Tampa before he reemerged in Damascus in 1995. The inspiration for the first attack against the World Trade Center, Sheik Omar Abdul Rahman, sought political asylum in New York. These are the shining stars of jihadism. But below them exist a whole layer of lesser-known imams, cadres, intellectuals, scholars, and operatives who, in different realms, were even more integrated into the system for years before September 11—and most of them still are. Lower-level Salafists have been infiltrating the American system and learning about it. This leads to a first conclusion: The jihadists know about the system, and know America's infrastructure very well.

But the best knowledge jihadists have of the United States—and of any other western country—is through the intellectual establishment, particularly the academic world. America has, fortunately for all, an open system where nothing is hidden and all public knowledge is transparent. In contrast with the Soviet Union, for example, or China or Cuba—let alone Saudi Arabia or Libya—the U.S. infrastructure on all levels is documented: finances, architecture, education, industries, legal and political institutions, and even to some degree, the military. Very few countries organize tours of their ministries of defense, as does the Pentagon.

The jihadists have seen what every American has seen but have studied the weaknesses of this country more than most Americans. One stream of information they count on is the mass of analysis and criticism produced by the academic elite against their own government, nation, and policies. In a democracy, criticism is absolutely natural. One major attraction of America and to a lesser degree the rest of the West is its freedom of thought. But the criticism the jihadists were interested in was the body of statements and literature that delegitimized the country while legitimizing jihadist doctrines and policies. It would take volumes to review the anti-American production of the intellectual elite, but that is not the real issue. Everyone can and should be critical in addressing all issues in domestic and foreign policies. Doing so is at the heart of the democratic process. The Salafists were not interested in this heart, but in the bad blood that could coagulate and kill the whole body: They selected from the anti-American literature, especially that written by Americans themselves, all that could constitute a basis for aggression against the United States. When infidels indict infidels for not endorsing the fundamentalists, naturally jihadists win. They see it as a sign of decline, the West's internal decomposition, and consider the time ripe for a holy war.

AL QAEDA'S READING OF AMERICA'S MIND

If you are a graduate from the Wahabi madrassas, listen to your Salafi preacher on a weekly basis, watch American movies at night and al Jazeera during the day, read only jihadi literature instead of social sciences, you will be convinced that America, the world center of *fisq and mujun* (depravity and physical pleasures), is undoubtedly going down. If you follow the logic of Osama bin Laden, Sheikh Yussef al Qardawi, and even the Iranian mullahs, you'll project that the United States is the sum of all *kufr* (infidels). Sheikh Mohammed Hussein Fadlallah, the ideological mentor of Hezbollah, has often said in his speeches: *"Amreeka sharrun mutlaq"*—America is evil in its essence.

These assertions show how the jihadists read America's mind. They postulate that evil brings its downfall by itself, because it cannot withstand the will of Allah on Earth. Hence all that jihad has to do is to help by administering the first strikes. The divine equation will do the rest. This also explains the jihad logic: Its only analysis of the enemy is its ripeness.

And by the jihadists' reading, that mother of all *kufr* was ripe in 2001. Seen from their angle, the United States bore the sins of Las Vegas, New Orleans, Hollywood, the presidential scandals, the pleasures, materialism, liberalism, sexual freedom, wealth, women's equality, and military arrogance worldwide. The jihadists believed that these signs of weakness and decadence indicated that America had lost its place among nations, that it was no longer legitimate. In addition, the Salafis considered how many times the United States withheld from reacting to jihad operations. Along with the "wisdom" coming from its own elites about America's illegitimacy, this view of the United States as unable to react led directly to the decision for the strikes.

AL QAEDA'S PLAN FOR THE BALANCE OF POWER

Once they perceived the United States as condemned by Allah, the jihadists planned accordingly. They decided to strike at the heart of the *kufr*, leaving the rest to divine will *(al irada al ilahiya)*. The direct consequences of the strikes would initiate America's collapse but leave open possibilities; how America collapses, how much time it would take, how many other strikes, by whom and when, and so on, are questions left to the "will" and the resources of the fighters. At least, that is the thinking on the ideological level; but what about the actual strategic context? How did bin Laden perceive the balance of power with America? Did he really think he would win a war against the United States, not just worldwide but even on its mainland? How could he be so ambitious unless he was certain that some allies, including divine ones, would intervene at the right time to give al Qaeda its final victory?

The answers may not seem logical by western standards, but they are by Salafi logic. If the United States is the main obstruction to the rise of Islamic fundamentalism and jihad worldwide, then all jihadist forces must muster to destroy it. And since the United States is no longer needed to destroy the communist threat posed by the Soviet Union, and if American society is not ready to respond to terror and its government is totally bound to oil threats and will not attack Wahabi-led regimes (the Taliban) nor mobilize its public against the jihadist ideology itself, then the United States will only grow weaker if it is hit on its mainland. In the eyes of the jihadists the balance of power is in fact a balance of terror. And as well explained by bin Laden and other commanders, "Terrorize them and they will run away; they only understand terrorism in terms of what they have to lose and they have no values to fight for."[5]

THE THREE OBJECTIVES FOR SEPTEMBER 11

For four years since the massacres in Manhattan, Washington, and Pennsylvania, Americans have been trying hard to absorb the strikes and understand their motives. Despite silly conspiracy theories that attempted to implicate the U.S. government itself (theories the terrorists themselves have discredited by taking direct responsibility), a universal consensus has accused al Qaeda of masterminding and executing the attacks in 2001. From there on, a lesser consensus, but still on a global scale, legitimized an all-out campaign against the bin Laden organization worldwide. The Taliban regime was removed from power and dozens of countries, including many Arab and Muslim governments, have engaged in the widest manhunt in history: to find and capture Osama.[6]

But beyond the worldwide campaign against al Qaeda, dubbed the war on terror, a single dramatic question remains mostly unanswered. And that is to know why bin Laden ordered these particular strikes, what he expected, and ultimately what place the attacks of September 11 have in his wider plans. In sum, what was he shooting for? Without a doubt, the answers to these questions are not just necessary on historical grounds, but crucial for the understanding of the war on terrorism and therefore for the emergence of a long-standing international consensus on collective action around the world. Answers to these questions will shed light on dramatic developments in Iraq, Afghanistan, the Middle East, and the Arab world as well as in Europe, and will shape the nature of what has been baptized Homeland Security in the United States.

To know what was in the mind of Osama when he engineered what he called "blessed strikes" *(al-darabat al mubaraka),* short of interviewing him directly or reading his memoirs, requires us to connect the dots from a combination of statements, over a span of a decade at least, and to read that material with the deepest possible knowledge of the movement that produced bin Laden. I will attempt to do that with as much caution as possible, while allowing raw data to interact with my instinct.[7]

FIRST OBJECTIVE: POPULAR CHAOS

It is a certainty that the man who ordered the destruction of the American centers of finance and of military and political power aimed to create chaos in the United States. The mass killing of civilians and persons in the military bureaucracy does not produce a battlefield defeat, as Pearl Harbor did. Although the element of strategic surprise was the most common characteristic of the two acts, Japan's ultimate goal was to break down U.S. military power in the Pacific, hence removing American deterrence from Japanese calculations in Asia. The direct outcome the jihad war room sought from the events of September 11 was to bring chaos to the American mainland, leaving U.S. forces around the world untouched. The real and first objective of the *Ghazwa* (jihad raid, as Osama called it) was to trigger a chain of reactions, on both the popular and political levels. Osama expected up to a million Americans to demonstrate in the streets against their government, as Israelis had done against their cabinets in the 1980s. He hoped that Congress would split in two and become paralyzed, campuses would rebel, and companies would collapse. He wanted chaos and a divided nation, scared and turning upon itself. He believed, for many reasons, that the time was ripe for the fall of the giant.

BACKLASH ON ARABS AND MUSLIMS

If you were bin Laden or the product of his political culture, you would anticipate revenge. Had similar events taken place in his region of the world, the majority or empowered community would have unleashed bloody punishments on the perceived kin of the aggressor. That is how things are dealt with from the Atlantic to the Indian oceans. Deep down, in his instincts, Osama was expecting Americans to attack Arabs and Muslims in some sort of pogroms. Not the 420 reported incidents—which by American standards were condemned at once—but the ethnic strife model, in which thousands of armed civilians wreak havoc on entire neighborhoods. He fantasized about Arab and Muslim blood spilled in the streets of American cities. Al Qaeda projected mass retaliations similar to sectarian backlashes in the Middle East and the Indian sub-continent. Ironically, in the first days after September 11 some jihadist callers were reporting alleged backlashes live to al Jazeera. Had such a nightmare occurred in America, al Qaeda would have ruled in Muslim lands and recruited hundreds of thousands of new members.

AMERICAN WRATH OVERSEAS

With chaos and ethnic wounds raging inside the country, the engineer of mass death projected that America would sow grapes of wrath abroad. Had he had such military power, and had his "*caliphate*" been attacked in similar ways, he would have unleashed Armageddon against the infidel world. Reversing the psychology,[8] bin Laden expected the U.S. military to carpet bomb Afghanistan and elsewhere. He thought he would draw the Yankees' raw power into the entire Muslim world and expected a global intifada to ensue. Interestingly enough, the jihadists anticipated millions of deaths in Afghanistan and the Middle East. Some indications lead me to guess that the sultan of the mujahedin wanted the "great Satan" to do the unthinkable and resort to doomsday devices.[9]

That is the war that Osama bin Laden wanted to instigate: a war that would drive America into chaos, shatter international law, and allow bin Laden to project himself as the new caliph. He would have come very close, had he calculated differently. His reading of human collectivities was highly ideological. He made the mistakes of his two predecessors, the Nazis and the Bolsheviks—but let us not project the course of future events yet, for the reasons that made bin Laden believe America was ripe are still deeply embedded in our collective tissue. Perhaps we need to take a hard look before another more tragic calamity would take us by surprise.

CONSEQUENCES

By understanding the above-described objectives, we can clearly see inside the jihadist mind. In the web site and al Jazeera debates that followed and continue to this day, we can see the emergence of three remarkably strategic conse-quences that al Qaeda hopes for. A long-term "internal" tension in the United States, one fed by actions such as sniper activities, dirty bombs, and govern-ment reactions, will lead to what they hope will become an "ethnic crumbling." Once that stage is reached, an irreversible mechanism will take over. In paral-lel, a world intifada will explode in several spots fueled by the jihadists around the world. With these two cataclysmic developments taking place simultane-ously, bin Laden or his successors will hope to witness the withdrawal of U.S. forces deployed worldwide and the general collapse of that nation. These end-of-times projections were made before September 11 and resumed afterward, and in fact continue today. They explain clearly the reasoning behind the at-tacks on September 11, and subsequent strikes elsewhere such as the March 11, 2004, bombing in Madrid, the Saudi attacks, as well as strikes in Turkey, Tunisia, Kashmir, Chechnya, Moscow, London, and the ongoing bursts in Iraq's Sunni triangle.

However, and as we will discuss later, what was not on the jihadist map of operations was the unexpected U.S. reaction and how the American public backed the government's counteroffensives, as well as the international solidar-ity with the war on terror.

Chapter Twelve

THE ROOT CAUSES OF
AMERICA'S FAILURE

A MAJOR STEP IN PREEMPTING FUTURE TERRORIST ATTACKS of the magnitude of September 11 was admitting that the United States failed to meet the first challenge. But the nature of the admission is more important than the act of contrition made by the government, even as it moves forward to equip the nation with needed institutions and infrastructure. The real question that the September 11 Commission should have asked is: What are we admitting to? That our Immigration and Naturalization Service failed to identify the terrorists? That the FBI was not communicating with the CIA? That the cabins of the airplanes were not locked and the pilots and stewardesses were not trained by the Navy SEALS? Are we admitting to the failures of high-ranking officers in Washington who dismissed whistle-blowers from the field offices? Or regretting that secretaries of defense and state have not listened to counterterrorism czars? How about the president's national security advisor, who did not respond to a memo that said that terrorists would use planes against buildings to hurt America? How about a president who did not order U.S. forces to mobilize because he received a memo stating that an attack might occur by a group that no one in the previous administration did anything about? How about a president who was served with a declaration of war and attacks on two U.S. embassies, but was discouraged from implementing his military command's war plans by his counterterrorism czar, who said "complications in international relations" would occur if the terrorists were removed?

In reality, the shortcomings of the experts led logically to failures of perception at the field level. Consider two examples: A U.S. pilot thought the Russians had bombed the Pentagon on September 11. Why? An FBI officer found it suspicious that Saudi men were training to fly aircraft but not to land, yet her superiors did not. Again, why? A truck almost destroyed one of the New York Twin Towers in 1993, but the government did not accuse the jihadists, let alone al Qaeda. Why? Bin Laden declared a jihad war against the United States and all infidels in February 1998, but no one answered him; al Qaeda destroyed two embassies in 1998, but the regime that protected the terrorists was not removed; al Qaeda attacked a U.S. ship in 2000 but no action was taken against the Taliban immediately and no recommendation to remove them was passed on to the next administration; a memo was sent to the U.S. national security leadership in August of 2001 about possible attacks, but no memo was sent to mobilize the government when the war was declared back in 1998. To all of these questions, we must ask, Why?[1]

At the September 11 hearings, the nation's national security and defense elite struggled to assign the blame for the failure. The waltz was opened by chief counterterrorism expert Richard Clarke, who began the dance by stating to the parents of the victims sitting behind him: "I failed you, your government failed you." But he stopped short of the big Godzilla in the room that no one had discussed, except by daring hints. A major question should have been raised about those who showered the U.S. government, media, and public with their "advice" as the threat was building.[2] So just who was it, who made sure that jihad stayed above the fray—for at least eleven years—until it descended in fire on the heart of Manhattan and Washington?

The hearings concluded with the publication of a voluminous book detailing an enormous amount of information about how the operation took place, from Pakistan to Florida. It warned of a repetition and prescribed a series of measures—which a declaration of war would have executed anyway.[3] So isn't the missing link the actual declaration of war and the mobilization of the public and the establishment of a Homeland Security branch? But how can you mobilize all the relevant agencies, alert the White House on time, and build coalitions to track down the terrorists if you are not at war with them? And how can you be at war with a network that exists because of an ideology if you do not identify it? Were the allies during World War II at war with the Wehrmacht, the SS, and the Panzer Grenadiers, or with Nazi Germany?

If America was not at war when jihad was striking, what was its status? Who knew we were at war but did not act, and for what reasons? In other words, where was the United States failing, and more important, why? These questions relate directly to the ultimate question of the shape of future jihad. Did the nation learn from the past, and is it mobilizing in the right direction? As important, are the jihadists and their allies aware of the strategies of the U.S. war against terrorism?[4]

SEEING BUT NOT LOOKING: JIHAD'S TRANSPARENCY

The debate about the U.S. government's handling of alleged warnings regarding the September 11 attacks deserves a close look. Actually, a review and analysis of the disaster, its causes, its root causes, the security failures, and the readiness of the whole national security apparatus will for years continue to be a historian's work.[5]

Multiple U.S. agencies had some type of information in their possession prior to the day of doom. And indeed, such data were shared within the constitutional pyramid of the United States, from the president on top to the various congressional committees farther down. Yes, various one-page reports sent to Pennsylvania Avenue and the Hill did mention[6] hijacking of planes and other plans. My first comment on these facts is this. For a superpower such as the United States in a post–cold war era, it was certainly expected that its agencies would at some point collect pieces of information related to activities by terror groups already listed as dangerous. Osama bin Laden's organization was under observation by the U.S. intelligence community abroad. Ever since the embassy bombings in Africa in 1998, America's national security leadership had allocated a specific amount of "time, money and energy" to deal with al Qaeda and its sister entities.[7]

Thus, whatever the combined efforts of the CIA, FBI, and other agencies had collected—regardless of their failure to exchange information—about bin Laden's activities the issue was the measure of "urgency" the U.S. national leadership granted to this matter as a whole over the past decade. In short, whatever reports the president and his teams were reading, as well as what the bipartisan committees in Congress were allowed (by law) to absorb, determined what the American strategic thinking of the time had devoted to potential attacks by jihadist radicals. And that, in sum, was very little.[8]

In the pre–September 11 mode of thinking, receiving information about bin Laden's plans to attack the United States was certainly a national security matter, but not yet a "safety of the nation" matter.[9] By this, I mean it fell under the attention of the various agencies and of the constitutional leaders of the nation, but it was not a matter of "national mobilization." One must distinguish between a prewar state and a state of war, even with terrorism. Short of having obtained the exact plans of September 11 from an al Qaeda defector, the administration and its friends and foes in Congress wouldn't have reacted differently in this decade and certainly not in the past decade. Because the United States was simply not prepared either culturally or psychologically for the attacks, no one would have reacted differently to reports of "potential or highly likely attacks by terrorists on U.S. soil" before the morning of the massacre. In the final analysis, various agencies saw "facts and trends" but were not looking for them under any overarching political guidelines. Experts saw them too, but covered them up to protect their sources of funding.

CULTURAL LOBOTOMY: BLIND BY CONVENTION

In the early 1990s, a number of observers, including me, lectured and wrote about the jihadist movement's plans and its willingness to "hit in the heart of the United States." The few of us who analyzed the evidence available knew that strikes were coming. We were culturally prepared for such a development. The overwhelming majority of the intellectual and political establishment of the country was not, however.[10]

Worse, a large segment of the academic and diplomatic circles in the United States was in fact preaching the opposite.[11] Endless numbers of scholars, opinion makers, and foreign policy bureaucrats were even blurring the vision of mainstream America. Hundreds of articles, books, panels, and shows played down the threat of jihad and its determination to engage in a "wholly and holy" war against mainland America. Remember the overwhelming "politically correct" punishments administered to the politically "incorrect" analyses by "adventurous" experts who warned of such possibilities years ago. A benchmark example is Steven Emerson's documentary *Jihad in America*. Produced in 1994 under PBS's sponsorship, the footage showed un-refuted proof of jihadi terror activities within the United States. Radical clerics were seen calling for violence on the tape. Mr. Emerson, once a correspondent for CNN, has since been banned from many outlets, including from public broadcast. As of the mid-1990s, Mideast expert Daniel Pipes, after he published an analysis about the surge of jihadi threats against the United States, was shunned by the Middle East studies establishment. As it appears years after, thousands of drafts and letters to the editors were rejected by dailies and weeklies, hundreds of scholarly papers were rejected at conferences, and dozens of applicants were turned down from academic and other jobs by the "lobby." Recall the huge power used by pro-jihadist lobbies in this country to numb the instincts of the public regarding terrorism.[12]

Before September 11, if the government had issued national "warnings" of potential "jihadist attacks," even by al Qaeda, it would have been faced with a barrage of apologists accusing it of bashing Islam. Investigating twenty men— or even one man—learning how to fly but not land aircraft would have brought on the wrath of the Saudi embassy and of numerous Arabist groups on the ground of "racial and ethnic" discrimination. Releasing sensitive information about "potential terror" attacks would have been exposed as "administration attempts to revive cold war ambiance and hunger for war at large." In the pre–September 11 era, the country, and hence its representatives, was simply not ready to imagine a holocaust-type attack on U.S soil. Its intellectual elite, who should have known better about the world of the jihadists, told the nation that such things were the products of our imagination.

So, if you were the president—any president—or one of his advisors, or a privileged member of Congress anytime before 8:40 A.M. on September 11, 2001, and unless you were given the exact scenario of the crime with proven data, you would react in the same way. You would ask for more information and call for continuous action against the potential aggressors. You would be conditioned by the political environment of the day.[13]

Osama bin Laden had that advantage over us; his ideology was protected by the intellectual elite of this country. His objectives were legitimized. His threat was concealed. Until he sent those planes into our buildings, he was not a "national threat" but a vague "security hazard" in the eyes of government and probably a potential hero in the eyes of the apologists.[14]

Therefore, I wouldn't blame the president or the opposition for not having been able to "read" those reports in their historic context. I do certainly blame the engineers of America's understanding of that specific global threat. And I do want to see the investigation into the events of September 11 evolve into the wider and more critical issue of how our collective mind refused to "see" what our eyes were seeing.

THE PENETRATION AND MOLLIFICATION OF AMERICA

As I described in an earlier chapter, the country's failure to respond was caused, by a jihadist penetration, among other factors. The question at hand is: Why did this penetration succeed? Why was the United States not aware of it and facing it from the beginning? A full review of the process of penetration will show a stream of events, one leading to and reinforcing another. For example there is the question of finances: The early Wahabi money targeted a number of nerve centers such as universities and community and religious organizations. If we examine that first wave from the end of the 1970s until the early 1990s, we find that not only was it not confronted, but it was not even on the national security agenda. The government's failure to act was caused by an overarching mechanism that mollified U.S. responses to terrorism if it was jihad related.[15] One can compare easily:

When the jihad terrorists hit the World Trade Center in 1993, it did not cause an all-out mobilization against the Islamist networks at home or around the world. When the Khobar Towers were attacked in 1994, again, there was no mobilization against Islamist networks. But when paramilitary units committed crimes in Haiti during the same year, U.S. carriers headed toward the island and performed a regime change, reinstalling Bertrand Aristide. That same year, half a million black Africans had already been exterminated in southern Sudan by the Islamist Front of Khartoum. No U.S. or western intervention saved them—a no-fly zone was not even established to stop the Sudanese Sukhoi sorties and napalm attacks against civilians. However, tens of thousands of U.S. soldiers did intervene subsequently in Bosnia to save "white" Muslim Europeans from being overrun by Serbian "Orthodox" militias. In America's courts, during the 1990s, jihadists from Egypt and other countries received political asylum—asylum that was denied to Christians from the Middle East. In 1998 and 2000, American diplomats and servicemen were massacred by al Qaeda, but the United States allowed the Taliban regime to continue in Afghanistan. By 1999 a million non-Arab Africans had been slaughtered in Sudan, but U.S. forces were intervening in Muslim Kosovo. The Islamist regime in Khartoum burned entire villages using Tupolev bombers; the United States sent Stealth bombers from Missouri to pound Milosevic's forces in Serbia. And by 2000, Islamist activists in the United States were targeting intellectuals who had exposed the jihadists during the 1990s; these same Islamists were arrested after 2001 as part of a roundup of a terror network.

These are just some failures at the national and international levels. In sum, it makes little sense to blame the foot soldiers of national security when the jihad influence had diverted the centers of strategic decisions from detecting or even conceptualizing their geopolitical plans. It was not just that the United States failed to prevent terrorism; jihad strategies have completely derailed national security for an entire decade.

THE MEDIA FAILURE

The media informs the public and teaches the nation on matters of national importance. It provides the world's headlines to go with the morning coffee and welcomes people with the nightly news when they come back from work. The media shapes the public's vision of world affairs and its priorities. But if we checked the archives back to 1990, what would we find on jihad terrorism? If we explore the *New York Times,* the *Washington Post,* the *Boston Globe,* the *Los Angeles Times,* the *Miami Herald, Newsweek,* and others, we will find many articles on terror, but very little analysis of the jihadi ideology, penetration, and manipulation. The archives of CNN, ABC, NBC, and CBS show the same trends. But more worrisome would be PBS, C-SPAN, and National Public Radio (NPR). Funded by U.S. taxpayers, these gigantic networks have dedicated less than 0.1 percent of content to what would become the main threat to the nation over the years. NPR would outdo every other medium: It actually aired more programs endorsing the apologists—those who denied a jihadi threat—than all other U.S. media combined. The pounding by NPR and the public networks over ten years further disguised the intensity of the Wahabi penetration.[16]

But can we blame the media for the ideas it receives from the intelligentsia? Journalists are, after all, the product of classrooms and reading. They rely on advice, research, and guests. Although many news analysts are also generators of ideas, these ideas start somewhere. The "central school" of ideas provides basic definitions of ideologies and political conflicts and descriptions of events overseas. This "central factory" consists of the elite, whose job it is to think, research, and categorize the world as it evolves: in other words, academia. Did it fail too?

THE ACADEMIC FAILURE

Now we are entering the heart of the problem: the sacrosanct space of a nation's collective mind. It is here where fresh brains come for intellectual sustenance and where the future cadres of a society are shaped, prepared, and sent to the real world. It is a web I know all too well, having spent two-thirds of my adult life in it. Colleges and universities educate students who will end up in the media, receiving information and processing it, choosing when to use it and what to use from it. A graduate from a department of history who isn't taught the evolution of the jihadist movements or their ultimate goals will write articles describing al Qaeda as a rebel movement. If a university president in south Florida defines Hamas as a "cultural" group, if a professor in a classroom could ignore the concept of "infidel" or explain jihad as "a sort of yoga," how can we blame the journalists who can barely pronounce these Arabic names or that fighter pilot who on September 11 thought the Russians were attacking?[17] How can an FBI agent spot a terrorist, if his teacher never mentioned the terrorists' ideology? How would it be possible for an analyst to understand the Salafis' views on *dar el harb* if his Middle East studies professor told him they were conservative reformers? How can a judge see the importance of a war fatwa if the apologist expert dismisses it as a legal opinion? How can juries decide if alleged terrorists are indeed conspiring against America if they have never been educated about *takiya?*[18] I could write a book on these questions and impossible answers. But let us paint the bigger picture that tells about future jihads from past failures in academia.[19]

Students are misinformed by their professors, who were misinformed by theirs—who were funded by the Wahabis. This is the center of the equation. From there, it is mathematical deduction: Graduates fill the positions and continue to be dependent on the factory. If you poison the factory, you devastate the streams and blur the nation's vision. From academia you reach the media, government, foreign policy, and eventually the military.[20]

America's failure to act is a result of a failure to educate Americans. The 9/11 Commission concluded that it was a failure of imagination. I disagree with the conclusion, if it stops there. Understandably, very few can review the result of academic smoke and mirrors if they are not on campus to see the subversion in action. How can anyone say that Americans are short on imagination? A nation that puts humans on the moon, invents the Internet, and captures the world's imagination with Hollywood is not short on imagination. It is education that failed Americans, failed Richard Clarke, and failed his government. And that is where I would look to see if we are ready to fend off the next jihad terror.[21]

Chapter Thirteen

PROJECTING FUTURE JIHAD

WITH THE RIGHT ANALYSIS OF THE HISTORY AND DECISION MAKING and with understanding of past developments, we can project a frightening image of the potential future of jihad war. But with no history and a wrong analysis of the root causes of jihad terror, we cannot move an inch in guessing the next development of this conflict. My very first statement in the futurology of jihadism may seem to take a page from genetics rather than political science, but it provides needed answers: The future of jihad terrorism is overwhelmingly inscribed in its own history and the history it refers to. Although technology and diplomacy can impact the course of conflicts, the organic link between the terror groups that follow Salafi or Khumeinist lines and their objectives is pretty much predictable. I and many other readers of the jihadist mind were in the unfortunate position to begin to predict the strikes against the West and, more important, the subsequent moves and countermoves in several spots around the world. As I have shown, al Qaeda and Hezbollah are seeking specific strategic objectives: The Wahabi current wants a caliphate in the Sunni world, and the Khumeinist current wishes for the establishment of an Imamate in the Shiia world. That is ideologically predictable. Even the routes traced by the jihadists to achieve these long-term objectives can serve as an encyclopedia of future Islamist strategies.[1]

Readers may be surprised by these statements. As I have shown, they are logically deduced from my studies into jihad, even though they have yet to get on the agenda of government research and academic programs. In the final chapters, I cross the line directly into the future and map the trends and events to be expected. However, as in any scientific methodology, one has to factor in

not just the decisions by the terror networks but also the strategies and decisions of the United States, the West, and, eventually, the majority of Arabs and
Muslims. Future strikes will be determined by how jihadists perceive the responses to their actions. They will also depend on how the coalition against
terror goes about its plans; finally and more important, they will be deeply influenced by the behavior, trends, and revolutions within the civil societies that
have witnessed the birth and growth of the jihadists. An analysis of the future
is neither unitary nor certain; it is a prediction of how the Islamists would act,
if circumstances permit.

VIRTUAL PROJECTION

I will start with a global assessment of what would and could happen had all
or most past jihadi plans actually succeeded. I will show here a picture of
what was intended from the September 11 attacks, only flashed forward to
2008. This fictive futurology of terror can help project what the jihadi plans
really are now and how they will develop in the next years and decades. The
exercise will start with one question: Had the events that took place in 2001
been delayed by seven years, what would have happened in the Middle East,
Europe, and in the United States? Would America have been sunk completely if we assume a time difference, an attack farther in the future, at a different point in the strategic vision of global terrorism? We have already begun
to derail this terrifying plan since 2001, because of those strikes, but we do
need to face future plans in order to take further steps in avoiding the aims of
terrorist organizations.[2]

A VISION OF A CHANGED WORLD

The two towers are down, the smoke covers New York's skies. The Pentagon is in flames, the president and his cabinet are dispersed, and al Jazeera
is accusing the CIA and Mossad of perpetrating a self-immolation of its citizens as an excuse to invade the Muslim world and take over its oil fields. But
in this scenario, it is not September 11, 2001, but 2008. But that is only a
part of the fictive picture. More targets were struck, more waves were
launched, and the world is radically different. Many developments have occurred before al Qaeda strikes: Here are some of these changes that would
have made a seven-year delay, or perhaps a decade, in the jihadist "landing"
a huge defeat for America. We need to see this played out in order to fully
understand what is possible.

AFGHANISTAN: MIDDLE EARTH GOES JIHADIST

In this scenario, the Taliban of Afghanistan has been able to invade the last free enclave of the Northern Alliance by the end of 2001. Ali Shah Massud was executed by al Qaeda in September of that year. (This actually happened.) Following the assassination of the most successful leader resisting the Taliban, the latter invade his strongholds in the steep valleys of the north. The Soviet-built Sukhois of mullah Umar pound the Kazak and Uzbek positions while their T–55 tanks overrun General Dustom's positions. The operations last for almost a month, generating few lines in the *New York Times.* There are no CNN crews covering the battles. Pakistan, Saudi Arabia, and al Jazeera applaud the "stabilization" of the country. In the White House and at the State Department, counterterrorism experts say it is better to have the Taliban, whom we can control via the Saudis, than people we do not know. We can talk with them about al Qaeda, which seems to have stopped its attacks for now, like Hezbollah in Lebanon has done. U.S. businessmen are received in Kabul to sign additional contracts on the oil pipeline—now possible after the end of the Afghan civil war. Taliban scholars tour U.S. campuses, at the invitation of Wahabi lobbies, to "open a dialogue" with the American intellectual elites (an invitation actually extended in July 2001). Al Qaeda establishes several bases in the country, trains thousands more core fighters of the caliber of an Abu Mussab al Zarqawi. Moreover, more than 400 men will be trained by Mohammed Atta (who did not perform the September 11 attack that year) for future operations in American cities, while awaiting further mollification promised by the "brothers" on the inside. By 2006, a second-generation network of jihadists is ready to move in on America and the West: They have passports and speak the language without an accent. Some among them are inside the armed forces. This part of the scenario is especially worthy of note, because if we do not pay attention to the new generation emerging in America, we will face disastrous consequences.

PAKISTAN: THE JIHADISTS GO NUCLEAR

The success of the Taliban in unifying the country, the extremist propaganda, and the multiplying madrassas in both Afghanistan and Pakistan deepen the influence of Salafism and al Qaeda inside the tribal areas of the country. Thousands of jihadists have "emigrated" toward the front lines with Kashmir, engaging in skirmishes inside India and launching many suicide attacks against the "Hindu" enemy. India's "nationalist" government retaliates inside Pakistan, prompting a Pakistani military response. The international community intervenes and the UN

Security Council issues resolutions. But the jihadist network moves faster: terrorist cells inside India provoke the massacre of thousands in a series of mass bombings, triggering a mass ethnic cleansing of Muslims by Hindus. A series of events (one can predict different versions) leads to refugees fleeing across the borders and mass disturbances inside Pakistan. Al Jazeera and other radical media incite against the "Hindu" Zionists, while massive demonstrations take the streets of Pakistan. The army is paralyzed by the Islamist intifada while a group of officers, mostly from the intelligence services and known for their allegiance to the jihadists, stages a coup. Radical militia and Salafist military groups take control of Pakistan's nuclear sites and weapons. A new Islamist regime is declared; it signs a defense pact with the Taliban, and mullah Umar is declared the "emir of the faithful" (*Ameer al Mu'mineen*). At first, the United States scrambles to secure Pakistan's nuclear sites but the "experts" rule against it as it would "complicate international relations." The Saudis rush to "fix the matter" and advise Washington that the new rulers, being Wahabis, "are under control in the same way Afghanistan is." In the United States, the academic and media elite blasts the Indian government, which because of "its relations with a Likud government in Israel," has been "poisoning the traditional balances in the sub Indian continent." The U.S. public, not really engaged in this complex situation in Asia, is still following the debate of the Florida vote counting. The Bush administration attempts to build a coalition to contain the "extremist nuclear power" in Pakistan and Afghanistan, but the domestic opposition resists these adventures in foreign policy while grave issues are not addressed at home. (Such statements were actually made during the 2004 presidential campaign.) By the end of 2003, al Qaeda and its affiliates have infiltrated the three Central Asian republics of Tajikistan, Turkmenistan, and Kazakhstan. Backed by the combined Pakistani-Afghan alliance, the Islamist movements are making progress in that huge regional Sunni triangle. Russia is sinking in a renewed and extremely violent intifada in Chechnya and severely criticized by the West. The Middle East Studies Association of America describes the jihadi movements in Central Asia as "transitional movements of change."

IRAN: A NUCLEAR REPUBLIC

Emboldened by the success of Hezbollah in southern Lebanon in May 2000, perceiving the subsequent Israeli withdrawal as a historic defeat, and counting on the al Aqsa intifada as a strategic advance for the Palestinian Islamists, Iran's mullahs move to a higher stage of regional mobilization. In 2002, and as soon as Pakistan and Afghanistan form a Sunni-Salafi alliance protected by nuclear capability, Iran declares its intention to become a nuclear power too. It argues that now that there is a "Sunni" bomb, a "Shiite" bomb must exist. The United States and some anxious nations in Europe attempt to intervene via the United Nations. One year is wasted because of blocks by the Arab countries, represented by Syria, on the Security Council. The western powers attempt to "contain" Iran's regime with a combination of economic sanctions and naval blockades, but three regional powers defeat the containment in 2004: Pakistan-Afghanistan from the east, threatening to fight the infidels with nuclear weapons; Saddam Hussein from the west, who is looking for any regional alliance against the United States; and, under growing Salafi influence, Saudi Arabia. By 2002, encouraged by the al Qaeda successes in Afghanistan, the neo-Wahabi clerics have imposed a more radical elite in the Saudi government and in the military.

Despite mounting criticism from Congress, the U.S. foreign policy establishment decides not to intervene, fearing that any action will "inflame the whole region." Government advisors rule against a policy of "incitement" and suggest an increasing reliance on underground "special operations" against leaders of organizations instead of an open "antiterrorist war." In contrast, the academic community and the Wahabi lobbies criticize Washington's foreign policy for having "oversupported Israel." By early 2004, America's foreign policy is paralyzed by the presidential elections. The administration's opponents are scoring points because of the "failures in international policies" and the still-unsolved legitimacy crisis of the Palm Beach ballots count.

In 2006, Iran tests a device and declares itself a nuclear republic. It puts Syria and Hezbollah-dominated Lebanon under its umbrella. The U.S. administration (most likely a new one) prefers a multilateral approach through the UN and mediated diplomacy via the Arab League. By 2007, Khumeinist Iran and Salafi Pakistan demand a review of international law and two permanent seats at the Security Council.

IRAQ: SADDAM OUT OF THE BOX

With the region shifting quickly toward the formation of a large jihadi block with two nuclear powers, a new Saddam Hussein–like figure frees his regime from UN sanctions, which as of 2003 were eroded by constant challenges from his forces on the ground. With the rapid domino effect coming from the east, strategic indecisions in Washington, and the European governments facing an increasing pressure by the Arab league, Iraq's Baath leaps out of the box. By the end of 2005, Saddam rejects the UN sanctions and the no-fly zones. With a

Turkish government formed by soft Islamists who refuse assistance to NATO (this also occurred in 2003), a nuclear Iran, and a Salafi-influenced Saudi Arabia that rejects a U.S. intervention in Iraq, a Syria that reconciles with Baghdad (which started to occur in 2002), a Hezbollah that threatens worldwide strikes if "American soldiers are deployed in the region," and a new Zarqawi for al Qaeda who is received at Saddam's palace, the ruler of Mesopotamia breaks his chains. Challenging Washington in the midst of its elections and escalating his campaign during early 2005, his forces move north.

Surrounded by Iranian, Turkish, and Syrian forces, the Kurds are forced to surrender their autonomy. Realizing that no air bridge is viable, the United States abandons the Kurds to their fate, absorbing thousands of refugees. A diplomatic and strategic assessment in Washington fears a regional war if a unilateral military intervention takes place in northern Iraq. Moving even further, Saddam strikes a deal with Iran and Syria: global alliance against the United States and its allies in return for Iran retaining Shiia spiritual leadership in Qum, instead of a Sistani preeminence in Najaf. By 2006, Saddam's regime escapes the sanctions, which are voted down by the Security Council, in return for an arrangement by OPEC to bring back Iraqi oil to the market (with American companies sharing in the operations).

With the new strategic situation regionally, Saddam speeds up his weapons of mass destruction program. Freed from sanctions and western pressures, his regime is expected to produce a doomsday device by 2007. The United States and Britain issue statements, but in view of the new regional reality and the mounting internal pressures in the West, a new doctrine is devised: long-range containment of the "rogue states." In 2004, the opposition had criticized the administration for not "building necessary alliances" and proposed direct talks with these regimes.

SYRIA AND LEBANON: HEZBOLLAH'S TENTACLES GROW

The domino effect rolling from the plateau of Afghanistan into Iran, Iraq, and the Arabian Peninsula impacts Syria and Syrian-occupied Lebanon. The Syrians have already acquired long-range missiles capable of hitting Israel and the eastern Mediterranean. Between 2002 and 2005, Hezbollah is equipped with long-range rockets that can reach two thirds of Israel. The organization, financed by Iran, establishes a wide cell network inside the United States (which had already occured by 2002). Taking advantage of the social and cultural tensions in America, Hezbollah links up with radical militants inside the country, infiltrates Lebanese communities in the diaspora, and widens its networks in Africa and Latin America.

SAUDI ARABIA: WAHABI JIHADISM

Tensions escalate between the hard-core Salafi networks and the monarchy. A number of emirs and members of royalty join the Salafis. Al Qaeda's sympathizers strike western and American interests. Washington and its allies threaten to respond, but the Saudis promise to "deal with the problem." America's Middle East experts advise that a direct confrontation with Salafi elements in Arabia would crumble the monarchy and threaten U.S. oil interests. A growing trend among academics and Washington's Wahabi lobbies recommends a positive engagement policy, including bringing more Salafi scholars to the United States to establish a dialogue. Europe's main democracies follow the advice and create a Permanent Forum for Western-Islamist Dialogue. But inside the kingdom, and as a way to satisfy the jihadists, more fundamentalists are appointed to sensitive positions such as those in the Ministry of Education. (This did occur in 2005.)

Internationally, the government takes advantage of the "dialogue with the West" to spend additional billions of dollars in funds on U.S. and European universities, think tanks, and public relations campaigns. The strength of the jihadist political power grows in the West. By 2006, 90 percent of American Middle East studies programs are run by Wahabi money, matched in many cases by U.S. taxpayer dollars. (Such facts were already verified in 2004.) By

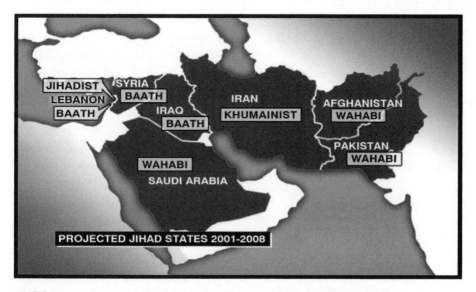

Had the war on terror not begun in 2001, possible emergence of a bloc of radical states.

2007, a coup (or a self-coup) brings the radical wing of the Wahabis to power in Saudi Arabia. The kingdom falls to the jihadists entirely.

SOUTH ASIA: THE DOTS CONNECT

In Asia, the Abu Sayyaf group in the Philippines widens its kidnapping operations and, by 2006, creates enclaves in the south, ruled by Salafists. Al Qaeda establishes bases. The Philippine government is criticized worldwide for its oppression of the "Muslim community." In Indonesia, jihadist networks are federated under the leadership of the Jamaat Islami, who link up with Laskar jihad. Their influence grows inside the armed forces. Al Qaeda's operations are omnipresent in the area: in Malaysia, southern Thailand, Bangladesh. American and western interests are attacked. The U.S. State Department reviews the cases of the terror threat, case by case, "making sure that the diplomatic relations are not challenged." In Australia, the jihadist cells expand and the terror networks infiltrate security forces by 2006 (assuming that the Bali attack didn't take place yet).

SUDAN: JIHAD GOES SOUTH

The National Islamic Front in Khartoum is emboldened by the events in Afghanistan and around the Muslim world, especially the changes taking place in Saudi Arabia. Despite internal tensions between militants and the military, jihad campaigns resume against the African south and develop against Darfur (a situation that occurred from 2003 to 2005). Massacres occur in large numbers, but the United States and the international community are not allowed to intervene. The "lobbies" in Europe and North America call criticism of human rights abuses "interference in Sudan's domestic affairs." And as ethnic cleansing peaks in 2005, Syrian, Iraqi, and Iranian expeditionary units and advisors arrive in the country. Sudan receives medium-range missiles by 2006, but denies having obtained weapons of mass destruction. Once more, the United Nations fails in its monitoring and the United States is blocked from preemptive activities from the inside. By 2006, al Qaeda is operating in Uganda, Ethiopia, Somalia, and Eritrea from Horn of Africa bases. U.S. special forces engage al Qaeda in covert operations in the area. American embassies and installations are hit again. Strikes are ordered, some are launched, but in America the "debate" on foreign policy is raging. Sudan is not an issue, despite the call by Sudanese exiles to put an end to slavery. The American intellectual establishment accuses Washington of meddling in Sudan's internal affairs, and the Nation of Islam organizes a huge rally to support the regime in Khartoum, "targeted by American imperialism and the Zionists."

EUROPE: DIALOGUE FOR THE JIHADISTS

The infiltration of Europe reaches a breaking point with the Salafists' takeover of most Muslim federations in Europe, with significant Saudi and Turkish backing. By 2006, the jihadist networks develop "political blocking powers" in France, Belgium, the Netherlands, Italy, Germany, Spain, Denmark, Sweden, and Great Britain. These powers, using the "representation privilege" of the communities, block antiterrorist legislation, force the hiring of their sympathizers in the various agencies, and put pressure on European foreign policy to distance itself from the United States, significantly before 2004 and continuously thereafter. The European establishment defines the violence perpetrated by the jihadists as "social crimes," not terrorism. Pressed between the growth of militant movements on the inside and the "forum of dialogue" on the outside, most European governments concede mainstream status to the Salafists. In Bosnia and Kosovo, al Qaeda proceeds with infiltrations, thanks to the Wahabi funding of sociocultural and financial centers. As of 2005, jihadist elements strike inside Serbia and Croatia to revive the conflict. Heavy recruitment is taking place in these areas to create a large contingent of White European terrorists.[3]

THE CULTURAL WAR

Worldwide, a massive cultural war is waged against the United States beginning in 2000. In August of 2001, a UN-sponsored Conference on Racism and Discrimination takes place in Durban, South Africa. There, the most radical rhetoric targets the image of America. Jihadists and their allies demonize the United States as a nation. In alliance with the extreme left wing internationally, they call for the "deconstruction" of the most powerful democracy in history. (This too occurred in 2001.) The tidal wave reaches the four continents. By 2005, the hate-America alliance becomes a political tsunami: Conditioned to hate by media and activist networks, millions march around the world. Embassies, consulates, centers, diplomats, and citizens are attacked. The jihad states from Pakistan to Sudan stage massive demonstrations, aired twenty-four hours a day on al Jazeera. Thousands from these "masses" are recruited by al Qaeda and Hezbollah. Hundreds among them are inside the United States.

The American debate turns sour after the 2004 campaign, and a majority of voters turn against their government, even if many feel danger gathering. The "lobbies" have manipulated the media and academia and have spread their influence inside the government. (This occurred by 2001.) In three more years, the political landscape of the country is transformed. A new administration imposes a radical change in foreign policy, but pubic tensions are high.

POLITICAL PREEMPTIVE WARS

From Durban on, the jihadists wage a global preemptive war against all potential opponents able to trigger resistance movements. It is as wide as their areas of influence and control. These activities against moderate Muslims had already been launched in the 1990s. (This did occur.) In several countries, jihadist organizations or regimes orchestrate the oppression of secular, humanist, democratic Muslims. The "preemptive and punitive" activities against Muslim intellectuals and dissidents reach the West, where liberal Muslim females in particular are targeted. The violence reaches western intellectuals, as well. Artists, filmmakers, authors, and academics are attacked, sometimes physically. (This occurred in the Netherlands in 2004.) The terror against critics widens worldwide, without serious international sanctions so that "prejudice does not alter the intercommunal relations."

The most devastating aggression by the fundamentalists takes place in the Arab and Muslim world, where writers, instructors, journalists, politicians, feminists, and cultural figures are persecuted. Minorities are increasingly oppressed. The suppression against the Copts accelerates in Egypt and increases against evangelicals in Iran, Chaldo-Assyrians in Iraq, and Christians in Aceh, Indonesia.

JIHADIST INTIMIDATION IN THE UNITED STATES

By 2005, the jihadist campaign waged against the opposition reaches an apex. A systematic harassment of intellectuals, journalists, activists, and Middle Eastern and Muslim dissidents turns into "persecution." (By 2004, this had already happened. An investigative journalist was banned from mainstream media under the pressure of the jihadi lobby for having produced a documentary exposing terror in 1994. The title of the film was *Jihad in America*.) One scholar, then others, are bashed, then harassed by the Wahabi network for publishing books on "militant Islam." The witch-hunt targets Middle Eastern Christians who have fled the region because of jihadist persecution. In Connecticut, a Coptic professor loses his job as a result of pressure from the Wahabi lobby and a Coptic family is savagely assassinated in New Jersey (these acts occured between 2002 and 2005). Minorities who flee from Pakistan, Iran, and other areas are under increasing pressure. Muslim dissidents who criticize radical regimes in the greater

Middle East find themselves victims of persecution in the freest land in the world. The court system is blinded by a mass of "experts" who describe these incidents as "racism" coming from Christian religious quarters and from "Zionists." Persecution or assassination of Middle East Christians is portrayed as "feuds between extremists." As most of the voices that can warn Americans about the advance of jihadism are silenced, the public at large no longer recognizes the threat. By 2006, the country's cultural warning system is taken out.[4]

JIHAD PHASE TWO ACCELERATED

By 2007, the jihadists have been able to secure two major victories.

First, Islamists took over or influenced a bloc of countries. Three of these regimes possess nuclear weapons: Pakistan, Iran, and Iraq. Three others have delivery systems: Saudi Arabia, Syria, and Sudan. In 2006, a summit of the six countries creates the "common front for jihad." The bloc is committed to respond collectively if one comes under attack. Collectively, these countries become the third nuclear power after China, the largest producers of oil, and the greatest state threats to the West. Al Qaeda has 100,000 fighters with 3,000 suicide bombers deployed around the world. Hezbollah has tactical nukes, 30,000 fighters, and 1,000 suicide bombers across the continents. A joint war room coordinates the two organizations.

Second, within the United States, the jihadists line up 5,000 "urban militants," deploy 400 suicide bombers, and infiltrate the main security agencies with first- and second-generation cells. Since the late 1990s, they have been training their followers in Afghanistan (facts verified) and within the United States. The followers are trained under the cover of paintball games in the country and in urban areas.[5] Religious schools are infiltrated and transformed into jihad madrassas. A network of "war colleges" is established around the nation, and two advanced training centers are up and running. At the top of the pyramid, Mohammed Atta and Ziad al Jarrah establish the national al Qaeda *Ghazwa* command.[6] It centralizes all other networks and oversees the infiltration of the FBI, CIA, and the military. It also disposes of a vast network of translators and analysts as well as operators inside the government.

SEPTEMBER 11, 2008

At twelve noon, twenty-four passenger planes are simultaneously slammed against the Twin Towers, the Pentagon, the White House, the U.S. Congress, the CIA, Disneyland, and targets in Las Vegas, Los Angeles, and Chicago, as well as nuclear sites, ports, and airports. More than 30,000 perish.[7]

Within the next hour, trucks explode simultaneously in front of the main FBI and federal buildings as security units mobilize to deploy. With the first wave, the national defense system is partially down, and the political leadership of America is essentially crippled.

The second wave targets military bases, airports, and ports. A thousand snipers and shoulder-fired missiles are deployed nationwide around military airfields, aiming at barracks and naval sites. Casualties among the U.S. military are high as the surprise is total and plans were never drawn against jihadist terrorism. An F–16 pilot, who dodges the missiles and reaches high altitude, screams on his radio: "God damn it, the Russians had us!"

It is total chaos when a third horrible wave strikes. This time, using the Beslan model of Russia, hundreds of urban terrorists led by Abu Mussab al Zarqawi, who married a U.S. citizen in 2004, ravages schools with bombs and machine guns, massacring children and provoking a mass hysteria among parents. Thousands of cell phone calls by survivors reach members of the military and security services who are rushing to their duty. Many among them run to save their loved ones. The third wave also targets the main hubs of national television in several cities. America is one-eyed, as local TV and radio stations become the only sources for news.

A fourth wave is launched at 4:00 P.M. An all-out computer attack devastates systems randomly, in the absence of a coordinated national response. In 2008, the bulk of the nation's communications, information, medical, and structural systems are entirely computerized. A "cyber war room" called *dar el harb* runs the computer attack operations. Its staff has been recruited jointly by al Qaeda and Hezbollah for about five years from departments of computer engineering and major companies across the nation.

A fifth wave has started already in different time zones around the world. The twelve U.S. task forces, the main military installations and bases around the world, experience a series of small terrorist activities perpetrated by jihadist personnel. Activated by the news of the strikes on the mainland, hundreds of operatives use small arms, hand grenades, and other weapons to sabotage the vessels, airplanes, and technological sites.[8]

By early evening, America's powers as an organized government are severely damaged. The legislative branch is shattered, and the main components of the executive branch are dislocated. Smoke covers many cities, and snipers paralyze many downtowns. In the late evening Osama bin Laden appears on al Jazeera and delivers the speech of *nasr* (victory). He warns the United States and declares his conditions for a cessation of hostilities. Among the conditions are two that would transform the United States forever. "You have one week to surrender your fleets and materiel overseas, sink them or destroy them. And you have one week to dismantle your own nuclear sites on the mainland." He follows it with another warning: "If you do not abide by these conditions, we will unleash Operation Yarmuk. [This is a reference to the first battle against the Byzantines led by Khalid Ibn al Walid on August 5, 636 A.D.] City after city, we will use our devices," most probably tactical dirty bombs, put together under the auspices of José Padilla over the past five years.

But the media ask a major question: "Why do they hate us?" Another one quickly follows: "Who are they?"

THE PATH TO IMPLOSION

Day 2: The regathered U.S. leadership rejects al Qaeda's conditions and vows a great retaliation. But the country's systems are terribly damaged. Chaos is spreading as the snipers and other terrorists are still at large, paralyzing large sectors of the main cities. The government has to deploy the National Guard and the armed forces over wide areas, for the first time since the American Civil War. Congress meets at another location and legislates "war acts" to fight the war on terrorism amid a growing protest movement on campuses and on the streets.

The paralyzed cities are in a state of siege. Suicide bombers, coming from urban zones, blast themselves against roadblocks, hospital entrances, and in supermarkets. A state of emergency is declared, soon to be rejected by "revolutionary coalitions" and radical factions from the extreme left and the extreme right, both attacking the government, calling for civil disobedience. The "jihad war room" of America has been able to mobilize and "fund" non-Islamist groups across the land. Armed groups emerge in different neighborhoods, prompting the military to deploy in the streets, which in turn triggers a wider terror wave, and countermeasures. Self-defense committees emerge.

Meanwhile the "threats" by al Qaeda internationally are growing and the menace of an "unconventional" explosion is imminent. Civil leaders, artists, and intellectuals form an "opposition to the war" and put pressure on the government to withdraw all U.S. forces from the various locations and bring them back home and to negotiate with the jihadists. Massive demonstrations against the government are launched, and incidents with "patriotic Americans" spread out. A backlash takes place within the United States against Arabs and Muslims, and confused social communities identify terror with immigrants, even from other backgrounds.

The military splits on the question. Some are convinced by the "opposition" while most put pressure on the government to unleash the counterattack. Plans are devised to strike back at al Qaeda's bases. But the organization has grown much bigger since the attack on the USS *Cole* with huge networks and headquarters in Afghanistan. Pakistan's jihadists vow to retaliate if an American intervention takes place. Iran declares it would stand by the Islamist bloc, as do Iraq and Syria. Saudi Arabia threatens to lead a second historic oil boycott to retaliate against the "backlash" against Muslims in the United States. Anti-American demonstrations cover most cities in Europe and the Middle East. And to add to the world tensions, Venezuela's "revolutionary" regime leads an anti-American uprising in Latin America, counting on Cuba and the "current" across the subcontinent.

Realizing that it cannot sustain a simultaneous war from the inside and the outside, unable to create an international alliance against such a large jihad bloc, and watching the Yarmuk operation wreaking havoc on the U.S. economy, the American leaders have two choices: Accept the conditions, with a negotiated solution, or unleash the greatest war ever, with the potential use of "unconventional" weapons. But American and western strategists soon realize that once the jihadist threat has taken root inside the realm of national defense on one hand and has gotten the opportunity to build a nuclear bloc of regimes on the other hand, it is too late. Any war on terrorism would become nothing less than a human disaster. Beyond that horizon, cataclysmic possibilities are open, including the old cold war fears of a nuclear exchange or of the terrorists using weapons of mass destruction as a way to crush their enemies.[9]

ALTERNATIVE FUTURE?

This logic is hard to accept but is irreversible: Either the United States would surrender its "power" internationally and take back its country from the terrorist threat, or it would have to wage a harsh war against unclear but growing enemies, while at the same time facing strife internally. The dilemma is inescapable, but in either case, the consequences will be tragic. Of course, the future will not occur in this way. This vision is virtual and based on models, but it shows what might have happened had jihadism been given a chance to pursue its desires fully. In this scenario, two parameters are permanent: a lack of perception leads fatally to a lack of decisions, and a lack of decisions in turn leads the opponent to an additional set of decisions.

This scenario of future jihad would be the result of three realities:

1. Not developing a clear national doctrine on resistance to jihad terrorism, even after the start of the jihad war against the United States and the West in the early 1990s.
2. Not mobilizing the national resources to withstand the threat of terror, but limiting the antiterrorist strategies to normal police and judicial processes.
3. Not preempting the rise of this threat by producing policies that would trigger counterterrorist forces, rooted in democratic ideas, within the societies where the jihadists have been produced.

In short, had the war on terrorism not been engaged as a result of the attacks of September 11, and had no decision been made to take that campaign to the enemy, the virtual scenario could have been close to reality—at the least, it was the future jihad the terrorists most likely planned for. Now that events have taken another course, we must ask three questions:

1. What are the real future plans of the terrorists?
2. Is America ready for them?
3. What are the prescriptions to avoid them?

Chapter Fourteen

THE CLASH
OF STRATEGIES:
AMERICA VERSUS JIHAD

L ET US NOW FOCUS ON THE CLASH BETWEEN THE STRATEGIES of the United
States and of the terrorists as it is developing. The current state of the war
on terrorism, when analyzed with the backdrop of what the jihadists had initially planned, can provide us with a projection of real future strategies to be developed by the terror networks. Let us see how the United States made and is
making its decisions for the future, compared with the jihadists.

U.S. STRATEGIES AFTER TORA BORA

It is very important to realize that the U.S. decision to go to Afghanistan in
2001 and remove the Taliban was in full contradiction with all the guidelines of
American foreign policy for at least the previous decade, if not longer. It was
simply a response to September 11—revenge against the "perpetrators" (al
Qaeda) and their protectors, the Taliban.[1] Practically, this meant that there was
no U.S. strategy for regime change as a part of a war on terror prior to the invasion of the Afghan plateau. More important, and stunningly, there was no
"war on terrorism" prior to the terrorist attacks against the U.S. mainland! Do
we actually have a strategy to counter future jihads against the United States?

U.S. forces went after al Qaeda in Afghanistan to remove it, destroy it,
and deprive it of real estate. That move was logical; but was it the only move
to win the war on terrorism? This question opens the wider question of just
what is the war on terror? Back in 2002, in the midst of the debate about it,

I repeatedly stated that we may be waging a war without a definition: Is it a war against the terrorists, terror, or terrorism? Is it a war against a method of war—terrorism—or is it directed at an ideology—jihadism—that lies behind that terrorism? Up to the moment of this writing, I still have not seen evidence that the United States, or the West as a whole, has been able to define the identity of the ongoing war against terrorism. We are still reacting to individual events rather than the strategy of terrorism in the long term.[2]

Is this to say that the U.S.-led war against terrorism lacks a global objective? The answer to this powerful question is yes and no. Yes, the war launched against terrorism has no identity objective—we do not really know who the enemy is, at least from what is announced publicly about this campaign. Who are the terrorists, and what do they want other than to terrorize? U.S. and western leaders have delivered many speeches since 2001 about the readiness against terrorism and the importance of this campaign for this generation and the future. Yet the texts do not really specify an identity for the enemy. In speeches, George W. Bush, Tony Blair, Jacques Chirac, and other prominent leaders referred to the Nazis, fascists, and Bolsheviks in the past, but speak of "terrorism" in present and future tenses only. One has to wonder why. Interestingly, Vladimir Putin of Russia was the only great power leader who named the terrorists with their actual ideological identification. He called them Islamic fundamentalists; he even mentioned their future goal, a caliphate, and rejected their method, jihad. But he was an exception. Let us keep this first issue in mind as we move forward in the analysis.[3]

It is only toward mid 2005, and slowly after the London attack of July 7, that President Bush and Prime Minister Blair started to use the term *"criminal ideology"* in an indirect indictment of jihadism.

Another unanswered question in the war on terror is a vital component to all planning: How can we win that war, and how will we know when it is being won? Is there a quantitative method that would allow us to draw such a conclusion? Is it the number of casualties on the terrorist side when an engagement takes place, cells dismantled, finances disrupted, geographical areas controlled, leaders captured, or other indicators? All of these questions are warranted now that the war on terrorism has become the official policy of the United States and dozens of governments around the world. I will revisit this question in the last chapter. But in reality, the declaration of war against terrorism made by President Bush on October 7, 2001, while addressing the U.S. Congress, in the presence of British Prime Minister Blair, and endorsed by France, the rest of Europe, and a very large number of countries around the world, was the response to the bin Laden fatwas of February 1998. The response came almost four years later and after thousands of lives were lost. This is the reality we need to reflect upon when we analyze the war: U.S. and western strategies are a *reaction* to terror actions. The strategies are developing as the war evolves and produces a global vision out of the experiments on the ground. However, and although the campaign is heading in the right direction(s), it avoids addressing the root causes of these terror wars. The elephant in the room has not been named yet. Most decision makers, policy planners, and legislators know the names of the threat, have an idea about its history, are able to project the general intentions of the enemy, and are devising the right guidelines to roll back the danger—but they are not educating their public as to the identity of the jihadists. And by failing to do so, they may risk stretching the conflict out longer. For only an educated public can produce a mobilized nation.

The international community gave the United States "license" to remove the Taliban as retribution for the massacres in New York and Washington. Under international law, retaliation in self-defense is permissible. Washington's leadership got an opportunity to strike back with full force against the jihadist terror, under the full extent of international law. But that was only a window of opportunity, which was supposed to close after the removal of the Taliban. The United States got its license to retaliate against the perpetrators of September 11.[4] During the Afghan war, there was a wide consensus behind U.S. operations and motives. But as soon as the last bastion of al Qaeda collapsed in Tora Bora in December 2001, the United States found itself at a crossroad. It had two options: Either remain within an international consensus, rooted in pre–September 11 thinking and interests, or cross the line into a post–September 11 world. The international political establishment, although supportive of the removal of the Taliban, had not yet licensed the indictment of an ideology, but of a government caught in criminal activities. The marriage of convenience was over after the battle of Tora Bora. After the ousting of the Taliban, most of Europe, Russia, all Arab regimes, and a number of Muslim governments opposed regime change anywhere based on preemptive logic. The U.S. administration, a majority in Congress, and a variety of countries around the world felt a major change had occurred historically. The principal question had become: Should the United States wait until a threat becomes evident before it acts against it, or should it act before the threat becomes evident? American strategists chose a middle way, but one closer to the second option. The United States would identify the threat before it acts, but would take action only when all other means were exhausted. Critics wanted to identify a threat as such only if there were both evidence of intent and a beginning of action. The dominant school in the administration and in Congress went the other way: When the evidence of the intention is clear, consider the threat to exist, but only act against it when the context allows. This school has the advantage of the strategic initiative. Such an approach was used after Tora Bora, including the intervention in Iraq and the war of ideas, which are discussed later.

Since Tora Bora, U.S. strategies have developed in two directions: defensive and offensive. The strategy has focused on the construction of a homeland security infrastructure domestically and an international network of alliances and activities to reduce al Qaeda and other threats as the global confrontation is taking place. The offensive strategy defines the mounting threats, evaluates their imminence, and initiates campaigns when the assessment of threat calls for action. One of the most salient parts of this offensive strategy has been and remains the "definition" of the enemy. President Bush, for example, declared the existence of an "axis of evil" during his 2002 State of the Union address: Iran, Iraq, and North Korea. This categorization signifies the potential threat emanating from these regimes. It combines two elements: the fact that these regimes have expressed a radical attitude toward international peace on one hand, plus, as important, the fact that they have or are about to acquire the means to threaten world peace. One element without the other would not define a regime as a member of the axis of evil. Obviously, opponents on the ground criticized this category because it indicts without proof of imminent danger. In reality, that was not Bush's aim. From what I can understand, based on the various speeches of the president and his team, the "axis of evil" was an announcement of deterrence rather than an indictment. It was a warning to these regimes not to cross the last line. As the international security system was unable to address global threats and the United Nations was not acting, the United States moved to redress the situation. In reality, Bush should have included more members in the axis: the Baathist regime in Syria, responsible for the occupation of Lebanon; and the jihadist power in Sudan, responsible for genocide in the south and Darfur. Both regimes have extensive records of human rights abuses and declared intentions to build, receive, and deploy weapons of mass destruction. However, they were not included, probably because the U.S. foreign policy establishment still hoped a mode of cooperation was still possible. This can be debated, as Syria was sanctioned by UN Security Council Resolution 1559 in 2004 and Sudan by a similar action in 2005—international initiatives to expose the "evil" perpetrated by the two regimes despite ongoing diplomatic initiatives.

With regard to terrorist organizations, the Bush administration and its critics, both domestically and internationally, found a consensus: al Qaeda, Hezbollah, Hamas, Islamic jihad, and a host of other radical Islamists—but also secular radical groups—were put in quarantine. What was a de facto policy in the 1990s became a legal reality after 2001. However, even though jihadist organizations were listed as terrorists, jihadism as an ideology was not equated with terrorism. This hole is precisely where future jihads will come from. Despite its advanced steps, American and western strategies have stopped short of the "factory," which is the ideology. They have decided to go after the products, but they are still being mollified from the inside.[5]

JIHADIST STRATEGIES AFTER TORA BORA

As Americans and westerners reassessed their war on terrorism and devised new strategies, the jihadists did the same: With the fall of Kabul and Tora Bora, the only "sovereign national space" in the hands of Salafi terrorists disappeared. From then on, the Islamists had to cope with the new realities: No regimes, including the members of the "axis of evil" and their potential colleagues, were available to officially host or endorse al Qaeda anymore. Iran and Syria continued to host and support Hezbollah, Hamas, and Islamic Jihad, but claimed no relations with bin Laden's group. Even Saddam's regime, which sought cooperation with the Islamists during the 1990s, denied ties to them in 2001. The radical regimes decided not to engage the United States on its terms and on its timing. Instead, they opted for alternative strategies: distancing themselves from the world's most wanted group, shielding their regimes and organizations, and preparing plans for future confrontations on their own timing and with their own tools. This situation deprived the Wahabi internationalists of any official recognition of the Taliban type. This new reality will force them to adapt to the "new order" and redeploy their assets worldwide. Meanwhile, while their geography changed dramatically, their political demography increased.[6]

The assessment of the enemy "losses" by western and American standards is mostly technical. It centers on the actual physical losses at all structural levels of al Qaeda. For example, the American evaluation of the war on terror factors in the depletion of the high-ranking officers of the organization, its killed and captured fighters, and the group's inability to retake the geographical positions they lost, such as Tora Bora or Fallujah (in Iraq). According to this method, the calculation is statistical, as in any classical war. But statistics can also produce other realities: There are more jihadists trained to fight today than at the beginning of the war on terror, and there are more suicide bombers today than in 2001. Besides, there are more areas of engagement and operations with the terrorists than four days after September 11. Does that mean that the terrorists are winning the war? Not necessarily; but the accounting by numbers can be matched with other numbers. The true story goes beyond statistics.

In order to revise their strategies, the jihad terror networks must evaluate the attacks and the counterattacks. Rationally, they should come up with an analysis that would guide their next actions. That would be the normal course of events—but with one difference: The jihadists are hyperideological, like all totalitarians throughout history (Bolsheviks, fascists, Nazis). And they even have a unique feature that distinguishes them from the previous currents. The Islamists do not fall back on rational choice theories. They do not see their losses as westerners see them, nor do they calculate their defeats as their opponents do. It is necessary to understand how the jihadists assess their own successes and victories in order to understand their strategies.

First, for the Salafists, and to a certain extent the Khumeinists, physical losses are not a main factor in their assessment. For example, losing one-third or half of the leadership is not seen as a defeat per se, but as a fact to note. So is the case with the foot soldiers. Losses are not defeat, say most jihadi spokespersons in their literature and websites. "They are all in Allah's paradise watching the battle with joy," write the clerics on al Ansar's sites. Being evacuated from land, a city, a position, or a stronghold is not defeat either. As long as there is a leading imam or emir, and as long as the "rings" of the *aqida* (doctrine) are safe, the battle goes on.[7]

Second, the jihadists' leaders and religious mentors usually explain victories and defeats with theological references in which the divine expresses satisfaction with regards to a particular confrontation. Drawing heavily from religious texts, often from the Qu'ran, the Salafist leaders "possess the entire truth." They can make a victory of their defeat and a defeat out of their enemy's victory. I analyzed their speeches, statements, and literature after the fall of Kandahar and Tora Bora in Afghanistan and Fallujah in the Sunni triangle; in both cases they had turned the facts into a divinely determined outcome. According to these speeches, "the infidels have been crushed and had to use greater technology, which signifies their weakness." They add in all similar cases that the jihadists had to migrate (*Hijra*) in the same way the first Muslims had to migrate—in order to come back and strike, in their own time and at the will of Allah. By referring to the Prophet's decision to leave Mecca and migrate to Medina, the jihadists have found a way to use theology to interpret modern-day battles. Note that both Osama bin Laden and Ayman al Thawahiri often say that the infidels do not dare face them on the ground but fight from afar, either from the skies or with long-range artillery. Al Qaeda frequently airs videos and audiotapes insisting on the higher courage of the "fighters on behalf of religion" over the "mercenaries on behalf of money and earthly materialism." However, al Qaeda rarely explains how its own brave mujahidin did not dare kill Americans face to face in the United States, but preferred to come to them from the skies without warning.

Hence, the jihadists do not calculate losses, victories, and defeats as their foes do. Their prism is the establishment of the caliphate—entirely, by pieces, by stages, and always going forward. A victory (*nasr*) usually comes in two ways. Either when they "recruit" a new fighter for jihad—that is a small *nasr*—or when an Islamist authority is established on some particular territory. Another form of *nasr* is when an infidel enemy surrenders, signs a *sulh* (temporary agreement), or collapses. But as long as the "factory" is producing waves of jihadists, there is no defeat. Only when the "factory" is broken or dismantled can defeat occur. But ironically, no jihadi authority will be there to admit it.

When al Qaeda and the Taliban fled Tora Bora, they started a new era in the war against the United States and the West. With no regime to provide them with cover and safe haven, the jihadists' first and foremost objective was to get a new one: in other words, to transform a Muslim government into a jihadi regime. The second objective was to acquire a global weapons system, one that can establish a balance of terror with America and the West. With the swift U.S. invasion of Afghanistan they learned that they cannot stop any similar military advance anywhere or anytime unless they obtain a weapon that can deter the Americans: nuclear, biological, chemical, or other. Hence, I contend that one major goal of the jihadists now is to buy, steal, or even build some sort of weapon of mass destruction.

Observation of al Qaeda's moves and statements and the evolution of other jihadists, including the Khumeinists, over the past four years reveals a number of elements in their strategies.

AL QAEDA'S RESTRUCTURING

A central command remains in effect, under the symbolic leadership of Osama bin Laden (regardless of his health, location, and even future survival), but managed primarily by Ayman Thawahiri. Others are in the line of succession if the number one and two leave the scene. But al Qaeda has structured its networks in "regional commands," such as Iraq (under Abu Mussab al Zarqawi), Saudi Arabia, south Asia, as well as North and South America. It continues to develop its central units, which it can move to remote fronts. Its recruitment is operated by the regional branches as well as central organs. Al Qaeda's initial body—the old-boy network of Afghanistan's camps—is physically present, but a new generation has already moved up the ladder. This second wave is younger, educated, as committed, but more realistic in its approach, and hence more difficult to detect. While the classical method of seeking new recruits was top-down, with al Qaeda cadres looking for new members among sympathizers around the world, a new type of growth has developed: a bottom-up approach whereby independent militants and self-formed cells are following the organization's ideology, path, and guidelines without necessarily being linked to it. These are satellites of al Qaeda—jihadi units that gravitate on their own, form networks and commands, and seek the same objectives, but are not bound to the hierarchy. At some point and when circumstances permit, the "satellites" look for the mother ship, find it, and join the fleet. In sum, what cements the greater al Qaeda is an ideology, and what holds the ideology together and feeds it is an elusive, fluid central fountain that continues to hold onto the rings, as yet unchallenged and unchecked by mainstream, moderate, and reformist Muslims.

AFGHANISTAN AND PAKISTAN

Al Qaeda's strategy is to continue to feed terror networks in Afghanistan until the Taliban can make a major comeback from the Pakistani battlefield. Al Qaeda's strategic objective in the region, undoubtedly, is power in Pakistan, achieved through the fundamentalist tribes and sectors of the armed forces. The ultimate goal is to secure Pakistan's nuclear weapons, with which the jihadist machine would enter the second stage of confrontation with its enemies, including the United States. Al Qaeda does not have to show itself at first; it would rely on jihadi followers and sympathetic elements in the military. It may use the Sudanese model of the 1990s, with Turabi the Islamist ideologue and Bashir the military president. The various scenarios I have provided in the last chapter are still on the table, but they are not the only ones. The Salafists would select any tactics, including regional conflict and terrorism, to trigger violent disruptions in Pakistan leading to a regime change.

SOUTH ASIA AND INDONESIA

Al Qaeda's strategy in South Asia and Indonesia is based on central terror operations against the infidels—Australians, Americans, British, and others—such as the 2002 Bali bombing, while local jihadists such as Jamaat Islami and Laskar Jihad operate inside the national fabric of the country.[8] The objective in Indonesia—the largest Muslim country in the world—is to push for an Islamist regime by forcing the moderates to choose between the Wahabis, or the West and the infidels (including Christians and Chinese). In the Philippines, the strategy is to support the Wahabi Abu Sayyaf branch to take the control of the Muslim south and establish a base for the international jihadists. In the mind of al Qaeda, an Islamic fundamentalist Indonesia would become the ally of a jihadi Pakistan and obtain nuclear arms from it, so that it could then threaten Australia. One development on the Indian subcontinent would roll like a tsunami in all directions. Similar strategies could be devised in Bangladesh, Malaysia, and southern Thailand.[9]

NORTH AFRICA

In North Africa, al Qaeda's allies in Algeria, Morocco, and Tunisia have separate strategies regarding their governments, but serve as conduits for the organization's recruitment and infiltration into the West, particularly Europe and North America. In Egypt, the lead will be taken by the Muslim Brotherhood, as the Mubarak regime is pressured to reform. But Egyptian members of al Qaeda serve internationally. In Sudan, the jihadists support the National Islamic Front of Hassan Turabi, but would use the front of Darfur with the Janjaweed to create a battlefield against international infidels.

SAUDI ARABIA

Al Qaeda's future strategy in Saudi Arabia has become clearer over the years. I call it: "Going home." Although the international jihadists have considered the Salafi power inside the kingdom as backers for the battlefields around the world, the equation has changed. Today's strategy, elaborated patiently, is to shift the balance of power inside Arabia toward the neo-Wahabis. In short: a takeover of power. Controlling Arabia has three benefits.

1. The jihadists would be in charge of Mecca and Medina, Islam's holiest shrines. This would shield them from any outside aggression.[10] A U.S.-led campaign into the holy areas of the Hijaz is unthinkable if an al Qaeda control develops. This is the home bin Laden or his successors would like to acquire to stage their grand plans against the United States and the West.
2. Oil resources would be instrumental to obtain arms and influence.
3. A radical Salafi state in Arabia would shift the world balance of power. It would become an overt launching pad for the jihadist ideology, multiplying tenfold at least what al Jazeera's effect is today.[11]

But does al Qaeda have the resources to provoke such a shift in the kingdom? Historically, the clerics have been sympathetic toward the aims of the organization. The Saudi government has begun to react to this strategy, but the regime does not know how deeply it has been infiltrated. Al Qaeda's objective is certainly to overrun the Saudis, but the most important issue is how. Considering that the main instrument of jihad in the kingdom is the kingdom's ideology itself, can the government adopt any policy to stop the neo-Wahabis from taking over, when the government itself was responsible for the spread of these doctrines? How can an establishment cut the bad branch it is sitting on if it does not want to fall?[12] The new king Abdallah could become a maker or breaker of neo-Wahabism.

THE WEST

"Our brothers and sisters in the West have a great mission," Sheikh Yussef al Qardawi has said several times on al Jazeera; the mission was to "prepare for the spread of the mission and also perform jihad in the ways they can." This sentence can be read in two ways: spiritual or political. Wahabi and Salafi spokespersons in the West state that the spread of religion is a right not only recognized by the international declaration of human rights, but also protected by the legal systems in the western world. And on that, they are right: Prose-lytism and evangelization are indeed part of religious freedoms. That Islamic centers proselytize for Islam as a religion is perfectly normal under any demo-cratic system. But that is not what the Salafists are calling for, or what they are strictly practicing. The strategies of the jihadists in the West are clearly outlined in the declarations made on the websites of Salafists and other radicals. They have an international body, even if they follow different paths, depending on their timetable and country of action.[13]

Evidently, the size of Muslim communities in the West is important to the ji-hadists, because it is the environment in which the Islamists can work. But more important than the plain demography are the numbers of Islamic fundamental-ists, because that is the pool from which the jihadists recruit. Hence, when the radical scholars and leaders call for the spread of religion, they are talking about their version of religion, which they deem to be the only version. Their literature and websites explicitly call for the "Salafization" of Muslims living in the West. Then and only then will the jihadists be able to use the "re-Islamized" commu-nities to advance their strategies. But can we summarize the main outlines of fu-ture jihads since the fall of the Taliban? Here are some sketches.[14]

They will pursue an aggressive strategy of "Wahabization" of Muslim com-munities in the West, including the United States, under the laws of the land. That would achieve 90 percent of the first stage. When the ideology of al Qaeda and or its sisters becomes the mainstream thinking of the dominant elites, the resources of the communities and their political weight would be used to serve the political objectives of Wahabism in western foreign policies and eventually shield the actions of the jihadists within these societies. In other words, the Salafists' and Khumeinists' first strategy in the West is to grow their presence within a shielded entity, which is protected by the legal system. This is the pregnancy phase. The system provides for all education, training, and facilities. It is only when the time comes for action that the jihadi creature would strike, regardless of the consequences for the community as a whole. The jihadi sword would strike and the community shield would absorb the counterstrikes. The terrorists would attack while the activists would absorb the reaction of the government and society in the media, courts, and public debate. In the United States, the Islamic radicals would focus in particular on ethnic minorities, such as new converts among Hispanics and the Nation of Islam. This layer of minorities is of particular interest to the jihadists since it can inflame ethnic and racial strife within society while it links up with jihadi views. Because of their high expectations jihadists will put more resources into them, particularly when jihadists move to phase two of their actions.

Their strategy is to build bridges with "objective allies," particularly with extremist forces on the left, such as Trotskyites, and on the right, such as neo-Nazis. The jihadists have expressed interest and demonstrated a will to play with the contradictions within infidel societies. They will (and have already) made inroads with non-Islamic radicals who share the same desire to destroy the enemy state. Instead of using their own troops at all opportunities, the jihadists will use the constituencies of other radicals to weaken the enemy and force it to spread thin.

The ultimate objective of the jihadist strategies within the West is undoubtedly to infiltrate the security and military bodies. This infiltration would provide them with important ingredients: It would grant them a spy network that would inform them of enemy strategies and tactics and above all provide a warning system. If jihadists can infiltrate the FBI, Homeland Security, or similar agencies in the United States and the West, they can foresee government moves and have invaluable information with regard to government weaknesses. For example, if Homeland Security is spending millions of dollars to protect planes, the jihadists will strike ships. If the government attention moves to ports, the jihadists would target the factories that build the planes to insert a long-range device at an early stage. Getting al Qaeda, Hezbollah, or other jihadists to become translators for the CIA, French, or British agencies is equal to a successful strike, for it is the first segment of an operation that would facilitate others. From there on, the infiltration process would become part of espionage manuals. The difference, though, is the fact that these networks are not necessarily or directly built by regimes, but by fluid networks. The ultimate fantasy of penetration of the western defense and security system remains the possibility of strategic sabotage; one that comes with D-Day–type operations.[15]

RUSSIA

The jihadist networks have been extremely clear in anointing Russia as a main enemy, despite the fact that it continues to supply Iran and to some degree Syria with weapons and assistance. But the Wahabi mother ship has ordered the destruction of the Russian empire in the same way it fought the Soviets. In the Wahabis' geopolitical perception, Moscow remains a major infidel power (*quwat kufr*) that occupies "Muslim lands." The Salafists do not see Russia as a nation with Muslim minorities; to them Russia is an occupier of Muslim territories. Fatwas have been issued online to "liberate these lands" from the occupation. The Wahabi network that follows up on the Russian front does not focus on Chechen national rights, inasmuch as it sees Chechnya as a part of the caliphate. And it does not limit its call for jihad to Chechnya, but encompasses also Dagestan and other areas within Russia. The jihadist plan for Russia is to dismember the country and bring down its power and economy.

To do so, the jihadists consider Chechnya a staging base for their Russian action. And in view of the wars that ravaged that area since the mid-1990s, the "Caucusus jihadists" have pushed their strikes into Russian mainland in Moscow and beyond. They have also adopted the mass killing of Russian civilians, such as the Moscow theater hostage-taking and the Beslan school massacre. From these strategies it seems clear that the jihadists eventually would use mass murder weapons or provoke incidents with genocidal consequences.

OTHER FRONTS

Al Qaeda, Hezbollah, and the jihad terror nexus have developed a series of other fronts *(jabahat)* around the world. Just to give important examples, I will cite a few cases in Latin America and Africa. In Venezuela, the jihadists have opened links with the government of Hugo Chavez. Chavez has been interviewed several times by al Jazeera and has been promoted in the Arab world as a leader who is anti-American and friendly to the jihadists. The promotion of Chavez on al Jazeera is a great indicator of the future moves of al Qaeda and Hezbollah. Jihadi bases have been reported on the island of Marguerita, Venezuela. Chavez has spoken about his "Arab roots," and has described al Jazeera as the best tool of communication between forces sharing the same views and strategies around the world. Note that he is a strategic ally of Fidel Castro, America's foe in the Caribbean. In Argentina, Brazil, and Paraguay, Hezbollah cells have formed a consortium in the triborder area. The jihadist strategy in Latin America is to open a southern front against the United States.

The aim is to incite local ethnic movements as well as the extreme right wing to join in a wide anti-American axis.

In Africa, jihadist groups are active in the northern part of Ivory Coast, northern Nigeria, and Mauritania. This is not surprising, as many among the cadres are recruited during the *Hajj* season in Saudi Arabia or by madrassas teachers, funded by the Wahabis. In West Africa as well, Hezbollah fundraisers are widespread among the Lebanese émigrés. Somalia has al Qaeda hubs, and South Africa is witnessing the expansion of local jihadists. Jihadist strategy in Africa is to inflame all local battlefields so that Wahabi regimes are installed, and when possible, to drag the West into military confrontations. Instead of one Afghanistan, the jihadists plan on claiming a dozen worldwide through the establishment of as many Islamist emirates as possible.

THE IRAQ CHOICE: AMERICAN DOCTRINE AND JIHADI COUNTERSTRIKE

One of the most debated wars in the history of the United States and international relations was, without doubt, the war in Iraq. The volume of arguments used by all sides is not only gigantic, but also and mostly indicative of the state of international relations with regard to the surge of jihadism. Had the jihad terrorists not attacked the United States in 2001, the debate about Iraq would not have taken place, or at least not in the shape it did. Even during the 1990s, particularly since 1998, the concept of regime change, inasmuch as it meant replacing Saddam Hussein with another leader, was accepted, even in many quarters of the Arab world. But what made the Iraq war a much more highly debated issue was less the fact of removing Saddam than it was the fact of replacing him with an Iraq-made democracy. But was this idea, and is it now, an American strategy against terrorism?[16]

Apparently it is. In 2002, after al Qaeda forces left Tora Bora, American policy planners were confronted with the dilemma of what to do next. One theory was to follow the policy of war against the terrorists, that is, the perpetrators of the September 11 operation. The other theory was to address the regional threat, which was also seen as global. Iraq was one open door to pursue the war on terror. In an article I wrote in 1991, I called the end of the first Gulf war the "unfinished symphony."[17] It was as an open wound that, if not fixed at the time, would re-open. The Kurds were put under a no-fly-zone but isolated and threatened by Saddam; the regime massacred the Shiites; and Saddam was boxed in by UN sanctions, but plotting to free himself and resume his previous strategies. The situation was a status quo that was drifting slowly toward the return of Saddam's power into the region. Had the events of September 11 not taken place, I believe that Saddam Hussein would have reconquered and oppressed Iraq's oppressed ethnicities. Moreover, projecting events based on the logic that "jihad fills a void" leads to a frightening conclusion: Saddam's Iraq was converging with al Qaeda and was heading to link up with Iran, Syria, and Sudan. And more importantly Saddam would have redeveloped his weapons of mass destruction program from scratch. The return of the flow of oil dollars, a devil's alliance with Damascus and Tehran, the collapse of the UN monitoring system, and the spread of jihad would have projected Iraq into the center of the emerging regional bloc. The American decision to go to war in Iraq used arguments from the pre–September 11 lexicon simply because the national and international context was not politically liberated. Secretary of State Colin Powell stated at the United Nations that the reasons for the Iraq campaign were, first, weapons of mass destruction, second, links to al Qaeda, and third, human rights abuses. In reality, Powell was not wrong. Analytical projection would have established these threats as real, but only when viewed through a prism of the global jihadist threat and strategies. The American public and international public opinion were not educated as to the nature of the long-term threat. Hence it was almost impossible for the U.S. administration to build arguments that national and international constituencies could understand. However, another door was there: human rights and genocide. By simply reversing the order of arguments, the U.S. administration could have made a solid case. As with Yugoslavia, the main issue in Iraq was the massacre of the Shiites and the Kurds. Powell should have focused on the genocide in Iraq, growing links to terror, and the potential threat of weapons of mass destruction.[18]

But as the intervention developed and as the United States was rebuffed on the weapons of mass destruction question, the American human rights argument surfaced as solid. Hence, in the process of liberating Iraq and helping its civil society to establish democracy, the third argument now takes center stage, by the power and intentions of the Iraqis themselves. And with the January 30, 2005, deadline for elections met, the leading drive for the U.S.-led Iraq campaign is now advanced democracy. So, U.S. strategy was initially to fight terror in its own region, therefore removing one threat at a time, starting with the most dangerous in the sense of future threat: That was the rationale for taking out Saddam. But once successful, the project shifted to democracy-building as a long-term strategy to counter future jihad terror.

On the other side of the conflict, al Qaeda projected that the United States was moving forward to remove Saddam Hussein as of 2002. Bin Laden de-

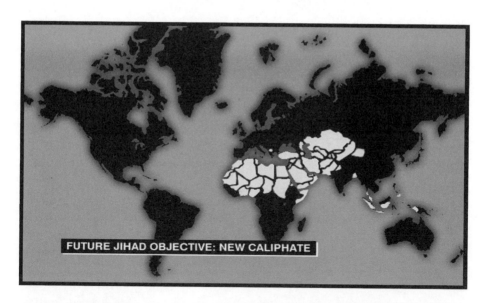

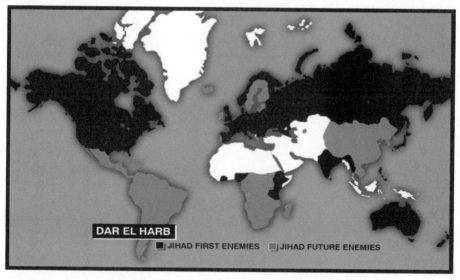

A jihadist vision of their projected empire and of their enemy states.

cided to move into the Iraqi battlefield even before the U.S.-led coalition invaded. By February 11, 2003, his troops were ready for the post-Saddam era.[19] On April 15, jihadists rose up in Iraq, and weeks later they launched the Fallujah operation. Al Zarqawi became the coordinator of their activities as soon as the Baath Party collapsed.

From a geopolitical perspective, both the United States and the jihadists viewed Iraq as a battlefield. Both got there at the same time, both had allies waiting, both had to fight for its future—the United States to allow Iraq's civil society to build a democracy, and the jihadists to establish a Wahabi state. The two strategies can be expected to clash in Iraq as long as the global war on terror lasts. The freedom strategy of the United States was able to establish a space for Iraqi democracy; the jihadist strategy was able to muster all its resources to block the latter, with unprecedented violence but without great success.[20]

In comparing the strategies of the jihadists to those of the United States you can see that the United States freed itself from the paralysis of the 1990s by striking back in Afghanistan, building a homeland security structure, and establishing an international cooperation with other governments. The jihadists lost one launching pad in Afghanistan but have restructured worldwide to generate a number of "Afghanistans" and engage the United States in as many battlefields as possible. U.S. strategies are now centering on "offensive mode," to preempt terrorist action, but they have not yet developed a full strategy to preempt future generations of terrorists. And jihadists have moved to future generations of jihadist strategies (generations who are born within the national fabric of the infidel world). This generation will be instrumental in the wider and deeper offensives of the future—the ones the jihadists were planning on accomplishing had September 11 not occurred in 2001.

Chapter Fifteen

AMERICA: JIHAD'S SECOND GENERATION

TERRORISTS HAVE STRUCK TWICE IN AMERICA, but as we have seen, jihadism has been striking at the foundations of the United States and the international community for decades in a patient buildup for a massive attack. If we analyze September 11, we see that it included not just the nineteen men as suicide terrorists but most likely a support system of up to three dozen others in a variety of complex networks. This brigade operated as part of a division, growing inside the United States, and linked to the international command of the organization outside the country. The division includes suicide jihadists, as well as operatives in different fields, including recruitment, espionage, reconnaissance, infiltration of agencies and technological industries, and also geographical cells.

Somewhere, the organization inside the United States and the West as a whole connects with the international Salafist pro-jihadi current. The organization and the current cooperate but do not necessarily overlap. The security operatives are a smaller circle within a wider militant circle. As is clear from historical studies on terrorism, activists involved in terrorism use covers within political organizations that support the same goals but still follow the laws of the country. For example, Ismael Royer, a militant convert, was a member of an Islamist lobbying organization known as CAIR (Council on American Islamic Relations), in the 1990s. While he was an officer of this organization, part of his mission was to track experts such as Daniel Pipes, investigative journalists such as Steven Emerson, human rights activists such as Charles Jacobs, and academics such as myself. Royer wrote several critiques about his adversaries, it can be argued, in order to discredit them and perhaps silence their opposing views. Similar attacks were directed at the small number of authors and activists who were warning about the jihadists before September 11, such as Swiss author Bat Ye'or, Coptic professor Shawki Karas, American cleric Keith Roderick, and others, accusing them of being anti-Muslim. In Holland, it can be argued that similar critiques led to the assassination of filmmaker Theo Van Gogh in 2004.[1]

The most significant aspect of this intimidation campaign was the fact that the same Ismael Royer who filled the Internet with ferocious writings against his targets pled guilty to terrorism-related charges. He was charged with being a member of a jihadist cell training in Virginia on ambushes and tactics, under the cover of paintball games, allegedly to be used in Kashmir. U.S. authorities also discovered other cells, including suspects who were members of the same militant group.

José Padilla, the alleged "dirty bomb" jihadist, was a member of an Islamic religious center, but one of his mentors was a member of an openly Wahabi lobbying group. The infamous "shoe bomber" had similar connections. The justice system caught other "respectable" members of lawful associations who were found guilty of being involved in terrorism. In Florida, the case of professor Sami al Arian is still pending, but his colleague Abdullah Ramadan al Shallah was a professor of Middle East studies until he vanished one day and reemerged as the head of Palestinian Islamic Jihad in Damascus. In Oregon, an al Qaeda cell was training under the guise of "games." Cases in Detroit and Idaho featured Salafists who were allegedly facilitating terror activities. There are too many cases of "terror jihadists" who are investigated, have been indicted, or are awaiting their trials as terrorists or supporters of terrorism to ignore. In many cases, they have links to legal organizations.

Not only in the United States, but also in Europe, Asia, Russia, Latin America, and obviously the Arab world, the big picture is clear: The terrorists thrive inside a certain habitat, either Salafi jihadist or Khumeinist. This habitat has been produced by the greater Wahabi infiltration of the United States and other countries. The Wahabist tendency stems from the same ideology but stops short of crossing legal lines. Before they commit their acts of terrorism, they are often connected to this wider network of militants. All that the terrorists have to do is to simmer inside the current until they receive instructions or decide to strike. As long as they live inside the body of Salafism and Wahabism (or Khumeinism) and abide by the laws of the land, they are safe. Even better, they can move freely, recruit, connect, meet, and develop their technological assets with impunity. During the day, as a mainstream journalist, Royer was a violent critic of his targets; at the same time he was training to be a sniper and an explosives expert. First-generation terrorists were well protected inside the belly of the dragon. They were so at ease in the United States that they could invite guests from the overseas community of jihadists. International terrorists such as Mohammed Atta and Ziad al Jarrah simply invited themselves to the United States and enjoyed its hospitality. No one really knows how many guests or hidden jihadists are circulating in America. No one knows how many active jihad terrorists are here, how many active and sleeper cells exist, or how many jihadists-at-large there are.[2]

But the first generation of infiltrated jihad terrorists is most likely dwindling. Those like Atta and al Jarrah had more freedom to act before September 11. At that time, Salafists, al Qaeda members, and Hizbollahis, even if not citizens, could come to this nation almost freely, cross most of its lines of defenses, scout all the desired targets, and travel back to Afghanistan or the Bekaa Valley without exciting any attention. America was totally open to jihadist infiltration from the outside and completely unconscious of the domestic infiltration. The question is: What has changed? Do the jihadists have a new strategy of penetration? Do they still have shields, and are they using them? Finally, have they adapted to the new era, and are they preparing for future jihadist offensives?

HOMELAND SECURITY: FIRST DETERRENCE IN THE UNITED STATES

By establishing a Department of Homeland Security, America leaped miles ahead in its fight against terrorism. It administered the first counterstrike to al Qaeda and the other jihad terrorists simply by opening the eyes of Americans to the fact that a national mobilization against the enemy was on. As simple as it may sound, the mere idea has set the holy warriors back one step. As primitive as it is, the concept of "homeland security" means even more than what any bureaucracy can do. The American people have been mobilized, even if only to recognize a concept. Millions of dollars, thousands of workers and officers, and several agencies, nationwide and on the state level, are now working, watching, and innovating. A much greater power is now protecting the American people. The homeland security structure is trickling down to schools, public libraries, city halls, and neighborhoods. At least 100 million Americans are reached in one way or another. This is a huge move ahead. Instead of three or four specialized offices in the FBI, State Department, and CIA, thousands of cadres are tracking terrorism and millions of citizens are empowered to identify the threat. Is homeland security ready to face all threats? No; it will need some time to catch up after the long decades of sleep. But today America has the single largest popular army against domestic jihadists—a huge body, but in need of accelerated education. Once this objective is met, the real war to reduce the terrorist threat will eventually be won.

On their side, the jihad terrorists are racing against the slow but global rise of homeland security. The free-for-all world of the 1990s is shrinking, not just because of the expansion of the homeland security structure, but because of the development of a consciousness, even if at a very early stage, among Americans. Even if Middle East studies are still blurring the cultural understanding of the threat, homeland security and terrorism studies are now coming to all colleges. Time is running out for the infiltrators and their recruits. Because of this reality, the jihadists have reorganized and are developing new strategies.[3]

Take this one example: Before September 11, if Americans or westerners had noticed a suspicious character trying to pull something from his shoes on a transatlantic flight, likely they would have done nothing. But after September 11, the minute the shoe bomber reached out to ignite his tennis shoes, civilians, not security, jumped on him. The terrorists have lost the total freedom of action they enjoyed. Hence they will act more sensibly and cautiously, and go underground. Jihadi elements will continue to pour through the borders of Mexico and Canada. The breach is too wide to ignore. The jihadists will recruit among non-Arab immigrants, including from ethnicities that have communities within the United States. They will keep coming until the doors are shut on them, not on other immigrants, and that will be the ultimate victory of homeland security. But meanwhile, on the inside, they will continue to use the system, grow under it, and attempt to infiltrate it further.[4]

How will the terrorists breach U.S. homeland security in the future? How will the next attacks materialize? Few can answer these questions with accuracy; but once jihadist global strategies are understood, their aspirations, planning, and medium-term objectives can be projected. We cannot use our minds to reason for them; by doing so, we would merely be projecting what we would do if we wanted to attack ourselves. We would project ourselves culturally onto the terrorists and fail to guess correctly. The government tries hard to look at all possible angles and holes in the system, but naturally within an American mode of thought; authorities still "think" as Americans when they plan for homeland security measures. They are bound by their cultural worldview of what it possible, impossible, or unthinkable. Certainly they are also bound by laws, which they can change if they wish to, but here lies the problem: Legislators, who shape regulations based on the experts' suggestions, are themselves bound (unless knowledgeable about the terror's ideology and history) by their culture.

Hence, one main problem in homeland security strategy is to think across cultures, that is, into the mind of the terrorists.[5]

Back in the fall of 2001, Florida authorities asked me to give a seminar statewide to law enforcement. I had the chance to interact with the audience and was able to measure the level of information and specialized education law enforcement had at the time. And that level was consistent with the general blockage existing nationwide. Since the 1990s, the jihadists were engaging an American giant with poor visibility. American manpower was among the best in the world, both technologically and mentally, but it was deprived of basic data about the war the jihadists had declared years ago against the United States. The questions the audience asked me were revealing: The officers knew little, if anything, about the entire history of the Middle East in general and particularly the actual existence of a jihadi movement. They were desperate for information. Yet, any faulty information could lead to a major disaster. For example, after I finished my presentation about the political culture of the jihadist, an officer, apparently from a Middle Eastern background, rose and said, "Female suicide bombers are not an issue, since in Islamic tradition women do not serve in the Muslim armies." With little other information at their disposal, the audience had no reason to doubt this assertion, which would have sliced the pool of jihadists by 50 percent. A few months later women perpetrated suicide bombings in Israel. A year later other women exploded bombs with their bodies in Russia. Yes, modern Jihadism produced what classical state jihad did not produce for centuries. I examine this phenomenon later. But my conclusion then was that failed education or wrong information served by experts, even from within the most equipped agency, could be at the source of a major security failure.

I kept observing the evolution of the intellectual capacity of U.S. counterterrorism personnel for years. The pace of transformation was significant. In February 2005 I had the opportunity to meet with an elite of former and current law enforcement and national security cadres at the first national intelligence conference in Washington.[6] The difference between 2005 and before was simply enormous. A revolution had occurred with the group of intelligence and security analysts and policy planners. They had educated themselves on jihadism, bypassing the classical teachings of the academic establishment. I was relieved, despite my constant worry: America's citizens are now protected by more and more self-educated officers and tactical planners. And from my European tours, I identified a similar pattern: The growth of antiterrorism education is rapid.[7] The West's intelligence community is catching up with the jihad terrorists. But in historical perspective, it is reaching level zero, for the simple reason that jihadist lobbies kept the level of intelligence so low for decades. But since the terrorists realize that their psychological space is being reduced, they will expend great efforts to try to break the nation's defenses before they develop to a very high level. The more U.S. homeland security improves and the more people become aware of the threat, the more it is likely that the jihadists will strike strategically by using unconventional methods and perhaps mass weapons.

I believe that the most important goal for current terrorist networks and for future jihads is to undermine, if not destroy, U.S. homeland security. This rationale is grounded in the Islamists' geopolitics. The main force preventing jihadists from taking over Muslim governments remains the United States. In simple logic, paralyzing the American capacity to intervene worldwide would allow the Islamists to overrun their foes and implement their plans. But facing the United States from the outside has proven difficult. Therefore, the jihad logic long ago shifted to igniting a breakdown within the nation. Unlike the Soviet Union, the United States has an accountability system that can change foreign policy (as al Qaeda was able to achieve in Spain with the Madrid March 11 terrorist strikes).[8] Before September 11, the strategic bet of al Qaeda and the jihadists was to strike deep on the U.S. mainland, so as to provoke through its democratic system a political reaction of withdrawal overseas. But that was before the establishment of homeland security nationwide and the unleashing of the policy of regime change overseas. Because September 11 did not produce the "Madrid syndrome" at the projected level, the jihadist strategy today and in the future will change with regard to America's mainland. Rather than striking to affect foreign policy, future jihads will plan on striking the United States to break down the country. Such a change in strategy will bring about different planning, tools, perpetrators, and objectives. This translates into a new reality: U.S. homeland security is not only a police security operation anymore; in the eyes of the new generation of terrorists, it has become the final frontier in the war against the infidels. If future jihad destroys or severely undermines U.S. homeland security, it would be winning the war against America; and if it does so, it would be the victor worldwide, because *dar el harb* would crumble in the minds of the jihadists—and perhaps in reality.

To achieve that objective, the terror networks—either organizations or regimes—have to act in a post–September 11 mode. The Mohammed Atta era is gone. The next waves will follow different paths. For example, they could still use civilian planes to provoke disasters, but not necessarily infiltrating as passengers. They may revert to "recruited" pilots, air marshals, mechanics, ground radar operators, or elements in the air defense system. In sum, they could penetrate any entity that has power over the flight network. Homeland security is fortifying the cabin doors of thousands of planes, but the next suicide jihadists may not even have to open cabin doors. They could be inside the cabin, on the tarmac, or armed with a surface-to-air missile near an airport. But in the larger scale of this scenario, an al Qaeda, Hezbollah, or other similar terror group may not trigger single strikes in the future, unless they are overwhelming. Why perform one or two acts of terrorism on American soil, engage precious resources, and so cue homeland security to harden its structures and unleash wider campaigns against the activists? Then again, smaller jihadi groups or individuals may decide to wage their own jihad inside the United States or western countries, isolated strikes launched by individuals, or by copycat groups. The "big ones" will be aimed at crippling national security in one major offensive, a multipronged attack when circumstances allow and preparations are fulfilled.

In at least two major speeches in 2001 and 2004, Osama bin Laden stated clearly that America's security is a direct and strategic target of the jihadists. His words have become a slogan around the radical Islamist world: "*Lan yakuna lakum amn ma lan yakuna lana amn*"—You will not have security as long as we do not have ours. But the English translation does not provide the full meaning. What bin Laden states is that *dar el Islam* (under his leadership, of course) has to acquire military and security defenses and establish a balance of terror with the West, or the wider *dar el harb*. Only then can there be a temporary truce and can arrangements be made. Al Qaeda and its sisters seek to continue to undermine western security, and particularly American national security, until the United States surrenders its military superiority overseas. Then international security, particularly in the Arab and Muslim world, will revert to the jihadists, who in turn will take over governments and assemble a military balance against the infidels. At first glance this strategy might seem unrealistic. Indeed, how can a bunch of terrorists, dispersed around the world, oblige the mightiest power in the history of mankind to surrender internationally to al Qaeda, Hezbollah, and their clones?

The jihadists believe that by crushing homeland security on the mainland they can defeat U.S. power worldwide. Al Qaeda's literature, jihadist chat room discussions, and past Hezbollah analysis indicate that they believe a massive pressure on the body of America will lead to its ineluctable surrender overseas. The 1980s attacks against U.S. targets in Lebanon; the 1990s attacks against U.S. interests, diplomats, and the military in New York and abroad; the massive raids of September 11; and the March 11 attacks in Madrid are considered enough evidence. Reactions to the kidnappings, beheadings, and torture of Americans and other citizens in Iraq's Sunni triangle indicate to the jihadists that at some level, the U.S. public will no longer tolerate the pain. That logic leads directly to the conviction that the jihad terror network is planning and executing a wider operation targeting America's first line of defense: that is, homeland security.

JIHAD IN COURT: THE SLAUGHTER OF JUSTICE

America's second line of defense is its justice system. Just below the security shield of the national agencies comes the sword that uproots a threat once it identifies it. This would be the main job of courts, prosecutors, and juries facing criminality at its apex: terrorism. But this is precisely where the problem was and remains: Was the justice system, and is it now, able to identify the presence of the enemy, namely jihadism? This could be the most sensitive ingredient in the war on terror as it signals the existence or not of the alertness, readiness, and the awareness of U.S. tribunals, judges, and lawyers in their most crucial mission since September 11. The question is grave and serious: Is jihad winning or losing the war in U.S. and western courts?

During the 1990s, and as an expert witness on conditions in the greater Middle East, I served in U.S. courts around the nation, meeting with the brightest judges and lawyers on both sides of the cases. Mostly on the side of the defense, I addressed the complexities of human rights, ideologies, and various claims of political asylum seekers. I must admit here that jihad was the winner in general terms until it was discussed inside a particular court. As a result of faulty education on campuses and lack of information in the media, the courts were not able to form a clear idea about the history, evolution, and rapid pace of the mounting threat. If people are not equipped from the classroom on, they cannot be expected to be able to use the sword of justice with precision. Some would argue that this is precisely the responsibility of the experts—which means that whoever educates the experts would influence the judicial process. That is the norm in all fields. But in the field of terrorism, the consequences are grave. The expert community can and has played a tremendously critical role. Was all expertise offered to U.S. courts over the past two decades about jihadism and its background accurate? Did all judges, lawyers, prosecutors, and juries obtain what they needed to form their opinions and render their sentences? In my modest judgment, they did not. For even if America has developed one of the best judicial systems in the world, serving the greatest democracy in history, a hole in that system can have and has had incalculable consequences.

One incident I witnessed in a political asylum case in the late 1990s is illustrative. The defendant, a Coptic woman from Egypt, claimed that she would be tortured by members of the jihadist Gamaat Islamiya if she was sent back to her motherland. The judge, surprised, turned to me and asked: "How come a group which is struggling for human rights against the government would persecute and torture a defenseless woman?" I asked why he considered this group a "human rights" one. He said: "Last week a political asylum seeker claimed he was from that group and that he was arrested by the government for his beliefs." I asked: "Your honor, did he state what the goals of the group were?" The judge said, "He stated that his group was persecuted because of his religion." I replied: "But this group and the government of Egypt have the same religion!" The judge was perplexed. In fact, the previous "seeker" had obtained his asylum status, en route to a green card and U.S. citizenship. The real question is: Over the years, how many jihadists claimed and obtained political asylum in America and the West? And the next one is: What were the accredited experts sharing with courts regarding jihad over the past twenty years? Most Americans would be surprised to learn how may people came through the justice system claiming political asylum based on jihadism from Egypt, Syria, Cashemire, Chechnya, and elsewhere. But these immigration decisions—unfathomable after September 11—make sense in view of the perceptions of the 1990s. If a university president described Hamas as a cultural group in 1996, why would you blame a judge who accepted jihadists as religious activists persecuted for their beliefs? Now, it was the mission of the expert community to inform academia and the courts that the ultimate objective of jihad was terrorism as a way to establish a system whereby both academic freedoms and secular justice would be banned. All it would have taken was a comparative legal analysis and an explanation that the jihadists ultimately want to establish a Taliban regime wherever they can.

But the most troubling area of jihad in court was certainly regarding terrorism. There too I had the opportunity to witness the legal and academic battlefield evolving, as did a number of my colleagues. I have been consulted on many cases by the government and think tanks, but I served in three trials: the Detroit terror case (2003), the Idaho Internet case (2004), and the Rotterdam terrorism case (2003). In addition, I reviewed the literature of many court cases dealing with terrorism with an emphasis on jihad as a motive. My conclusion: Same ideology, different cases; same expert defense, different facts. In sum, from Rotterdam to Detroit, the material I have reviewed comes from the same ideological roots: jihadism. I can even generalize and state that every single case related to jihad-inspired terrorism that I have looked at provided propaganda and ideological material drawn from Salafist, Wahabi, and jihadi doctrines. (The number of websites is enormous. The main sites belong to the Salafists:

al ansar; ansar al sunna; al khilafa; al muhajirun; al jihad; al tawheed; etc.) The
trail leads to almost the same teachers and similar objectives, and is at some
point intertwined within a network of websites. All my colleagues had similar
findings: the same people were justifying jihad, providing a smokescreen, and
all were connected to the same teachings, websites, and the like. Clearly, and
regardless of the battle or the physical evidence in question before the defense
and prosecutors, the ideology of violence was omnipresent. In reality, the primary role of academic experts in Islamic fundamentalism and jihadism within
U.S. and western courts is to determine the actual meaning of the documents
found with the alleged terrorists. Do they or do they not endorse, legitimize,
and call for violence?

The courts want answers to two questions: Is there physical evidence that
incriminates the defendants? And does the material found on them constitute
evidence of terroristic intent? The matter under most western systems depends
on the various legal systems in each country and in each particular case. But the
common trend that has impeded the fair process of many cases was the constant attempt to conceal the nature of the material found. In every single case I
witnessed and in all cases I reviewed (on both sides of the Atlantic), one pattern is dominant: There is a clear and firm attempt by a political faction to deny
essential information and education to juries, prosecutors, and judges. The Wahabi lobby did all it could to block basic facts from reaching the United States
and the western justice system regarding jihadism. In each case, where the defendants were tried for alleged terrorism, the defense and their experts would
claim that Salafism is not jihadism and that jihad is not violent. The question
was not whether their clients were jihadist, but rather whether jihadism was illegal. This was the gist of the court struggle with jihad terrorism.[9]

When tribunals look into cases of neo-Nazis perpetrating violence, the defense does not defend the ideology or attempt to change it. It may try to use
freedom of thought and the First Amendment in the United States to claim that
ideology alone cannot be indicted. This is a valid debate. But that was not the
strategy used in U.S. and European courts in defense of alleged terrorists. In
most jihad cases, the offensive was to "clear" the ideology by using the legal
cases: not to prove the innocence of the defendants by denying their affiliation
with the violent ideologies, but to make sure that no one blamed the ideology
itself. The critical point was not the actual link between the defendants and
their action: That is basic legal work. An alleged terrorist is either proven guilty
or not. Justice would decide. But the dangerous offensive aimed and continues
to aim at declaring the innocence of jihad terrorism in courts. By declaring that
jihad is *not* holy war—even though the texts and documents presented to

courts say so—defense lawyers and their experts are obstructing justice, not serving it. Rather than simply acknowledging the nature of the terrorist material but stressing other issues, such as the weak link between their clients and the material, the Wahabi lobby proceeds to further blur the understanding of both the judges and the juries. And the juries—the most important component of criminal justice—are already deprived of basic information about the subject in the classroom and by the media, so they are ultimately denied full knowledge in the courtroom. In the end, the opinion about the material at hand will be determined by a faceoff between the two expert sides. The rest is easy to guess: All that the defense attorneys have to do is to bash the credibility of the government's expert. The battle is almost won, since the nation has more than 1,000 academics with expertise favorable to the Wahabis, versus a handful of those who are attempting to explain historical realities.

In the Rotterdam case in Holland, a number of Salafis were accused of preparing violent activities against Dutch forces in Afghanistan in 2002. The accused terrorists had been using jihadi literature consistently, material that links them directly to al Qaeda and the international network. The defense team hired a Dutch professor who claimed he had expertise in Islamic studies. He rendered an opinion stating that the jihadi material is "just religious texts." Translation in this case becomes everything. The case stumbled on procedural matters, but what remained standing in the media was the "expert opinion" about jihadism. It can be argued that the Dutch people were denied the truth: that jihadist networks are developing in the country and propagating extremist material. In the fall of 2004, the first physical evidence of this fact stunned the Netherlands. A jihad terrorist savagely assassinated a well-known liberal filmmaker.[10] The terrorist had in his possession the same Salafist material found with the Rotterdam cell two years ago; thus the ideological rings have struck.

In the Detroit case in 2003, a group of Salafists were arrested on different charges. The prosecution found a basis for indictment on terror-related grounds. The legal battle raged for a whole year. But the most relevant issue was the material found with the alleged members of the cell: a series of audiotapes, all of which in my opinion were related to jihadist ideology. The clerics on the tape and those cited were part of the Wahabi Salafi network worldwide, the hard-core body referred to by al Qaeda and its allies. The defense team attacked the government on the grounds of post–September 11 bias against Arabs and Muslims. Although the material was crystal clear in its adhesion to *takfir* and jihad, the experts brought by the defense stated the opposite. They affirmed that these were "mere religious discussions." In my opinion, they were standing in the way of intellectual justice in a court of law.

The jury, representing the American people, was faced with direct disinformation twice: first in the classroom and then in the courtroom. The case again crumbled on procedural grounds—some say under local political pressure. But more important than the result of the case is the message resulting: Courts were and continue to be jihad-blind, as a result of "lobbying pressure."

The Idaho case of 2004 revolved around the prosecution of a Saudi student who was accused by the prosecution of "building websites to recruit jihad terrorists." In fact, the defendant was indeed building sites and recruiting fighters for a jihad overseas. The Saudi embassy hired experts to state that Salafism is not jihadi. Instead of distancing the defendant from jihadism, those experts— some of whom had been hired in the Detroit case as well[11]—focused on denying the terrorist factor in jihad ideologies, which their client was promoting online. Here again, another defense approach could have been to separate their client from terrorism or state that spreading terror ideologies alone (apart from acting on them) is protected by the U.S. Constitution. But they went further, by alleging that jihadism is not terrorism. And here lies the tragedy. For case after case, across the country and all over the West, jihad ideologies are legitimized as acceptable doctrines. Painted as mere religious teachings, or described as spiritual inner struggle, the doctrine of jihad against the infidels, in all of its clarity, is hidden under a thick camouflage.

The determination by the Wahabi lobby to win the battle for the sanctification of jihad in western and U.S. courts has no limits. If one single case is tried on the basis of jihadism, the winds of change would overwhelm the jihadist networks across the land. Once tribunals come to consider the material as an indicator of jihadist ideologies, and correctly identify those ideologies as terroristic, even though final sentencing must remain based on tangible evidence only, the tide would turn. To avoid this ideological defeat, the lobbies have concentrated their fire on the tiny minority of accredited experts who can prove that jihad is a form of terrorism under current international law. That realization must be blocked if the terror jihad is to survive within the West and worldwide. The jihadist sympathizers have used court cases to put jihad on trial—in order to find it innocent.[12]

The battle in courts has extended to the so-called prisoners of war, many— but not all—of whom have been sent to the U.S. base in Guantanamo, Cuba. The Bush administration classified the al Qaeda fighters from the battlefield of Afghanistan first as enemy combatants. Not members of armed forces, they were nevertheless considered combatants as if they were part of a regular army. Other internees were captured on the U.S. mainland but sent to the island as well. A significant debate has raged since. Lawyers for the Guantanamo detainees and anti-American activists have been insisting on the illegality of the status under which they were and are detained. The critics argue that these suspects must be processed within the U.S. court system, as alleged common criminals. The reason behind this movement is easy to absorb: It would kill the concept of war on terror, and therefore of combatants. And by doing so, the activists would succeed in stopping any investigation of the political motives of the al Qaeda members. Therefore, unless they were caught shooting against U.S. or allied troops and killing or wounding servicepeople, the detainees are not guilty of nor are they participants in a war. And even if they are found guilty of murder, the ideology that fueled them for such acts would dodge the prosecution. The defense aims to extract jihadist ideologies from the whole equation, even if their clients would fall under other indictments. Last year, as I was interviewed on al Jazeera along with Guantanamo lawyers, I made the point to ask if the mujahidin were performing jihad or not, or if they recognized international law or not. I added, to the consternation of the panel, that all that they have to do is to prove that they are not members of al Qaeda. The objective of the other side is to force the debate in a different direction: Members or not, their use of violence is legitimate.

And while the confrontation is raging in courts and the same material is found in cases in Virginia, New York, Oregon, South Carolina, and elsewhere, prominent academics put their weight behind the blur campaign.

JIHAD ON CAMPUS: THE ROOT OF DEFEAT OR VICTORY

In the past few years many articles, studies, and websites have been dedicated to addressing the clash of trends on U.S. campuses. The issue is hot, but also central to the American national debate on the war on terrorism. Eventually, over time, American universities will decide the final outcome of the war on ideas. Future generations will fill the ranks of the three branches of power and the media and draw the outlines of thinking for the next decades. Hence, major developments in the academic world would have a great influence on the battle with jihadism. Jihadists and their allies well understand this. Terrorism has two interests to advance in that world: a general one and a specific one. Let us start with the specific.[13]

The American public and many in the media assume that the threat growing on campuses was and is embodied by the actual presence of terrorist cells within educational establishments. In fact, that is only the minor threat. But that threat was able to grow because of the omnipresence of a greater problem.

The presence of terrorists or of militants who could launch jihad terrorist activities when the time was right has been a public issue since the mid-1990s, but came under further scrutiny after September 11. The highly publicized cases of professors Abdallah al Shallah and Sami al Arian in south Florida have brought to the attention of the government and the public the concept that members or alleged members of terrorist organizations can hide under faculty status. But that is not unique to universities—it could also be true to all other institutions and agencies.[14] Two issues arise. One is the question of whether there are more similar cases in the United States, or if the south Florida cases are the only ones. If there are others, what are the implications of such a presence on U.S. campuses? And more important, what would be the mission of such cells, particularly in hard science departments? It is widely believed that a main source of information on sensitive areas related to defense matters can be obtained from universities, especially the ones that are contracted by the Defense and Homeland Security departments. Some believe that this is an area of natural interest for terrorists to infiltrate. But even beyond finding refuge, fundraising, building cells, or acquiring scientific knowledge for their enterprises, a much higher objective could be reached by actual infiltration of the university system: that is, to send "graduates" to the market of their interest: government, security, or military agencies. The presence of jihadists hidden behind the robes of academics could produce a fundamentalist madrassa within a secular madrassa—that is, college. Instead of recruiting them after graduation, indoctrination would be part of their educational process, and afterward would accompany them into whatever sphere of interest they migrated to. This would be the habitat par excellence of the second generation of American and western al Qaeda, Hezbollah, and future integrated jihadists.

But that is only the minor field. There is a wider one.

As mentioned earlier, the most efficient jihadi thrust into the American system is the penetration of the U.S. academe by Wahabis. For decades, phenomenal and sustained funding has created a dominant current in the majority of all higher education establishments in the United States. The epicenter of the current is within the Middle East studies programs in most universities, particularly the most visible and prominent ones. In his book on the subject and on his website, professor Martin Kramer describes with accuracy the tidal wave that took over the teaching of Middle East studies in America, Canada, and Europe. Arabist, Islamist, and apologist influence has covered the teaching and research in political science, international relations, history, sociology, economics, geography, and all related fields of art, literature, and subfields such as peace studies and film. The ensemble is under the auspices of the Middle East studies elite assembled under MESA, the national association of Middle East studies. The organization, which has been shown to be tightly controlled by academics sympathetic to the Saudis or the Arabists and has received funding from the Wahabis, has limited research investigations into human rights abuses by Islamists or radical regimes.[15] Its annual meetings, especially since the early 1980s, have rejected academic papers dealing with significant democratic changes under Wahabi, Baathist, and similar regimes. Its panels have excluded serious discussions of the fate of ethnic minorities in the Middle East, such as southern Sudanese, Berbers, Kurds, Assyro-Chaldeans, Copts, and the Christian communities of Lebanon. It denied the genocide of Shiites in Iraq and the Massalit in Darfur and attempted to dilute the massive persecution of women under the Taliban or in Saudi Arabia. But more importantly, in my opinion, MESA has heavily influenced the study of jihadism and led to the confusion over what it means. This contributed to America's failure in preventing the September 11, 2001, attacks.

The Middle East studies elite in the United States and the West is supposed to be the prime institution responsible for guiding nations in their encounters with Arab, Muslim, and Middle Eastern societies and cultures. The group's ethical and academic mission is to tell the truth, all the truth, and nothing but the truth about the historical and contemporary facts of the region. It must relate that history without distortions, describe the realities of the region accurately, and explain the variety of ideologies without exclusion. Unfortunately, it has failed to do so. Reasons are multiple, but one is salient: the influence of the Wahabi funding. Since the 1973 oil crisis, a gradual stream of funding increased the programs in Middle East and Arab-Islamic studies in the United States and the West. The direct result of this Wahabi funding was a perversion of the academic mission. The elite in charge of teaching, guiding, and recruiting covered up for the regimes supporting this funding. The rest is a series of logical consequences.[16]

Because the teaching of Middle East history in America and the West was twisted to accommodate contemporary militants and regimes in the region, decades of scholarly camouflage built a wall between the public and historical realities overseas. This explains how basic questions about terrorism, jihadism, and cross-civilizational crisis were unanswered for most Americans. "Why do they hate us?" "Who are they?" and "Why didn't we know?" were disturbing questions after September 11. Until now they are still unanswered, for the simple yet disturbing reason that the academic elite that produced the crisis is unwilling to diffuse it. By blocking mere historical information and contemporary political knowledge from reaching students and future teachers,

the Middle East studies establishment created a hub of miseducators. The hub
has been co-opting new colleagues, selecting more of the same, and rejecting
candidates who think otherwise. In that regard, MESA's elite acted like an academic "regime," suppressing the "scholarly opposition." And to purify the field
from "other voices," especially the older generation of knowledgeable scholars,
the apologist lobby campaigned year after year against intellectuals such as
Bernard Lewis, Samuel Huntington, Bat Ye'or, Daniel Pipes, and others on the
grounds that they were "critical of Islam." In return, the Wahabis encouraged
establishment praise of the role of Arab regimes in "supporting" the field and
narrated their achievements. In addition, the establishment produced a new
leading elite for the field: shining stars like Edward Said, John Esposito, and
Juan Cole setting the agenda for Islamic and Middle Eastern studies.[17] At the
same time they attempted to delegitimize other scholars' views when they presented a critical position on jihadism.[18] In ten years, the new regime dominated
millions of dollars in grants, new open lines for hiring, search committees,
graduate programs, and of course the ultimate tool—letters of recommendation. In his book, Kramer showed that this has had profound influence on intellectual endeavors overall: You are more likely to get a good grade if you're
critical of the United States; you can't present a paper at key conferences if it
addresses human rights abuses under the funding regimes; and getting a teaching job is nearly impossible if your research concentration is on jihad ideologies as "root causes for Terrorism."[19]

The dominant elite controlled the official line of Middle East studies for
decades. With it came the consequences. Its graduates were hired in the public realm: foreign service, intelligence agencies, legislative branch, national security, and media. In short, the blinding process was produced on campus and
exported to the real world. Hence—and as much as this statement would be
an unpleasant shock to uninformed citizens—it is a fact that an intellectual
coup d'etat gradually took place within the realm of Middle East studies and
policy. Thus not only was the ideology of jihadism and its derivatives not reported and analyzed, it was excessively distorted. The early warning system,
which usually starts on campuses among America's thinking elite, was working against the nation's interest and security and against the people's basic
right for information. In the same way, the government trusts its academic advisors to enlighten it with the most recent research in the domain of technology and national security; it did the same with regard to the understanding of
the Greater Middle East region. But it was failed by its own advisors. During
the September 11 Commission hearings Richard Clarke got the high-profile
treatment when he stated that "your government failed you." I added later, in

media and community appearances, that in fact if the government failed its public, it was because it was failed by its advisors and academic consultants.[20] What should we expect from presidents, secretaries, and analysts who are supposed to decide policy toward jihad terrorism if researchers have rejected the concept that jihad is an ideology that threatens the United States and international society? That was and is the heart of America's dilemma with its war on terrorism. The academic establishment refused to consider jihad's doctrines as a threat or to report on its abuse of human rights worldwide before it hit the U.S. mainland and attacked dissenting scholars and blocked their words from reaching the public and leaders.

By blocking opposing views in the classrooms, in the professional conferences, in the hiring process, in the media, and finally from the decision makers, America's defenses would not be able to detect the threat. This helps explain how intelligence analysts saw the data, but did not come up with the right explanation or the policy. Doesn't it tell us more about the "whispers" in the ears of U.S. leaders not to engage al Qaeda, Hezbollah, and the other jihadists, "because this would create complications in international relations"? Aren't these "complications" in fact a change of policy that would have identified jihadism at least one decade earlier and allowed pro-democracy policies to surge years before the rise of the Taliban, the massacre of the Shiites in Iraq, or the Syrian occupation of Lebanon? These were "complications" that would have opened the eyes of Americans to the spread of Wahabism, madrassas, and jihadism in the region and eventually triggered a policy of reform abroad. Ironically, jihadist movements and regimes became the providers of education to the United States. Some argue that an alliance between the Wahabi lobbies and the extreme left wing, naturally thriving on campuses, caused this drama to take place.[21]

The imminent question today is: Is this state of affairs still prevailing in the academic world? The answer is yes and no. Yes, the curricula, programs, and related activities and teaching philosophies are still the dominant ones in most Middle East studies centers and departments. Yes, the "political culture" developed by Wahabism and company still prevails wherever the stream spreads. And yes, despite September 11 and the mounting requests for reforms on behalf of students and the public, the "regime" still obstructs changes. But academic opposition to jihad-in-residence is on the rise. Other views, unable to be expressed through existing programs, are developing in their own fields, such as homeland security studies, terrorism studies, and conflict studies.[22] It will be a while before the general student population has access to the larger picture. Hence, although jihad has been able to penetrate the sacrosanct centers of

American learning for two decades, it is being detected and hopefully will be addressed intellectually through a future reform.

JIHAD AGAINST U.S. FOREIGN POLICY

Between 1973 and 2001, the Wahabi lobby and its allies were successful in heavily influencing U.S. policy toward the Middle East in general and the interests of the fundamentalists and the Arabists in particular. However, and while oil influence was growing within the West and the U.S. strata of power, the lobbies and their networks constantly accused Washington of unconditionally submitting to the will of Israel and Jewish pressure groups. This charge, with legendary roots in the Arab world, and sometimes flirting with anti-Semitism, claimed that pro-Israel lobbies had full control of U.S. foreign policy. The charge of pro-Israeli influence made by the Islamists and Arabists was a mixture of myth and reality. The myth was the so-called Jewish cabal inside the U.S. government—a classic tableaux of anti-Semitism. But the reality was that, indeed, organized Jewish communities and their pro-Israel supporters did have significant influence with regard to U.S. Middle East policy and definitely regarding the Arab-Israeli conflict. It does not take a political scientist to figure out that in an open democracy, especially the American system, the better organized and better funded a lobby is, the more clout it can wield inside the government. This is true in domestic politics and foreign affairs. Hence, pro-Israel advocacy had a higher influence than that of Arabists from 1948 until about the early 1980s. Jewish lobbying organizations were efficient, politically educated, and had little competition when they made the case for Israel when presented as an island of democracy and western values in a sea of dictatorships and extremism. Between the 1940s and late 1970s, Israel's friends in Washington would be consulted on what type of weapons Arab allies could get, as was the case, for example, with the airborne warning and control system (AWACS) episode. At the end of the 1980s, pro-Israel pressure groups made sure Saudi Arabia would not obtain the early warning planes that could have spotted all air traffic in Israel.

But things had already started to change after the 1973 Arab oil boycott. Leading the campaign, Saudi Arabia and its allies were able to rectify the balance of power in Washington by pushing back pro-Israel influence within the confines of security issues and the peace process. After the Lebanon war in 1982, the Hezbollah suicide attacks of 1983, the first Palestinian intifada in 1987, and the changes taking place on American campuses throughout the 1980s, Israeli influence shrank to the Jewish state defense issues and the peace process. By early 1992, the administration of George H. W. Bush and the State Department under James Baker were putting significant pressure on Israel's Likud government and threatening to cancel the loan guarantee agreement. That period saw a weakening of Israeli influence in Washington. By the mid-1990s, and because of Israeli political division over the peace process with the Palestinians, there was no more American endorsement for Israeli action outside its borders. Although still committed to Israel's security, the Clinton administration confirmed and strengthened deals with a number of totalitarian regimes, including Saudi Arabia, Syria, and Sudan, while tolerating most of the others. By 2000, and with the exception of Israel's strategic security, Wahabi power was practically inspiring, if not dictating, U.S. policy in the Middle East. I provide some examples later. One of the most prominent is Lebanon. From supporting its western and pluralist character in the mid-1970s, the United States abandoned this little country to the PLO, Syrian occupation, and later Hezbollah's dominance. With one exception, during the Israeli intervention in 1982 and the brief rise of President Bashir Gemayel (who was assassinated by pro-Syrians), any careful review of the advice given to the State Department during recent decades would show a deep Wahabi influence.[23]

JIHAD AGAINST AMERICA'S MAKEUP

In some of Osama bin Laden's speeches and in a number of chat room discussions over the past few years, a very interesting yet indicative line of thinking surfaced: undermining America's ethnic makeup as a way to crumble the country's national security. This strategy, applied all over the world by regional powers, has been adopted by the jihadists against the United States. The leader of al Qaeda said America is not strong on the inside. He sees it as a collection of a variety of ethnic groups emigrating from different nations and religions. He called the United States "*innahum tajammuh umam*"—"gathering of nations," not a true nation. He says the "*rajul al abiad*," the white man, controls the black (African), the red (Indian), and the yellow (Asian). He goes on to say that he will create a coalition against the white man of America, which, along with the mujahidin, will help him defeat the soon-to-be-minority whites. These propositions by bin Laden are unusual and not in conformity with the mainstream jihadist thinking. In the Salafi universe, the world is divided into *dar el Islam* and *dar el harb*. In principle, no races or ethnicities supersede the Islamic divide. But a thorough analysis of the jihadist strategies, especially modern ones, shows an intelligent adaptation to the infidel challenge. In other words, to defeat the *kuffars*, jihadism can adopt tactics and strategies at will. If the infidel (in this case America) has a perceived weakness, it is permissible to use their weakness to defeat the greater power of the infidel. In short, since the country's ethnic makeup can serve as an instrument for strife, jihadism will seize on it as a weapon.

Bin Laden and other jihadists speak of the worldwide battle against the "white man." Strangely, their discourse is sometimes similar to that of Louis Farrakhan, the Nation of Islam's leader. Both talk about the world's 17 percent "white Europeans," against whom the rest of the world should unite. But al Qaeda and its allies have an attitude toward the "white man" that is full of contradictions. For example, they fail to mention that jihadism is also attacking other ethnic and racial groups around the world on religious grounds. As mentioned, the National Islamic Front of Hassan Turabi has conducted "Arab" ethnic cleansing against the blacks of southern Sudan, massacring about a million people. So the Islamists are also racists themselves. And at the same time, the Wahabis support white, blue-eyed Muslim Slavs against non-Muslim members of the same ethnic group (the Serbs). So the jihadists will support white Europeans, as long as they are Muslims. In West Africa, the jihadists support Blacks against Blacks, siding with the Muslims against the Christians and animists. In America, the jihadists would support the Nation of Islam against the White Christians, but they would also support Farrakhan against Black Christians. Had Farrakhan's own community been located in Darfur, the jihadists would have sided with the northern Arab (read White) Muslims against these Black Muslims.

The tactic has its own logic. First, all non-Europeans should unite against the "Whites." But meanwhile, the Islamists would support the White Muslims versus the non-Muslim Whites. Afterward, as the Whites are defeated or Islamized, the turn of the non-White non-Muslims will come at the hands of all Muslims, both White and non-White. So, at some point we can expect the jihadists to use blue-eyed White Muslims to attack non-Muslim Blacks.

The jihad strategy to destroy America's ethnic makeup targets the minorities, starting with the African Americans. Significant studies have been made on the infiltration of black communities. The jihadists are taking advantage of the normal phenomenon of conversion to recruit for their own movement. There are two circles in the process. The first one, wider, is the circle of religious conversion. But the second one, smaller, is the circle of ideological recruitment. The Wahabis conduct the mainstream efforts for religious conversion: It is believed that Islam is the fastest-growing religion among African Americans. In the United States, as mentioned, proselytizing is part of the political culture and is entirely protected by laws. All religions can proselytize. However, it is in the second circle that jihadism develops, when radicals and jihadists recruit converts to staff their own groups. I make that distinction between radicals and jihadists on the ground of academic accuracy.

The Nation of Islam, for example, is an American-born, ethnically centered movement. It follows the teaching of a nonorthodox brand of Islam. Its prophet is Elijah Mohammed, in addition to the seventh-century Messenger of Allah, Mohammed, who received the Qu'ran.[24] On that ground alone, mainstream Muslims consider Nation of Islam's dogma heretical. But it is the political ideology of the group that is sought by the jihadists. In the 1990s, Muammar Qadhafi of Libya promised to deliver $1 billion to Louis Farrakhan in support of his struggle. The grant did not go through, but indicates how radical regimes and organizations fantasize about the existence of an American-born ideological group that would undermine the United States from the inside. Farrakhan was on a tour that took him to, among other destinations, Libya, Sudan, and Iran, three regimes that have a record of massive human rights abuses. Sudan's National Islamic Front is responsible for the genocide against the Blacks in the south. Yet the Nation of Islam stood firmly with the Khartoum regime against the campaigns aimed at exposing that genocide. Farrakhan went as far as to deny the existence of slavery in Sudan and Mauritania in the 1990s, lining up with pro-jihadist lobbies such as CAIR in Washington and pitting his group against the black victims of jihad in Africa.

The jihad lobbies and the overseas regimes see radical Islamic groups within the African American community as precious allies in their attempts to weaken interethnic relations in the United States. The more powerful these radical groups are, and the more supportive they are of the grand jihadist designs, the deeper the jihadist lobbies can insert their influence within the African American community. The ultimate objective of the wider jihadi strategy is to use the racial factor to protect their agenda. Hence any political criticism against Nation of Islam is denounced as a political attack against the African American community. One of Nation of Islam's most ironic attempts to defend the Sudanese regime was to stand against the issue of liberation of Black slaves in Sudan. Farrakhan's group went so far in its alliance with the Islamic fundamentalist regime in Khartoum that it found itself defending the "Arab masters" against the "Black slaves"—at least, until former Sudanese slaves showed up in the African American community starting in the mid-1990s and told their stories directly to American Blacks. One major launching event I attended (and was a speaker at) was at Columbia University in 1994. There, for the first time in modern history, Black Sudanese confronted Arab lobbyists and Nation of Islam militants face to face. "We are blacker than you, and we were former slaves," they told the apologists for Khartoum. From that moment on, the community heard the other side of the story and started to identify with the Black resistance to jihadism. But in 2004, the fundamentalists ravaged the Sudanese area of Darfur, showing the world again that even black Muslims cannot escape racist-based jihad when the time comes. Still, jihadists have and will continue to use the influence of Wahabism and radical offshoots within the African American community.

In a general scheme, the Wahabis continue to fund conversions (by extending grants through local centers) within the African American community, making sure that the converts are educated by Salafists. This will ensure a wide pool of Islamists, from which the jihadists will recruit their own cadres. The terror networks—not a secret anymore—aim at building a network of pro-jihadist militants within the community of converts. They project this scenario: While recruiting and indoctrinating recruits, they will be under the shield of "ethnic protection." If confronted with national security inquiries, they will turn the matter into a "racial tension." In other words, the recruitment process will take place under the shield of civil rights and religious freedom. Once the process is completed, the African American recruits will be among the most precious elements in the larger pool of jihadists. They can detonate an ethnic bomb. From the Los Angeles riots in 1992, the jihadists have learned that the ethnic factor, if well manipulated, can cause social and legal order to disintegrate. They have since doubled their efforts to increase its possibilities. Infiltrating the African American community and indoctrinating isolated elements or supporting existing radical groups is the single largest strategic threat the jihadists are developing within, but ultimately against, the Black community itself and of course against the larger national community of the United States.[25]

In the fall of 2001, al Jazeera aired so-called video clips from Afghanistan, showing, among others, an African American al Qaeda member calling on his "brothers" in the United States to join the fight, insisting that the struggle would soon come to their cities. A couple of years later, the Washington sniper John Allen Muhammad—an African American—was arrested after days of terror in the greater capital area. He had received ideological training with jihadist material. Other cases indicate that a special effort is being put in this direction. Several times, Nation of Islam leaders reminded the government, especially before the war in Iraq, that a large number of African Americans serve in the armed forces—a very strange statement in American politics, because the U.S. military is not a forum for foreign policy. Was this Farrakhan hinting of potential action by Black Islamists inside the corps? Many noted that the incident of the Black soldier who tossed hand grenades at his comrades in Kuwait just before the 2003 Iraq invasion was an example of what the jihadists are planning for the future.

But the "ethnic bomb" the jihadists hope to explode is not limited to African Americans. Another group is Hispanic Americans. Again following the path of conversion first, indoctrination after, the network aims at recruiting terrorists-to-be from that growing community. One high-profile example is José Padilla, the alleged dirty bomb maker. With Padilla, the first seed was planted at the early stage of conversion. Once the ideological seed was planted, political recruitment followed. The dilemma in the counterterrorism community has always been how to distinguish between a normal religious conversion into Islam—one protected by freedom of religion—and recruitment for jihad terrorism. One side of the debate states that *all* conversions are protected by the law and terrorists should be tracked on evidence of preparations for violence; the other side states that *all* conversion to Islam are basically a mobilization by Wahabi-like groups. In fact, the situation is more complex, depending on who oversees the "conversion." If a moderate cleric—such as a Sufi—is in charge of the process, the convert is not submitted to jihad indoctrination. But if a Salafi imam is in charge, the convert is taught a version of Islam jihad terrorists could use at a later stage. Jihadist interest has also developed within other immigrant ethnic groups, such as Asians, with a particular emphasis on ethnicities from Muslim areas such as Pakistan, Bangladesh, Indonesia, the southern Philippines, and so on. Interest is also focusing on Europeans, especially from the Balkans, such as Bosnians and Kosovars.[26]

Jihadists also use the ethnic warfare system to incite white extremists against the government and other groups, such as the Jews. The link between supremacists and jihadists is no secret anymore. Forging a new version of the old Nazi-Islamist alliance of the mid-twentieth century, the white extremists and the jihadists have recognized common goals: The weakening and the bringing down of the U.S. government. In 1981, I witnessed the arrest of a right-wing fascist cell in East Beirut by the local authorities. Its members, German neo-Nazis, were heading toward the Bekaa Valley to link up with radical Islamic groups. A few visits to websites can show you the convergence of interest between the two tendencies. The white supremacists do not have to be converted into Islam and indoctrinated into jihadism; they already hate the authorities. Interestingly enough, the jihadists could and are building ties to extremist groups that are archenemies of each other. Consider that they are able to ally themselves with white supremacists and with black Islamists!

The sum of all fears, for national security, would be the capacity of the "mother ship" to trigger mass actions by a coalition of groups mentioned above. Such an action, launched before, during, or after a massive terrorist strike, would fuel ethnic unrest on a nationwide scale. These scenarios have often been mentioned in chat rooms. To jihad terror groups this is a grand plan for the erosion and then collapse of America's ethnic makeup. As noted in the last chapter, had September 11 taken place seven years later, the jihadists might have had enough time and tools to provoke a widespread ethnic civil unrest. The ultimate scenario of al Qaeda and sisters are for many U.S. cities to look more like Sarajevo, Beirut, and Belfast at the peak of urban wars. They have combined the images of the Los Angeles unrest with those of Waco (Texas) and the D.C. sniper and merged them in one scenario: the fall of *kuffar* power from the inside.

JIHAD AND U.S. DEFENSE

If jihad against America's ethnic makeup is the ultimate way jihadists plan to defeat their foe, their ultimate weapon to attain that goal is the subversion of the U.S. military. The Trojan horse method is not new to military planners— but the United States is not well enough prepared for a horse of this kind. In past decades, American defense systems were targeted by either Nazis or Communist operatives, for either spy or sabotage missions. U.S. counterterrorism agencies were successful in general terms in dismantling these networks, despite grave misses. But overall, since 1941, Washington's intelligence force knew what and who it was facing. It was able to factor its counterespionage tactics into the global conflicts of both World War II and the cold war. American strategies to defend its armed forces from infiltration and penetration were part of its wider strategies to win the wars against the axis and the Soviets. Practically, the defense of its military from the inside succeeded because of the global victories overseas. With the collapse of the German Nazis and Italian and Japanese Fascists in their home countries, the axis threat faded away. A similar situation resulted with the end of the cold war. With no more Soviet Union to feed and back the communist moles and agents within the western defense apparatus, most of the networks that existed melted down. But in the jihad war waged against the United States, the questions are more complex: How deep is the penetration? What are its objectives? Is the U.S. defensive system affected so far?

These tough and sensitive questions cannot be answered fully but can be addressed analytically. Short of tangible data, no one can say just how far jihadist networks have penetrated the U.S. intelligence community. I raised this matter during a panel at the Intelcon Washington Conference of January 2005:

How can analysts determine if there is a jihadi penetration of the military or other defense agencies? Are we talking about foreign power intelligence services, for example, Iranian, Syrian, Lebanese, or Sudanese? Are we talking about friendly countries whose agencies are infiltrated by Salafists or Khumeinists, and who are using the diplomatic or cultural structures abroad to serve the tactics of their own independent organizations? In other words, are al Qaeda, Hezbollah, or other groups infiltrating Arab and Middle Eastern regimes and governments so that they can use their assets in turn to penetrate the West and the United States? Is there a possibility that a military attaché or a diplomat for an ally is in fact a mole for al Qaeda or Hezbollah? Could Islamist moles penetrate the diplomatic services of Indonesia, Egypt, Turkey, or others, ending up under protection in the United States or a western country? These are powerful questions, but they fall under classical counterespionage cases. However, beyond the classical spy warfare, we can examine the deeper jihadist thrust into the U.S. defense system.

Jihad terror groups have a long history of penetration of Arab and Muslim governments and military. Perhaps the best trained and sophisticated in this area are the Muslim Brotherhood and their offshoots. Islamic fundamentalist elements have penetrated the military in Egypt, Syria, Sudan, and Pakistan for years. This is a fact of life in these Arab and Muslim regimes. But in these contexts, detecting the jihadists has ups and downs. Counterintelligence agencies have an advantage of language and sociological skills on one hand, but on the other hand, the Islamists blend much more easily into Muslim armed forces. Besides, the standards of human rights and sensitivities are much lower under these regimes than in the West. From that angle, how would jihadists aim to penetrate the U.S. military, and for what reason?[27]

To infiltrate the United States, jihadists would first manipulate the need of the defense apparatus for experts in the region, culture, and habits—translators, analysts, mentors, religious leaders, trainers, and country experts. In a pre–September 11 state of mind, this first corridor into the belly of the defense system would be efficient. The jihadists would be servicing the armed forces or other agencies and therefore would be at the forefront of the knowledge regarding their own struggle.[28] Imagine a vast early warning system made up of infiltrated jihadists in the U.S. defense system. They would be able to learn about the tactics, trends, and practical steps to be taken. This first generation of infiltrated jihadists would be able to warn the outside as to the upcoming moves and also blind the inside with regard to important information circulating within the defense network. However, at this stage, the jihad structure inside the military is not yet able to affect the whole defensive body strategically.

The jihadists' credentials, even with security clearance, will not allow them to move up the ladder to high positions.

But the damage that can be caused by the jihadi penetration can only grow further. Once a presence is established inside the military and security structure, removing it would be practically impossible without a full-fledged knowledge of its ideology. Because of the *takiya* tactic (simulation and deception), the jihadists can afford to remain inactive for a long period, until the right moment for jihad comes. The aim of this first generation of jihadist infiltration is spying, limited sabotage, and development of a wider network of jihadism within the system. Ultimately, these groups can participate in a large operation like September 11 but with wider scope, as projected in a previous chapter. Some argue that because these types of operatives have no regimes to coordinate with, they would be easily noticed and suppressed if they attempted to act collectively. That is a rational argument, but I believe the penetration is not necessarily organizational: The hundreds of jihadists do not have to be connected. Because of their ideology and their easy access to outside sources and guidelines (including from the jihadist media and websites), a general call for action, not necessarily a direct order, could trigger their attack. Jihadists would engage in action in response to a fatwa or a call by their leaders; no special mission order would be needed. This is indeed the most difficult challenge the U.S. and western intelligence agencies have ever had to address. But there is an even more dangerous threat: the second generation, whose members believe in the ideology but are part of the national culture.

This type of jihadist would be born in the United States or the West, speak the local language with no accent, know the culture and be part of it, and grow up within the system—but would be indoctrinated by jihadists early in life.[29] This is the ultimate weapon that Salafists and Khumeinists are dreaming of and waiting for. Inserting cadres into an immigrant country is one thing; recruiting individuals who grew up within the social fabric is something else. Al Qaeda's next generation is more sophisticated. It will be the product of a patient process of recruitment by existing networks. The long-term objective would be to place these proto-jihadists deeply within the institutions, in positions of power. This second generation would be able to practice *takiya* with efficiency. Its ultimate objectives would be:

1. To have access to the highest type of information affecting the country's strategic security: weapons of mass destruction, operational plans, and members of high command.

2. To block the policies against the jihadists at large, to pass knowledge of the policies to the outside, and/or to propose less effective alternatives.

3. Ultimately, to affect the strategic plans of the United States and its allies.

A historic achievement of a second-generation penetration of the defense system would be to cause it to break down during the war or at a crucial point in a confrontation. A culmination (based on dramatization of the scenario) would be to create a strategic dissidence among the military at a high point of a conflict, an ingredient needed to bring about chaos and collapse.

Jihad against the defense system is not exclusive to the armed forces, but is primarily targeted at U.S. domestic and international intelligence and security. Focusing on the FBI and homeland security agencies is the first logical area for the jihadists, especially those of the second generation. Once they deploy inside these agencies—in the midst of a gigantic bureaucracy—the capacity of national security to act independent of the penetration is almost impossible. Outside a legal framework and without a massive education of the personnel nationwide, the doors are pretty open to the second generation. Once the domestic agencies are compromised, the international arms, such as the CIA or State Department, will be at the mercy of who is on their backs.

Perhaps this description seems overly dramatic, but I contend that careful study and projection of jihadist strategy leads ineluctably to this conclusion. Given their doctrines, there is no logical reason why the jihadists would stop short of pursuing all possibilities to bring down U.S. and western defenses. And because there is nothing in existence to prevent such penetration, the areas discussed are likely targets. The practical question is how to make the U.S. public and bureaucracy aware of the likelihood of such scenarios. Forewarned is forearmed.

Chapter Sixteen

MUTANT JIHAD

SO FAR, WE HAVE EXPLORED THE HISTORY OF JIHADISM, its current state, and a projection of both what the movement could have achieved and wishes to achieve. This brings us to the final analysis of the most extreme transformations of the threat. Such a short but informative exploration is necessary for the projection of future jihads. Indeed, had these types of analysis been performed in the 1970s or even in the 1980s, the surge of the 1990s would have been better understood, and the logic of the events of September 11 would have been absorbed earlier. At the 9/11 Commission hearings in the summer of 2004, the most haunting query in the room was the issue of "why we did not know anything was afoot." And in many other investigations and debates, the question kept coming back to "why." Evidently, it is difficult for a democratic society to answer such a question clearly, given poor knowledge of the adversary. Israeli, Turkish, Lebanese, and now Afghani and Iraqi societies can understand it; so can Americans of the post–September 11 era, as well as Spaniards and Britons. But the one major difference across the Atlantic is history and its teachings. In the Middle East and the Arab world, national and ethnic communities have experienced jihadism through two channels. First, they've encountered it in the political culture, at school and at the mosque. But second, they have seen it in action, in wars and disturbances. As I noted in chapter one, few Arabs and Middle Easterners debate the meaning of jihad. They discuss its relevance and its necessity, but not its meaning.

In America, we have two barriers to our understanding of jihadism. One is the lack of historical experience: Unlike France, Italy, Spain, Greece, the Balkans, and others, the United States has never been invaded by armies chanting "jihad."[1] Unlike Britain and Russia, American forces have never conquered the lands of jihadism and *fatah.* Until modern times, American soldiers, their diplomats, and their teachers back at home did not need to consider how to confront jihadism. Jihad did not impact the collective psyche of America. Until the events in 1983, jihad was an alien phenomenon to the U.S. military. Until September 11, and despite previous attacks, it was an alien concept to most Americans. But now things have changed. The U.S. public has been transformed into students of jihad by the images of the collapsing Twin Towers, the videotapes of Osama, the beheadings perpetrated by Zarqawi's followers in Iraq, the murdered children of Beslan, the victims of Madrid and London, and expanding literature on the subject. But if America and the West are "learning," so are the jihadists. Indeed, as Sun Tzu reasoned, if it is raining on you, it is also raining on your enemy.

The Wahabis, Salafists, and Khumeinists know about the self-education Americans and other societies are undergoing and recognize that the era of blindness is gone. Despite the raging battle in the academic world to maintain the foggy state of affairs regarding the study of jihad, a page has been turned. Most enlightened Americans have realized that something went wrong in their encounter with the "enemy." Hence, a natural effort is underway to learn and acquire the means to win the war on terrorism. But at this critical stage of the conflict, the jihadists are adapting. Future jihad is being built now. A mutation is also underway within the worldwide movement, or at least among its elite— it is becoming a mutant jihad. What are the main characteristics and challenges facing jihad today that will determine its future fate?

THE BATTLE OF THE DEBATES

The debate about the war on terrorism in the West is wide and open. The jihadists and their supporters are part of it, attempting to divert it, camouflage it, move it in different directions. The apologists are fighting an intellectual rearguard action, blasting any improvement in public knowledge made by jihad experts and authors.[2] The Middle East studies elite and Wahabi activists are fiercely fighting new courses on the subject in a desperate attempt to deny information to students through academic channels. This battle will shape the future of student generations in the United States and the West. Today's textbooks and research will determine the ability of the future American public to absorb new realities. And beyond the scholarly arena, a similar debate is taking place in the media. While some are gearing up to investigate jihadism, other media has been frozen in the pre–September 11 era. In 2002 I was invited to debate the war on terror with David Gergen on MSNBC's *Hardball with Chris Matthews*. The minute I mentioned the new era, I was dismissed as a neo-conservative. Evidently, my sociodemocratic credentials were not taken into consideration. The divide is too deep in the foreign policy public debate in the United States, and is nonexistent in European media. Ironically, a large segment of self-described "liberal" media acts conservatively, insisting on the old order of ideas. This segment resists the change of intellectual parameters: It finds it difficult to reverse the past analysis that partitioned the world into right wing and left wing only. It cannot absorb the realities of today, in which the world is jihadist and non-jihadist. The apologists and the Wahabis have a common agenda: Maintain the old debate and refuse to address the root causes of jihad terrorism. This "reactionary" attitude has influenced and is still influencing the debate on foreign policy, the war on terrorism, and the various issues the United States is involved with, such as Afghanistan, Iraq, and the war of ideas. While one segment of the American intelligentsia is "getting it" and is moving forward to widen its scope of understanding, the other segment is unable to provide sensible answers to grave questions about jihadism. The two sides of the debate mirror the two traditional camps: liberal left and right-wing conservative. In fact, mutant jihad wants the debate to remain as it was before September 11: sinking in a universe of ignorance, to borrow the Salafists' rhetoric.

But from the remote lands of the Arab world and the greater Middle East, another debate is exploding—one that is of great concern to the radical regimes and organizations. From Afghanistan and Iraq, and lately from Lebanon and Syria, indicators of rejection of jihadism are emerging. Elections in Afghanistan in 2004, elections in Iraq in January 2005, and the Cedars revolution in Lebanon have sent unmistakable signs to Salafism and Baathism that, in the region, the debate is shifting significantly. Women, students, and human rights activists are on the rise in the Arab world and in Iran. Although the "reactionary" western elite is stuck in its pre–September 11 mindset, the post-Saddam Middle Eastern youth are rebelling against jihadism. Ironically, a dose of new reality from the Middle East is helping to awaken the western public. Mutant jihad wants to break down this connection before it happens. That is what will determine the new intellectual tactics of the Islamic fundamentalists. We must expect more subtle and adaptive arguments from their propagandists. Surprisingly, the jihadist propaganda will do better in the West than in its birthplace, the East.

BUILDING DEFENSES

A rather stunning reality of mutating jihad—one that will not go down well with the U.S. and international public—has to do with the building of current and future defenses against terrorism. In view of the foregoing analysis and simple projections, I have shown that although American and western efforts are underway to build a global defense system to prevent future attacks, we must assume that the jihadists are already infiltrating the system. With the present state of laws, political culture, and low level of awareness, jihad terrorists still can place themselves in all sites and fields of the war on terror. Take, for example, the various projects of the Department of Homeland Security. Jihadists may have been recruited to work on every single one. The defensive wall designed to protect Americans is partly being built by, or at least under the observation of, the terrorists. Very likely they know every single measure Homeland Security is taking.[3]

Similar situations may occur in other national agencies, such as the FBI, CIA, and to a certain degree the State Department. As already noted, a different form of mutant jihadist can move inside the defense system. Is this idea too alarmist? I do not believe so. Islamists can and will adapt to changes and learn from the evolving systems to develop their own countersystems. What can be done to avoid the development of the jihadist threat within the system as it is being built? A possible answer requires an intellectual revolution. In this book's conclusion I describe its outlines.[4]

NUCLEAR JIHAD

Lots of ink and megabytes have been dedicated to the "sum of all fears": that is, the nuclear threat posed by the jihad terrorists. The one overarching question that has an answer that no one wants to hear but everyone knows is this: If al Qaeda or its sisters obtain a nuclear weapon, or an equivalent doomsday device, will they use it against America; against a western nation; against a Muslim nation? Why and how? This is the single most urgent strategic issue on the face of the planet today. All world security hangs in the balance of three scenarios:

1. An exchange of blasts between countries such as Pakistan and India, which only could happen if the jihadists take control of Islamabad's military.
2. A unilateral nuclear attack by North Korea against its southern neighbors or across the Pacific on the United States. (A frightening scenario, but a rational analysis shows that Pyongyang would lose any type of nuclear conflict and hence would be less rather than more likely to engage in such a risk; it would rather use the threat as leverage.)
3. Most haunting: the use by jihadist organizations of a nuclear weapon to achieve their goals.

Two of the three apocalyptic scenarios feature the jihadists as initiating parties. With Iran's completion of its nuclear power, the Islamists would have three options—and possibly more if the Salafists overwhelm Saudi Arabia or the central Asian republics. But would a future al Qaeda nuclear device actually be used, and if so, why?

In an interview with *Time* conducted in 1998, Osama bin Laden said, "Acquiring nuclear weapons for the defense of Moslems is a religious duty. If I have indeed acquired these weapons, then I thank Allah for enabling me to do so." During the fall of 2001, bin Laden appeared on al Jazeera television and stated that "the wonderful nuclear weapons of Pakistan are ours." He meant that they belong to the jihadists even though they are in the custody of the Musharraf government. In other parts of the same speech, Osama said he would use all the arms and resources at his disposal to defeat the *kuffar* (infidels)—an indirect announcement that al Qaeda or another jihadist group would have recourse to weapons of mass destruction. Suleiman Abu Ghaith, al Qaeda's spokesman, also said that same fall that "American cities will be under smoke." In November 2001, Abu Ghaith made the infamous statement, "We have the right to kill 4 million Americans, two million of them children" in what he argued was a retaliation against American policies that killed many in the region.[5] Back in August of 1990, Saddam Hussein (radical but not fundamentalist) declared openly that his missiles could "burn half of Israel." Iranian Khumeinist leaders have often threatened that their ballistic missiles would reach Europe, Russia, and beyond. On the whole, a culture of nuclear jihad is pervasive among the radicals in the region. Thus, should a cataclysmic weapon fall into the jihadists' hands, its use is more than just possible; it is almost a certainty. The clearest statements in this regard are made in the al Ansar chat rooms. Clerics frequently visit the subject, arguing that "Allah will decide how to use this man made power, the *quwwa al thirriya* or nuclear power." Publication of such statements indicates that a divine intervention—read a decision by the radical clerics—will decide how and when the bomb will be used. There are important conclusions to be drawn. One is that the jihadists will use the nuclear weapon in offensive mode; if they calculate that they can achieve their goals through such a strike, they will trigger it. But is there a jihadist rationale for nuclear warfare, similar to the Soviet Union's? Not exactly. And will a balance of terror work? Unfortunately, it is not likely. The reasons why go back to the core of jihad ideology.

The Soviets, being communists, were atheists, and therefore did not believe in the next life. Hence they factored into their strategies the "survival" equation. The mutual assured destruction (MAD) balance of power with the United States sufficed to deter Moscow. But the jihadists are Islamists, and one of their major doctrinal pillars is sacrificing for the other life. Suicide bombers are a chilling reminder of this ideological reality—which directly leads to one conclusion: Unlike the Soviets or even the Chinese or North Koreans, the jihadists do not fear death, let alone fear mass death. Fear of nuclear retaliation is not a determining factor in a jihadi state of mind. The decision to attack is in the hands of radical regimes or clerics acting as mentors of the jihadic organizations. Ideologically and strategically the latter would choose a nuclear posture based on their beliefs about how close nuclear use would bring their objectives rather than beliefs about likely retaliation by the enemy. During the fall of 2001, a prominent U.S. senator told me that "in the case of a September 11–like second attack, expect the United States to go nuclear"—it would retaliate with nuclear capabilities. I of course asked, "Where?" He answered, "Where the attackers are coming from." In 2004, a report named countries that could be targeted for retaliation.[6] The report was described as "theoretical." But debate about the subject still rages behind closed doors and sometimes in public. There are no set answers how the United States, Russia, and the West would respond to jihadist nuclear attacks. The response might be linked to the magnitude of the attack, and would largely depend on the public's reaction as well. But beyond or before the question of response is that of how the jihadists would decide to launch a nuclear attack in the first place.

The most important factor in the jihadist nuclear strategy is the day after. If the jihadists were to detonate a device, either tactical or strategic, on an infidel land, what would their goal be? The matter is worth speculating on for the simple reason that no theological answer has ever been provided—not during the seventh-century A.D. *fatah,* nor by Ibn Taymiya during the Crusades, and not even by Hassan al Banna today. Neither the Prophet nor the early caliphs were ever confronted with the possibility of destroying the actual country of the infidels. Thus, the decision-making process for such a use must be contemporary. In fact, jihad theoreticians' eyes only opened to the possibility in 1945. Since that time, they have been trying to put Hiroshima and Nagasaki in a jihadi perspective. Two signs of the jihadist will to use such a weapon were the 1993 and 2001 attacks on New York. In 1993, Ramzi Yusuf and Sheikh Omar abdul Rahman knew that by exploding a truck inside the World Trade Center's underground parking garage at least one tower might collapse, killing tens of thousands, the equivalent of a nuclear detonation. In 2001, bin Laden said he had expected tens of thousands to die in the Twin Towers, with their faster collapse. Both operations aimed at casualties of nuclear magnitude. Therefore, if the jihadists were to obtain the bomb, they would not hesitate to use it against their enemies, since they are already aiming at nuclear-level casualties in their terrorist acts. A nuclear device would simply make it a certainty.

But what would be the strategy of the clerics issuing fatwas licensing a nuclear genocide? There are two options: Either they would want to destroy America or another western society, or they would want to dominate it. From analyzing the general trends in Salafi thinking, the first priority is to resume *fatah* (the conquest) and ultimately establish their version of religion around the world *(Iqamatu eddine)*. Therefore, it would be contradictory to destroy what they wish to conquer. A leading Muslim Brotherhood thinker, Sheikh Yussef al Qardawi, has often stated that America is too beautiful, rich, and full of resources to destroy, and is a great land of opportunity, including the "expansion of Islam."[7] Here again, one would hardly project that massive strikes would maintain this "beauty" or attractiveness for any sort of expansion. Sheikh al Nufeisi, a Salafi cleric who appears frequently on al Jazeera television from Saudi Arabia, focuses constantly on strategies against America and builds psychological momentum for great losses that the "U.S. would draw to itself." The clerics have not expressed completely formed opinions, at least not in the open. Bin Laden once stated that when considering the nuclear option, "one has to be very careful in the use of these weapons. Their consequences let us think about their use." This sentence is very revealing, for it shows the following: One is that the jihadists have indeed considered the use of nuclear weapons, but that they have geopolitical considerations to watch out for. A fair assessment leads me to believe that al Qaeda and its international allies may want to use all conventional capabilities before moving to the greater options. And if they do use the greater options, they will want to use strike(s) to provoke a collapse of the system. Their eventual goal is to reestablish the caliphate and extend it into the western hemisphere. A possible scenario of nuclear jihad war may also be included in a combination with classical terrorist strikes, the generation of internal tensions, and the spread of chaos. The fertile imagination of the jihadi mind is vast but it is also contained by its own ideological goals. However, the desire to see mass destruction in America—even at the hands of nature—were made clear after Hurricane Katrina's devastation of the Gulf areas in August–September 2005.[8]

The first generation of al Qaeda has taken the conflict to the heart of the infidels, but the second generation is growing inside *dar el harb*. It is adapting to its systems and adopting new ones. Mutant jihad will conduct a new type of warfare and will take it to more sophisticated levels. It has time on its side, in the sense that it is a generational conflict. But time is not a long-term commodity for the new jihadists. Back in the greater Middle East, political and ideological change may well affect their sources of legitimacy.[9]

Chapter Seventeen

GUIDELINES AND PRESCRIPTIVE POLICIES

In this last chapter, I will use the findings from our journey in the jihad world to suggest a few guidelines for policymaking. It is obvious that analyzing an ideological movement throughout history and modern times does not provide full answers for current political strategies. A global overview of jihadist thinking can help draw conclusions from past trends and benchmarks to future directions. But it would be difficult to prescribe precise policies and agendas to counter jihadist strategies or contain them. To be able to do so, one would have to possess a higher knowledge of executive powers or intelligence data. Hence the following points are strictly guidelines for U.S. and international policies, based on historical findings and strategic assumptions. They can change if abrupt diversions or a wider flow of information is made available.

DEFINING THE ENEMY: ANTI-JIHADISM LAWS

Perhaps the most important and overarching obligation to execute in the ongoing war on terrorism is to define the enemy. Short of such a political declaration, the massive efforts to win that conflict will be hampered and the final outcome will be remote in time and costlier in resources. The U.S. president, the U.S. Congress, and by extrapolation world leaders, including those in the Arab and Muslim world, must without any hesitation designate jihadism, as defined by Islamic fundamentalists (both Salafists and Khumeinists), as an enemy of world peace. Yes, it is a war on terrorism, but it is also a war against an ideology that legitimizes and produces terrorism, that is, jihadism. An American national declaration and an international declaration on jihadism will constitute the basis for three important achievements:

1. An understanding that the war on terrorism is not a war against a religion, Islam, but against an ideological movement that uses religion in its doctrine.
2. The unification of Americans and international society in a vision of the conflict and its solutions.
3. The establishment of a necessary legal framework that can separate the crucial set of liberties and civil rights from the ideological terrorist movement.

Congress must produce laws that prohibit jihadism to allow law enforcement to concentrate on the terrorist network, instead of reducing the freedoms of everyone in order to find the guilty ones. The drama of the USA PATRIOT Act of 2003 was simple. In the absence of legislation on jihadism, all citizens had to pay from their personal and collective freedoms and comfort because of the principle of equal treatment for all. The principle of equality must remain and be fortified, but in return, the law must isolate jihadism in the same way as it singles out racism and Nazism. Once this is accomplished, Muslim communities need not be afraid and will not be harassed because of the jihadist activities of a few, and the national community will not be put under extra pressure because of the inability to isolate the jihadists.

On the international level, a consensus must be achieved among western nations regarding jihadism. France, Great Britain, Spain, the Netherlands, Russia, Argentina, and India have enough dramatic experience with jihadism to be able to agree on one definition. Many Arab and Muslim countries have better capacities to confront the jihadists in their own languages and cultures: Afghanistan, Iraq, Jordan, and Morocco, for example, can lead an in-depth reform of historical and world political perceptions of jihad and reject the jihadist ideology. Saudi Arabia, Egypt, Indonesia, and Pakistan can make additional efforts to isolate the radical Salafists by mobilizing moderate clerical authorities. With democracy and freedom reinstalled in Lebanon, Syria, Iran, and Libya, the balance would shift increasingly to win the war of ideas. In short, the Islamic fundamentalists can continue to claim their view of history and society, but can foment strife only when they have the political means. Any religious vision of the world should adapt to international relations, law, and above all recognize peace. The United Nations should legislate in that direction and equate jihadism (as advanced by the jihadists) with terrorism.[1]

HOMELAND SECURITY: UNDERSTANDING JIHAD STRATEGIES

With new legislation in hand, the Department of Homeland Security would be able to design new strategies based on addressing the roots of the terror. Instead of dealing with the last 10 percent of the process—starting from the moment when jihad terrorists were ordered or decided to act—U.S. action would commence during the first 20 percent of the process, when people are being indoctrinated into jihadi belief. Rather than focusing 100 percent of its resources on reactive and security measures, the Department of Homeland Security would be able to dedicate about 40 percent of their resources to preemptive policies. Why wait for a person to become a terrorist, if you can influence the process that transforms him or her into one? By focusing on the materials, structures, and diffusion of jihadism, the department can and should prevent its formation. "Social worker"–type offices can adopt a plethora of methods and programs to engage the most targeted sectors. Homeland security education can and should be provided to the public as well.

But the Department of Homeland Security should also anticipate the next acts of the terrorists. Besides focusing on efforts to shield public and critical sites from attacks and dedicating significant resources to react to strikes on medical, biochemical, and other public facilities, a special emphasis should be put on public participation in homeland security.

AMERICAN RESISTANCE TO JIHAD IDEOLOGY

The concept of national resistance to jihadism is fundamental. Educating U.S. and international public opinion about the root causes of jihadism, its identity, and mechanisms, would create the first shield of defense against terrorism. Before the attacks of September 11, jihad militants roamed freely in America and in most western societies; since, potential aggressors have had a much more difficult time in the *dar el harb*. The buildup of public awareness can multiply the resources of a government tenfold. Just as local communities and authorities cooperate in fighting criminal and racist activities, everyone should be involved in fighting terrorism. Recall the French revolutionary adage *chaque citoyen, un soldat* (each citizen a soldier); today more than ever, all adults should be alert and intellectually equipped to understand the threat at their level. A network of tens of millions of aware citizens around the country would shield society from penetration by an ideology that promotes violence.

Enabling Americans to understand the threat would unleash important talents. On the popular level the culture of counterterrorism would spread, and communities would mobilize for debates about it. The more citizens and communities discuss the subject, the less likely it is that terrorists will be able to induce people to embrace the ideology and thereby become susceptible to recruitment for violent action. When the population lacks information and is not mobilized, terrorists are able to fill the void. Going further, educating the public would trigger the artistic and cultural elites to participate in the mobilization. Movies, books, plays, articles, and documentaries can enhance the capacity of the public to absorb the new challenge and reverse the process of mollification to which it has been subjected for decades. A more educated public would generate teachers, students, executives, lawyers, judges, government employees, and juries who would enable society to make the right distinctions and the right choices.

SUPPORTING MUSLIM HUMANISTS

Jihadism was produced within Arab and Muslim societies by radical ideologues. That is a historical fact. Therefore, the antidote to these radical ideologies must and can be produced by the same societies that witnessed their surge. Democratic, pluralist, and humanist Muslims from various social and political backgrounds are the appropriate figures to debate and counter the arguments of the jihadists. As ironic as it may sound, peaceful human-rights and democracy activists can blunt the surge of jihadism better than national and international security. Not that resistance to terrorism is obsolete. Just the opposite: Without counterterrorism strategies, social and intellectual antidotes will have no chance. But security and military strategies alone cannot reverse the long-term tide of jihad ideologies.

As a reminder, since the fall of the caliphate under the Ottomans, a number of ideological currents claiming ownership of jihad have asserted themselves as the true representatives of the Muslim community worldwide. With this self-legitimization, they gradually obtained power and influence within their societies. Their civil societies, suppressed by dictatorships and jihadist movements alike, have not been able to produce either the normal functioning of pluralist democracies or the appropriate intellectual responses to the fundamentalist arguments. Clearly, the most natural responses to jihadism are freedom in civil societies and empowered democracy movements in the Arab and Muslim world. Civil society and democracy movements are the arch-opponents to religious fanaticism in all societies, and particularly in the communities where jihadism appeared. Such movements are best equipped to counterargue, respond, and organize opposition to jihadi violence within their societies. These civil groups can be from left-wing, liberal, or even conservative Muslim backgrounds. They can be opposed to each other with regard to future policies and government structures, but as believers in civil society, they can produce the historical antidote: Book for book, website for website, and radio station for radio station, they can open a debate with the jihadists and provide an alternative vision for the youth of the region to choose from.[2]

Therefore, the United States and the West should offer a constant policy of support to Middle East and Arab civil societies. Such a strategy, the essence of which has been adopted by the U.S. government over the past two years, must provide international backing to nongovernmental organizations, human rights groups, educational forums and institutions, and intellectuals so that they can pursue sustained campaigns of mass education. Democratically elected governments that are pledging to support pluralism must also be encouraged to enable their peoples to achieve self-expression. Democracy, of course, is not only elections; support to civil society should not be limited to the organization of the democratic process, but should also empower democratic movements and the free circulation of ideas. The international community must help indigenous liberalizing elites to have equal access to the younger generations. It is only with the young that the war of ideas will be won in the long term.

The war of ideas is a confrontation between the culture of democracy and the culture of jihad. It will be won when most Muslim institutions reject jihadism as a tool of international relations. The Islamists used to raise the slogan of "*al Islam huwa al Hall*"—Islam is the solution. In reality, it looks like Muslims are the solution to jihadism. Shepherding humanist Muslims internationally and supporting them in their own quest for peace is the appropriate response to the threat of future jihads.

CONCLUSION

A T THE END OF THE NEXT DECADE, HISTORIANS WILL BE ASKING many questions and will face the dilemma of hindsight. The war against terrorism will be seen as archaic compared to what will have by then become a worldwide conflict with jihad terror. And it may also be possible that the war of ideas will have been won by stages. But a stalemate could have been reached as well, if by the middle of this decade several opportunities have been lost. Among the most important questions historians will be asking, there are at least five whose answers we ought to be searching for now.

HOW BIG WAS THE 9/11 DAMAGE?

Can we assess today how big was the damage caused by the September 11 attacks against the United States? Specific answers vary with the philosophical, ideological, and political views of the respondent. But one can find common answers, common ground, and common feelings. Starting with the latter, without any doubt, not only the nation's life was shattered but each individual's life was affected. Beyond the lifestyle change that had to take its toll—including increased security measures—the main personal ravage was and will continue to be the feeling of loss of peace. To average Americans, the simple sentiment of not being fully secure and free to enjoy their lives is damaging. I myself share these same feelings. An era has ended. The peace of the 1990s, a quick respite between the end of the cold war with its nuclear nightmares, and the new jihad threats, was reminiscent of the 1920s and early 1930s. That peace is over, and that is the greater damage. The idea that we are at war is stressful, especially because most among us haven't grasped its beginning or its stakes. They see the horrific pictures of the falling towers and the barbaric beheadings; they hear the arguments of the debate and their government's warnings about harder days. But the one thing they can't perceive clearly is the outcome and, above all, what it is that will win the war against terror and restore the peace of pre–September 11.[1]

Actually, what most of us don't know yet, or may not want to accept, is that the pre-9/11 peace is not coming back soon, and may not come back at all. For, as we begin to understand the historic challenge we are facing, two horizons are possible: One is a longer war with jihad, harder than the engagements of the 1990s and of the last few years; and the other is a real peace, better than that of pre-9/11. It is not a secret anymore that what we lived, here in America and overseas, before bin Laden's war, wasn't even peace. It was a peaceful *hudna,* or armistice, at the discretion of the jihadists. That feeling is even more stressful. It is the equivalent of realizing that universal civilization survives only at the discretion of a much higher power that can erase us at will. History is full of these examples. If you were a citizen of Constantinople in the fourteenth century or a pre-Colombian Indian of the Americas in the fifteenth century, you wouldn't know that your world was to end soon at a particular juncture in history. These examples may well be too extreme, but the feelings could be comparable. One difference is definite: Civilization today can still win over the threat.

And yet there are also those among us who refuse to acknowledge reality. There are two extreme ways of thinking. On the one hand, there are those who still don't accept the idea that the nation was attacked for what it is. Mostly concentrated in the intellectual elites and among their followers, this group doesn't accept the idea of a war on terror to start with. Some among them do not see jihadism as a threat or as a terror movement. Stuck in a different era and unwilling to accept historical realities beyond the ones they favored years ago, they consider every development since 9/11 as unhistorical. In the movie *Independence Day,* they would be the equivalent of the highly "mediatized" elite that refuse to believe that the extraterrestrial ships are actually the enemy—until they are blasted to pieces atop the highest Manhattan tower. The Hollywoodian tale is farfetched, but the attitude is somewhat familiar. Ironically, the relativism of those who cannot see a threat in jihadism didn't help them develop an alternative analysis, as if relativism is in itself relative.

On the other hand, we have those who realize the danger, but who refuse to have hope. They understand the challenge and see its threat historically, but believe it will never be solved. Such people are convinced that no change can take place in the Arab and Muslim world and that, eventually, jihadism will win the doctrinal debate on the other side. They conclude that a massive cataclysmic confrontation is bound to happen, with the West having to take the most extreme measures. This school of thought would rather opt for the "besieged fortress" attitude than for a global effort to spread freedom and democracy. The two opposing perspectives can be summarized simply: One rejects the war on terrorism and surrenders the world to jihadism. The other fights back against terrorism but doesn't believe in the outside world. My view, and that of those who share a strong belief in human nature and potential, is that the war against terrorism is real and is being fought; it can be won; and that the main shift will occur when democracy and human rights improve in the Arab and Muslim world.

A dramatic side of 9/11 is definitely its human victims: the losses that occurred on September 11, since that date, and over the years around the world, from Afghanistan to Iraq. Although every single human life is beyond value, both in the eyes of the loved ones and philosophically, casualties bear a chilling message. The more than 3,000 victims of the 9/11 attacks were killed without a legitimate goal, but their deaths created a purpose. It prompted the ill-prepared American nation to wake up, mobilize, and find itself in a world of creeping threats. It is hard to admit it, but the Manhattan, Washington, and Pennsylvania victims, in their deaths, probably saved the lives of millions of others. Even harsher to face is that jihad killed 3,000 in 2001 instead of 30,000 in 2005, or maybe 300,000 in 2008. Random the numbers may be, but bin Laden himself named the figure of tens of thousands and his aides openly called for three million victims in America alone. The jihadists are so focused on the destruction of America and the infidel world that they have enlisted Allah and nature in their quest. For as soon as Hurricane Katrina devastated New Orleans and coastal Mississippi in August 2005, al Qaeda and other Salafi voices declared victory and rejoiced. They announced it as a victory and hailed Allah's "smashing of US cities."[2] They were immediately joined by their "objective allies" inside America. Many political, academic, and activist figures, known for their sympathy to U.S. foes, grabbed the opportunity: "We had a disaster at home, because we are engaged in a War on Terror," said a number of scholars at the American Political Science Association (APSA) Convention in Washington, days after.[3] As if the weather was retaliating against Washington for having dared to defend its nation against the jihadists. The jihadists' intention to destroy America is there, undoubtedly—but the success of the terrorists is not in their hands alone.

The 9/11 strikes wounded the American body but didn't kill it. And that is the main lesson from that dark day at the dawn of the twenty-first century.

WHAT DID IT TRIGGER?

The attacks by Osama bin Laden sent shock waves through the American soul. It stunned Americans, mobilized them, and forced them to rise. It prompted the U.S. president, the U.S. Congress, and the public to move forward. It shattered the wall of blindness that surrounded the collective mind of the nation. There was a challenge to meet, an enemy to face, and a future to plan. The 9/11 assaults crossed the red line. Instead of further mollifying the body of the victim, America, it awakened it. It also sent tremors around the globe: Europe, Russia, India, Latin America, and Africa firmed up their attitudes against terrorism. In the Arab and Muslim world, it created two camps, one of which stands with the international campaign against terror, and more importantly with the push toward democracy.

Wars are always bad, with no exceptions. But each war has a signature, an effect on history. The war on terrorism, launched indeed ten years late, has however gained a decade in time. Homeland Security today is better than homeland collapse would have been in the middle of this decade; the removal of the Taliban in 2001 is better than facing off with a nuclear sultanate years after; removing Saddam in 2003 was better than confronting three equivalent regimes bound together. But more important, triggering the war of ideas now is better than giving free space to the jihadist ideology forever. The new geopolitical situation since 2001, if the appropriate strategies are applied, could be a gift from History. It is true that events since 9/11 have been dramatic, and that they resulted from past errors and oil greed, but the post-9/11 window is a chance for survival and for a better future. Prospects will depend on how U.S. and international leadership use the precious time ahead to defend the public, defeat the terrorists, and help the societies of the Greater Middle East rejuvenate themselves. But the condition sine qua non for a successful campaign is the understanding of it. For if you do not act in the right direction, the outcome is doomed. Even if you head in the right direction, without a global vision of the outcome the result will be the same. This decade is still wide open for the United States and other democracies to use all their resources to achieve a historic outcome; but are they, in fact, winning the war on terror?

WHERE ARE WE IN THE WAR ON TERROR?

If the aim of the war on terror is to run after the terrorists, find them (particularly Osama bin Laden), dismantle their cells, bring them to justice (which system of justice?), and restore the pre-9/11 order, then no one really knows where are we in that war. But if the war on terror is redefined as a campaign to reduce jihadism as a mean in international relations and trigger democracy dynamics within the societies dominated by jihadist and totalitarian ideologies, then one can precisely determine the course of such a campaign, project its future, and provide a rationale for its stages. If this is the case, then here is where we are in the war on terror and the war of ideas:

In America, a slow but vast increase in consciousness is taking place. More Americans today understand the global geopolitics of the war on terror. Most poll responses, mass reactions, and public answers to basic questions related to the mounting threat are coming from the right direction, even though the official discourse isn't yet as clear as it could be. The blocking systems—the ones that blurred the vision of Americans in the past—haven't been removed, but increasingly are being identified as things that undermine American and western resolve. More important, the removal of the Taliban and of the Iraqi Baath has unleashed the energies of millions of men and women who believe in democracy and pluralism and oppose dictatorship and jihadism. The Cedars revolution of Lebanon is moving forward despite the dangers, and the reformists are on the rise in Syria. Dissidents are becoming more outspoken in the Arabian Peninsula, human rights activists are bolder in Egypt, and the plight of the black Africans of Sudan is at least on the political map now.

The jihadists are stalling in Afghanistan; shedding blood but unable to reverse the course of events in Iraq; and unleashing their historic reserves in Saudi Arabia. They are recruiting more supporters among Islamists, but the latter aren't recruiting from among the democratic forces. The Islamic fundamentalists took advantage of the cold war, the authoritarian regimes, the 1990s, the Arab-Israeli conflict, and the lack of freedom. But with several spots of pluralism appearing in the region, with others to follow, the democracy movement will meet the jihadists in the widest encounter in "Middle Earth." From Iran to Algeria, Wahabis, Salafists, and Khumeinists will be confronted by women, students, minorities, and democratic masses. It will be a long, tenuous, and harsh struggle, but *alea jacta est,* the dice are rolling. The jinni of jihadism was haunting the region and the world unchallenged. Progressively the wind of democracy and humanism will spread as well. All will depend on the vision and the determination of the free societies and the international democracies. Either they will extend their support to the Greater Middle East's surging democracies, as they did for South Africa, Eastern Europe, and Latin America, or they will watch them struggle alone. Future jihad depends on this equation.[4]

CAN WE AVOID THE SECOND GENERATION OF AL QAEDA?

We certainly know that a second generation of al Qaeda and its sisters is brewing worldwide and within the West. We assume that it will be more sophisticated, but also more lethal.[5] However, can it be averted? Can an increased awareness in America and the West of the global phenomenon of jihadism reduce its risks and spread an alternative democratic culture instead—and before the second generation engages the international community in future jihads?

There are various answers to this question. The wrong answers have already been given in an abundant literature that has dominated the mainstream scholarly work: They call for an ostrich attitude, or worse, a rapid retreat into the pre-9/11 mindset. These types of answers have failed, but they continue to occupy the public intellectual debate.

The right answers are on the table, but limited, experimental, and lacking enough academic volume. I summarize them as follows: The war on terrorism is winnable if the war of ideas is won. In layman's terms, a necessary condition of victory is to see clearly in the war on terror. But the sufficient condition is to be clear in the war of ideas. For if you want to reach out to the future generations of jihad, they must hear you, read you, and see an alternative to the jihadi teachings, madrassas, and vision. It boils down to simple propositions. The clearer the campaign, the more it will reach future youth. The truth will set you free, it has been said, and the truth will set these captive minds free, too.

ARE AMERICANS READY FOR FUTURE JIHADS?

The spread of accurate knowledge is not perfect yet, thanks to the classical and dominant educational establishment, which is now becoming an isolated bastion of denial. But, like water, air, and life, the drive to learn among mainstream Americans and international opinion-makers is finding its own way. By a simple review of recent literature, one can see that there are as many publications indicting jihadism as a terrorist ideology as those that still apologize for it. In three years, the debate has become an even 50/50, where it was once entirely dominated by the apologists. If you compare the renaissance of the American and western mind since 2001 with the gigantic efforts by the Wahabis and the projihadist elites since the 1970s to blur the vision, you will conclude quickly enough that an intellectual revolution is underway. In a few years, what was very difficult to learn and absorb will become mainstream learning and thinking.

"The Earth is flat" said the mainstream scientists centuries ago. It took strenuous effort, sacrifice, and vision to prove that assertion wrong.

In trying to warn, understand, and propose the best possible policies to avoid the ineluctable rise of future jihads, I seek to contribute to an effort of reasoning so that the future Earth will be more peaceful than ever. It is going to take the hard work of many courageous people to ensure a happy ending to this millennial quest for conflict: Many visionary people in the West and many more brave people in the Muslim world will contribute. This will decide if future jihads end up with mushroom clouds around the world, or if peace, democracy, and freedom mushroom worldwide.

NOTES

INTRODUCTION

1. *"Nous sommes tous des Americains"* (We are all Americans), *Le Monde Diplomatic,* September 12, 2001.
2. *Al Taadudiya* (Pluralism) (Lebanon: Kaslik University Press, 1979). For other publications since, go to CV at www.walidphares.com.
3. Interviews with the author on local NBC, ABC, and CBS affiliates in Florida between September 11 and 18, 2001.
4. See Lewis, Bernard, *What Went Wrong? The Clash Between Islam and Modernity in the Middle East* (New York: HarperCollins Publishers, 2002), "The Lessons of the Battlefield," p. 18.
5. *The 9/11 Commission Report, Final Report of the National Commission on Terrorist Attacks upon the United States,* "Foresight—and Hindsight," p. 339.
6. Intelcon, National Intelligence Conference, February 8–10, 2005. See http://www.fbcinc.com/intelcon/agenda.asp.
7. *The 9/11 Commission Report,* "Policy," p. 348.
8. Al Jazeera, February 22, 1998. Al Hayat, February 23, 1998. Also, "Jihad against Jews and Crusaders," World Islamic Front Statement, February 1998. See http://www.fas.org/irp/world/para/docs/980223-fatwa.htm.
9. The statements were aired on al Jazeera between September 11 and 15, 2001.
10. See *The 9/11 Commission Report,* particularly "September 11, 2001," p. 285.
11. See for example Esposito, John, *The Islamic Threat: Myth or Reality?* (New York: Oxford University Press, 1995).
12. From Dr. Richard Clarke, chief counterterrorism advisor at the White House, Testimony to the 9/11 Commission, August 2004.
13. See *The 9/11 Commission Report,* "Imagination," p. 339.
14. After the terrorist attacks in Madrid on March 11, 2004.
15. Adapted from an op-ed by the author. See Phares, Walid, "The 9/11 Hearings and the Failures of the 1990s," *FrontPage Magazine,* March 26, 2004: "The 9/11 Commission could have transformed the country into an adult nation, if the debate had concentrated on the investigation of the real root causes that allowed the jihad terrorists to massacre thousands of Americans on that fatal morning of September 2001."
16. Adapted from an op-ed, Phares, Walid, "Blinded by Convention: How America Missed the Jihadist Threat," *Washington Times,* June 9, 2002.

CHAPTER ONE

1. Too many texts push for a dominant spiritual meaning of jihad. But see for example Hossein, Nasr Seyyed, "Islam as Religion," *Islam: Religion, History, and Civilization* (San Francisco: Harper, 2003), p. 25; also "Doctrines and Beliefs of Islam," 59; and "A Brief Journey through Islamic History," 115.
2. One of my op-eds on the subject addressed the issue by clarifying that jihad cannot be changed at the will of politicians. See "Jihad Is Jihad," *Palestine Times,* June 1997.

3. Pipes, Daniel, "What Does the Arabic Word 'Jihad' Mean?" *New York Post,* December 31, 2002.

4. See Streusand, Douglas E., "What Does Jihad Mean?" *Middle East Quarterly* (September 1997).

5. See Sauders, J. J., "Arabia and Her Neighbors," *A History of Medieval Islam* (New York: Routledge, 1972–2003), p. 1.

6. See Chaudry, Rashid Ahmad, *Stories from Early Islam* (Islamabad: Islam International Publications Limited, 1989), "The Holy Prophet" and "The Religion of Islam," p. 9, 11.

7. See Lewis, Bernard, "In Search of Islam's Past," *Islam in History* (New York: Open Court Publishing, 1993), p. 103.

8. See Azzi, Joseph, "L'Islam avant l'Islam," *Le Pretre et le Prophete: Aux Sources du Coran* (Paris: MaisonNeuve et Larose, 1992), p. 134.

9. See Chaudry, *Stories from Early Islam,* op. cit.: ; "Sword of Allah," p. 60; "Non-discrimination," p. 71. See another approach by Ye'or, Bat, *Islam and Dhimmitude* (Madison, NJ: Fairleigh Dickinson University Press, 2002): "Jihad," 42; "The Tactics Adopted," 239; and "The Tactics of Dhimmitude," 239; "Silence," 239.

10. See Sauders, "The Prophet," *A History of Medieval Islam,* op. cit., 18.

11. See Sauders, "The First Conquests," *A History of Medieval Islam,* op. cit., 39.

12. It is ironic to note that British-based al Muhajirun used this reference before the London attacks on July 7, 2005, and al Qaeda Europe used the same terminology after the attack when claiming responsibility.

13. See Ye'or, Bat, *Juifs et chretiens sous l'Islam* (Oxford: Berg International, 1994): "L'orient à la veille de L'Islam," 11; "Naissance de l'état Islamique," 14; "Les conquetes," 21; "Le Jihad," 23; "Le Jihad historique," 31.

14. Series of interviews with scholar and historian Fuad Afram al Bustani, 1983–1984.

15. See Ostrogorsky, George, *The History of the Byzantine State* (New Brunswick, NJ: Rutgers University Press, 1969): "Arab Invasions," 110.

16. "Jurists' texts" (Ibn Abi Zayd al-Qayrawani, Ibn Khaldun), 161, and "Conquest," 162, in Ye'or, *Juifs et chretiens sous l'Islam,* op. cit.

17. See Valognes, Jean Pierre, *Vie et Mort des Chretiens d'Orient* (Paris: Fayard, 1994): "L'Histoire des Chretiens en Terre d'Islam," 55.

18. For an extensive literature on the subject see Ye'or, *Islam and Dhimmitude,* op. cit., particularly "The Orient on the Eye of Islam," 33; "The Seventh-Century Religious Context," 33; "The Birth of the Islamic State," 35, "Conquest," 40; "Jihad," 42.

19. See Ye'or, *Islam and Dhimmitude,* op. cit.: "The Tactics Adopted," 239; "The Tactics of Dhimmitude," 239.

20. See Sauders, "Civil Wars," *A History of Medieval Islam,* op. cit., p. 59.

21. See Momen, Moojan, *An Introduction to Shi'i Islam: The History and Doctrines of Twelver Shi'ism* (New Have, CT: Yale University Press, 1987), p. 11.

22. See Saunders, "Mongol Disaster," *A History of Medieval Islam,* op. cit., p. 148.

23. See Pipes, Daniel, *In the Path of God: Islam and Political Power* (New York: Basic Books, 1980): "The Medieval Synthesis," 48.

24. See Lewis, "Ottoman Empire and Aftermath," *Islam in History,* op. cit., p. 233.

25. See Ostrogorsky, *The History of the Byzantine State,* op. cit.: "The Collapse," p. 401.

26. See "Turkish Irruption," p. 141, in Ostrogorsky, *History of the Byzantine State,* op cit.

27. See Saunders, "Breakup of Caliphate," *The History of the Byzantine State,* op. cit., p. 106.

28. The debate about the real spread of Islam divides the researchers. Read for example Szumski, Bonnie, *The Spread of Islam* (San Diego: Greenhaven Press, 1999). Also, in it, Lippman, Thomas W., "The Spread of Islam in Arabia," p. 49; Eaton, Richard, "The Geographic Expansion of Islam," p. 71; Martin, Richard C., "Political Growth of the Islamic Empire," p. 78.

A bolder view on the expansionist spread is developed by Warraq, Ibn, in *Why I Am Not a Muslim* (Amherst, NY: Prometheus Books, 1995): "The Origins of Islam," p. 34; "The Problem of Sources," p. 66; "Arab Imperialism, Islamic Colonialism," p. 198.

29. See Payne, Robert, *History of Islam* (New York: Marboro Books, 1990; reprint). Also Lewis, Bernard, *Islam in History* (Chicago: Open Court Publishing, 1993).

CHAPTER TWO

1. Clarke, Richard, *Against All Enemies: Inside America's War on Terror* (New York: Free Press, 2004).
2. Bergen, Peter, *Holy War Inc.: Inside the Secret World of Osama Bin Laden* (New York: Touchstone, 2001).
3. On Islamic fundamentalism see Husain, Mir Zohair, *Global Islamic Politics* (New York: HarperCollins College Publishers, 1995), particularly "The Muslim Fundamentalists," p. 44; "Puritanical Muslims," p. 64; "Emulators of Prophet Muhammad and His Pious Companions," p. 68.
4. See Bostom, Andrew (ed.), *The Legacy of Jihad: Islamic Holy War and the Fate of Non-Muslims* (Amherst, NY: Prometheus Books, 2005).
5. See Spencer, Robert, *Onward Muslim Soldiers* (New York: Regnery Publishing, 2003).
6. Schwartz, Stephen, *The Two Faces of Islam: Saudi Fundamentalism and Its Role in Terrorism* (New York: Anchor, 2003).
7. Spencer, Robert, ed., *The Myth of Islamic Tolerance: How Islamic Law Treats Non-Muslims* (Amherst, NY: Prometheus Books, 2005), particularly "Radical Muslim Theorists on Non-Muslims," p. 52.
8. From "al ansar" chat room on Paltalk.com, January 12, 2005; argument also found on multiple Salafi websites, in debates in al Sharia websites, and in debates in al Sharia wal Hayat on al Jazeera TV.
9. See Algar, Hamid, *Wahabism: A Critical Essay* (New York: Islamic Publications International, 2002), particularly "From the Writings of Muhammad b. 'Abd al-Wahhab," p. 71; also "A Near Contemporary View of Early Wahhabism," p. 77.
10. All able adult Muslims must perform the duty of pilgrimage, *Hajj*, once in a lifetime at least. The Saudi monarchy has the exclusive privilege of being the custodian of the ceremonies and hosting process of millions of pilgrims coming from around the world.
11. For more on the Muslim Brotherhood, see Mitchell, Richard P., *The Society of the Muslim Brothers* (New York: Oxford University Press, 1993).
12. See Qutb, Sayyid, *Social Justice in Islam* (translated) (New York: Islamic Publications International, 2000; revised ed.).
13. See Burke, Jason, *Al Qaida: Casting a Shadow of Terror* (New York: Tauris and Co., 2003), pp. 31, 36, 45.
14. See Lewis, Bernard, *Islam and the West* (New York: Oxford University Press, 1993), "The Shiia in Islamic History," p. 155.
15. For more on Shiite doctrines see Momen, *An Introduction to Shi'i Islam*, p. 246.
16. See Algar, Hamid, "A Shi'i Response to Wahhabism," *Wahabism: A Critical Essay,* op. cit., p. 81.

CHAPTER THREE

1. See Lewis, Bernard, *The Crisis of Islam: Holy War and Unholy Terror* (New York: Modern Library Edition, 2003): "Defining Islam," p. 3.
2. See Lewis, Bernard, "The House of War," *The Crisis of Islam*, op. cit., p. 29.

3. See Khomeini, Ruhollah, "The Form of an Islamic Government," *Islam and Revolution: Writings and Declaration of Imam Khomeini,* translated by Hamid Algar (Berkeley: Mizan Press, 1981), p. 55.
4. See Keppel, Gilles, *Jihad: The Trail of Political Islam* (New York: Belknap Press, 2002).
5. Interview in *al Diyar* (Beirut) August 18, 2005.

CHAPTER FOUR

1. See Hanson, Victor, "Jihadism and Nazism," *Biography,* Arts and Entertainment Network, November 27, 2005, http://victorhanson.com/article/hippolito111404.htm.
2. From a forum on Paltalk.com in the "al-ansar" discussion room, September 23, 2004.
3. From a forum on Paltalk.com in the "ansar al sunna wal Jihad" discussion room, January 20, 2005.

CHAPTER FIVE

1. Lewis, Bernard, "Satan and the Soviets" *The Crisis of Islam,* op. cit., p. 82.

CHAPTER SIX

1. See Lewis, Bernard, "An Ode against the Jews," *Islam in History,* op. cit., p. 167.
2. Littman, David, "30. Judeophobia Today = Anti-Judaism/Anti-Zionism/Antisemitism: A Growing 'Culture of Hate,'" in Spencer, ed., *The Myth of Islamic Tolerance,* op. cit.
3. The Ladinos were the Jews who emigrated from Spain as of the fifteenth and sixteenth centuries to the Ottoman Empire, particularly Istanbul, to seek refuge after the Inquisition. The Sultanate opened its doors to the Jewish immigrants principally because of their skills.
4. Other issues included the theological debate in the Muslim world between Sunni and Shi'a and among Sunni as well.
5. "Fatah" is also the name of a main Palestinian organization founded by Yasir Arafat in the late 1990s.
6. See Kuntzel, Matthias, "Jihadism and anti-Semitism," in www.matthiaskuentzel.de/texte/matthias_kuentzel_-_djihad_english.pdf.

CHAPTER SEVEN

1. *Jahiliya,* literally "the era of ignorance," is the period preceding Islam, according to Muslims.
2. See Lewis, Bernard, "Secularism and the Civil Society," p. 96, in *What Went Wrong?* op. cit.
3. See Pipes, Daniel, "Fundamentalist Muslims between America and Russia," *Foreign Affairs* (Summer 1986).
4. Saudi Arabia was the only Arab country to recognize the northern Turkish separatist republic. As a Wahabi regime, it followed "religious solidarity" while Turkey asserted "ethnic solidarity."
5. See Phares, Walid, and Rabil, Robert, "The Ideological Roots of Terrorism Can Be Traced," *The National Interest,* May 5, 2004.
6. For an extensive study of the jihadist networks in France, for example, see Sfeir, Antoine, *Les Réseaux d'Allah: Les filières islamistes en France et en Europe* (Paris: Plon, 2001), particularly "Du Tabligh au terrorisme," p. 63; "France: Le Réseau des Mosquées," p. 66.
7. I was an expert on behalf of the U.S. government on Islamic radicalism in the Detroit terror case (2002–2003), in the Idaho website terror case (2003–2004), and on behalf of the Dutch government in the Rotterdam terrorism case (2003).

8. Among the 115 audiotapes I reviewed as propaganda material in the Detroit terror cell case, August 2002 to June 2004, this sentence and identical ones on several audiotapes called for the spread of the "culture of Jihad." Most of the tapes featured Salafi Sheikh al Qussi.

9. On the strategies of the Salafist Islamists, see "The Salafist Movement, The Revolutionary Ideology—Salafi Jihadism," CBC News, December 1, 2004.

10. Professor John Entelis. See his subsequent chapter on the subject: "Islam, Democracy, and the State: The Reemergence of Authoritarian Politics in Algeria," in Ruedy, John, ed., *Islamism and Secularism in North Africa* (New York: St. Martin's Press, 1994).

11. I analyzed the long-term strategies of the Iranian jihadists in a book published in Arabic in 1987. See Phares, Walid, *Khalfiyat al thawra al khumainiya al Islamiya* (The Background of the Islamic Khumanist Revolution) (Beirut: Dar al Sharq, 1987).

12. See Roy, Olivier, "The Iranian Islamic Revolution: How Politics Defines Religions," in *Globalized Islam: The Search for a New Ummah* (New York: Columbia University Press, 2004), p. 83. Also, Emerson, Steve, Prepared Testimony before the Senate Foreign Relations Committee, Subcommittee on Near Eastern and South Asian Affairs. Subject: Tehran and Terrorism, Iran under President Muhammad Khatami, May 14, 1998.

13. See "The Islamic Revolution in Iran," p. 217, and "The Genesis of a Revolution," p. 218, in Husain, *Global Islamic Politics,* op. cit.

14. Husain, "Exporting Revolutionary Islam," p. 227, *Global Islamic Politics,* op. cit.

15. Sfeir, Antoine, "Les Réseaux des mullahs," *Les Réseaux d'Allah,* op. cit., p. 109.

16. Roy, Olivier, "The Iranian Islamic Revolution: How Politics Defines Religions," *Globalized Islam,* p. 83.

17. Sfeir, Antoine, "Les 'Afghans,'" *Les Reseaux d'Allah,* op. cit., p. 123.

CHAPTER EIGHT

1. In Arabic, m*adrassa* literally means "school." The current public use of the term in the media and research is in reference to the *Madaress al Qur'aniya,* the Koranic schools, strict religious schools. Most of these entities are controlled, funded, or influenced by the Wahabi scholars of Saudi Arabia, and most of them receive funds from the kingdom.

2. On the interpretation by Wahabis of Islam's history see Schwartz, Stephen, *The Two Faces of Islam: The House of Sa'Ud from Tradition to Terror* (New York: Doubleday, 2002), particularly "Permanent Jihad: The Shadow of Afghanistan," p. 152.

3. "The Taliban Phenomenon—Arab Fighters Amid the Taliban," in *APS Diplomat Redrawing the Islamic Map* (newsletter) (New York: Pam Stein/Input Solutions, November 2001).

4. Jalali, Ali Ahmad, Grau, Lester W., and Rhodes, John E., *Afghan Guerrilla Warfare: In the Words of the Mujahideen Fighters* (Osceola, WI: Motorbooks International, 2001).

5. Nojumi, Neamatollah, *The Rise of the Taliban in Afghanistan: Mass Mobilization, Civil War, and the Future of the Region* (New York: Palgrave Macmillan, 2002). See "Sword of Dishonor: The Wahhabi International," in Schwartz, *The Two Faces of Islam,* op. cit., p. 181.

6. A number of researchers have warned about the rise of mystical jihadi commanders in the 1980s. See the work of one of them: Peroncel-Hugoz, Jean-Pierre, *The Raft of Mohammed: Social and Human Consequences of the Return to Traditional Religion in the Arab World* (New York: Paragon House Publishers, 1998), especially "The Holy Strike," p. 23

7. Lewis, Bernard, "The Marriage of Saudi Power and Wahabi Teaching," *The Crisis of Islam,* op. cit., p. 120.

8. On the surge of Islamist terrorism, see Lewis, Bernard, "The Rise of Terrorism," *The Crisis of Islam,* op. cit., p. 137.

9. For more on the ideological root of "Jihadi Terror," read original texts of offensive jihad in Kotb, Sayd, *Milestone* (American Trust Publications, revised ed. 1991).

10. Sfeir, Antoine, "La Nébuleuse Ben Laden," *Les Réseaux d'Allah,* op. cit., 209.

11. See Furnish, Timothy R., *Holiest Wars: Islamic Mahdis, Their Jihads, and Osama bin Laden* (New York: Praeger Publishers, 2005).

12. Another opinion in the Islamist debate was: "No universal Jihad as long as there is no caliphate." See *Jihad After the Caliphate,* Special Dispatch—Jihad & Terrorism Studies, No. 435, October 30, 2002, http://www.memri.org/bin/opener_latest.cgi?ID=SD43502.

13. Olivier, Roy, "On the Path of War: Bin Laden and Others," *Globalized Islam,* op. cit., p. 290.

CHAPTER NINE

1. See Roy, Olivier, "The Peripheral Jihad," *Globalized Islam,* op. cit., p. 312.

2. See Pinto, María do Céu, *Political Islam and the United States: A Study of U.S. Policy towards Islamist Movements in the Middle East* (Reading, U.K.: Ithaca, 1999), p. 340. Pinto finds that the "real" leading experts did not consider Islamism as a threat but a "healthy grassroots response to the failure of Arab governments to tackle growing socio-economic problems." However, she admitted that a shorter and generally less specialized group of writers argued that Islamism "is inherently hostile to the Western world and is on a collision course with it."

3. See global analysis on the oil crisis impact on jihadi influence in Europe in Ye'or, Bat, "The Oil Embargo: The Trigger," *Eurabia: The Euro-Arab Axis* (Madison, NJ: Fairleigh Dickenson University Press, 2005), p. 47.

4. See Baer, Robert, *Sleeping with the Devil: How Washington Sold Our Soul for Saudi Crude* (New York: Crown Publishers, 2003), "The Seduction," p. 73.

5. On OPEC's politics see Husain, *Global Islamic Politics,* op. cit., "OPEC, OIC, and Islamic Politics," p. 201; "Prelude to OPEC's Ascendency," p. 202.

6. See for example Phares, Walid, "9/11: A Failure of Academia," *FrontPage Magazine,* July 28, 2004.

7. See for example Pipes, Daniel, "Jihad: How Academics Have Camouflaged Its Real Meaning," *New York Post,* December, 2, 2003.

8. See Kramer, Martin, *Ivory Towers on Sand: The Failure of Middle Eastern Studies in America* (Washington, DC: The Washington Institute for Near East Policy, 2001): "Said's Splash," p. 27.

9. In her book on U.S.-Islamist relations, she mentions the names of the leading intellectuals who espoused this view, including: John Esposito, James Piscatori (author of the introduction to her study), Hooshang Amirahmadi, John Voll, James Bill, John Entelis, Richard Bulliet, Charles Butterworth, and Augustus Norton, as well as some nonacademics: Graham Fuller, Shireen Hunter, Richard Murphy, Leon Hadar, Robin Wright. But she also provides a list of those with opposing views, whom she described as alarmists: Samuel Huntington, Martin Kramer, Judith Miller, Bernard Lewis, Peter Rodman, and Daniel Pipes. See Pinto, María do Céu, *Political Islam and the United States,* op. cit.

10. For an example of an academic analysis that criticized other academic warnings from jihadism, see the various publications of Professor John Esposito of Georgetown University. In particular, Esposito, *The Islamic Threat,* op. cit.: "The West Triumphant: Muslim Responses," p. 47.

11. Phares, Walid, Congressional Briefing on 9/11: "Four Years Later, Are We Safer?" September 8, 2005, co-sponsored by the Counter Terrorism Blog. On the subject see also Kushner, Harvey, *Holy War on the Home Front: The Secret Islamic Terror Network in the United States* (Sentinel HC, 2004).

12. On universities' "infiltrations" see Kushner, Harvey, with Davis, Bart, *Holy War on the Home Front: The Secret Islamic Terror Network in the United States* (New York: Penguin Group, 2004): "Universities," p. 1.

13. See the MacKenzie Institute, "A Review of Overseas Terrorists in Canada," August 12, 2005, http://www.mackenzieinstitute.com/2003/other_peoples_wars11.htm.

14. For a comprehensive reading on the deployment of jihadists within the United States, see the pioneering work of Emerson, Steve, *American Jihad: The Terrorist Living Among Us* (New York: Free Press, 2002), especially "How I Made Jihad in America and Lived to Tell about It," p. 5.

15. See Phares on the "Great Story" on Fox News, August 5, 2004: "The arrests in the New York mosque open the file of the infiltration of these religious sites. How large and how widespread are these infiltrations is the question. Are these arrests important, or just a small piece? In fact they are a main tip of the iceberg. Now we know where they may be and how they operate. However, beyond the security agencies, the wider issue is to see Congress and the administration addressing the matter of ideology behind terrorism. The U.S. public must be informed of the kind of literature and material found in possession of the suspects."

16. See Emerson, Steve, "Anatomy of Infiltration," *American Jihad,* op. cit., p. 27.

17. Phares, Walid, on CNN: "Bomb Scare, Terrorist Probe Jolt Florida University," April 26, 1996, http://www.cnn.com/US/9604/26/univ.terror/.

18. On infiltration of charities and the prison system see Kushner with Davis, *Holy War on the Home Front,* op. cit.: "Charities, p. 21; "The Prison System," p. 35.

19. See for example the legal essay by Elaine Cassel criticizing U.S. counterterrorism efforts: "Is Playing Paintball and Firing Legal Guns Terrorism? Three Disturbing Convictions Strongly Suggest Discrimination Against Muslim Americans," *Findlaw Legal Commentary,* May 25, 2004.

20. See al Jazeera forum with Walid Phares, Radwan al sayyid, and Muntsir al Zayat on the Thawahiri's tape in reaction to Dr. Rice's speech at the American University in Cairo, July 4, 2005. Phares: "It shows that al Qaida is afraid from the spread of democracy among the youth in the region. The jihadists resent the doctrines that oppose their ideology, regardless of liking or disliking America": http://www.aljazeera.net/NR/exeres/EE6FB5DE-2872-495F-AB1E-8E37EBE799C1.htm.

21. For a significant analysis of Arabist lobby influence in the U.S. foreign policy establishment, particularly in the 1990s, see Kaplan, Robert D., *The Arabists: The Romance of an American Elite* (New York: Free Press, 1993): "Mr. Foreign Service," p. 85; and "Mugged by Reality," p. 181.

CHAPTER TEN

1. It took courageous citizens to ask for answers about the reasons behind the massacre that had obliterated the lives of their loved ones, fathers, mothers, family members, or children. They wanted closure, and who could blame them?

2. See Fukuyama, Francis, "No Democracy without Democrats," *The End of History and the Last Man* (New York: Avon Books, 1993), p. 131.

3. See *The 9/11 Commission Report,* op. cit.: "Bin Ladin's Appeal in the Islamic World," p. 48.

4. See Fouad, Ajami, "A Thwarted Civilization," *Wall Street Journal,* October 16, 2001.

5. See Peroncel-Hugoz, Jean-Pierre, *The Raft of Mohammed: Social and Human Consequences of the Return to Traditional Religion in the Arab World* (New York: Paragon House Publishers, 1998): "The Hidden Feathers," p. 163.

6. Emerson, "Osama bin Laden, Sheikh Abdullah Azzam, and the Birth of al Qaeda," *American Jihad,* op. cit., p. 127.

7. See "Bin Ladin's Appeal in the Islamic World," in *The 9/11 Commission Report,* op. cit., p. 48.

8. See Emerson, Steve, "World Trade Center I," *American Jihad,* p. 43.

9. See Phares, Walid, "Attack against US Marines in Beirut led to 9/11," *FrontPage Magazine,* October 23, 2003.

10. On the spread of Wahabis internationally, see Schwartz, "Sword of Dishonor: The Wahhabi International," *The Two Faces of Islam,* op. cit., p. 181.

11. Declaration of War against the Americans Occupying the Land of the Two Holy Places by Osama bin Laden, August 1, 1996: http://www.defenddemocracy.org/research_topics/ research_topics_show.htm?doc_id=185673&attrib_id=7580.

12. See *The 9/11 Commission Report,* op. cit.: "A Declaration of War," p. 47, and "Building an Organization, Declaring War on the United States," p. 59.

13. Response by more than one official during the 9/11 hearings in 2004.

14. See Stalinski, Steve, "CAIR Silences Its Critics," *FrontPage Magazine,* August 4, 2005; McCormick, Evan, "A Bad Day for CAIR," *FrontPage Magazine,* September 24, 2003; also Stalinsky, Steve, "CAIR Anti-Muslim Hysteria," *FrontPage Magazine,* November 5, 2004; and Spencer, Robert, "CAIR's Lynch Mob," *FrontPage Magazine,* July 23, 2003.

CHAPTER ELEVEN

1. See for example Roy, Olivier, "What Is Bin Laden's Strategy?" *Globalized Islam,* op. cit., p. 55.

2. Baer, Robert, *Sleeping with the Devil: How Washington Sold Our Soul for Saudi Crude* (New York: Crown Publishers, 2003): "The Honeymoon," p. 91.

3. One of these concepts is the "neglected duty." See Phares, Walid, and Rabil, Robert, "The Neglected Duty: Terrorism's Justification," *The National Interest,* May 5, 2005.

4. See Qutb, Sayyid, *In the Shade of the Qur'an* (*Fi Zilal al-Qur'an*), translated M. A. Salahi and A. A. Shamis (The Islamic Foundation, 1999).

5. See Moore, Robin, *The Hunt for Bin Laden: Task Force Dagger* (New York: Random House, 2003): "Tora Bora," 233; "After-Action Reports: The Hunt for Bin Laden," p. 309.

6. Statement often made by al Qaeda reporters on al Jazeera and on jihadist websites.

7. I developed these three parameters as of October 2001, and I had the opportunity to comment about them on MSNBC, Fox News, and radio shows in 2002 and also during my FAU-LLS lectures. See Phares, Walid, "Usama's Strategic Reasons behind the Attacks," *TownHall,* September 13, 2003.

8. In his first major speech aired on al Jazeera after September 11, Osama bin Laden was issuing threats to preempt what he projected as a much wider and irrational reaction by the United States. See bin Laden, Osama, "Warning to the United States," October 7, 2001, http://news. bbc.co.uk/1/hi/world/south_asia/1585636.stm.

9. Early al Qaeda reactions show the initial projection of the jihadists: They looked for crumbling inside the United States as they issued strategic threats. See for example Sulaiman Abu Ghaith, official spokesperson of the organization in a message aired on al Jazeera, October 14, 2001, "Retaliation for Air Strikes on Afghanistan," http://news.bbc.co.uk/1/hi/world/middle_east/ 1598146.stm.

CHAPTER TWELVE

1. See Gertz, Bill, *Breakdown: How America's Intelligence Failures Led to September 11* (Washington, D.C.: Regnery Publishing, 2002): "The Loud Bang No One Heard," p. 21; "The FBI: The Decline of Domestic Intelligence," p. 83; "Technical Spying," p. 127.

2. In his pre-9/11 book *The Arabists,* op. cit., Robert Kaplan suggests that the U.S. foreign policy establishment was providing wrong advice to the top policy makers because of the Saudi Wahabi influence.

3. See the relevant sections of *The 9/11 Commission Report,* op. cit.: "The Law Enforcement Community," 73; "The Federal Aviation Administration," 82; "The Intelligence Community," 86; "The State Department and the Defense Department," 93.

4. I raised these issues in a series of lectures at the University of Miami IRP series, "September 11: The Root Causes," during the fall of 2001 and at the annual Phares lecture of the Florida Society for Middle East Studies in March 2003.

5. See Phares, Walid, "Tracking the Terrorists," The Discovery Channel, November 18, 2004.

6. See *The 9/11 Commission Report,* op. cit.: "Before the Bombings in Kenya and Tanzania," p. 108.

7. For example, in August 2005, Pennsylvania congressman Curt Weldon revealed that a formerly secret military intelligence unit called "Able Danger" had identified Mohammed Atta and three of the other 9/11 hijackers as U.S.-linked al Qaeda operatives as early as 2000. See Shenon, Philip, and Jehl, Douglas, "9/11 Panel Seeks Inquiry on New Atta Report," *New York Times,* August 10, 2005.

8. See *The 9/11 Commission Report,* op. cit.: "Responses to al Qaida's Initial Assaults," p. 108, and "Crisis: August 1998," p. 115.

9. See *The 9/11 Commission Report,* op. cit., "From the Old Terrorism to the New: The First World Trade Center Bombing," p. 71.

10. I published a monograph of my op-eds during the first part of the 1990s under the title *Radical Islam* (Miami: IRP Press, 1995–1999). In that essay, I made the case that the jihadists aim to "hit mainland America" as a strategic target. Also, I developed this thesis through the lecture series "Jihadi Terrorism and the U.S.," IRP, University of Miami, November 1995. As early as 1987, I developed the thesis of "international jihadism" leading to assaults on *dar al harb,* including the United States (in *Mashrek International Magazine* [Beirut, 1987], and Mashrek Institute Forum [Winter 1987]).

11. The blurring of vision was initially intellectual. If a public opinion leader does not name the threat, he or she will be morally contributing to the consequences. See for example Ye'or, Bat, "Historical Amnesia: Naming Jihad and Dhimmitude," in Spencer, ed., *The Myth of Islamic Tolerance,* op. cit., p. 107.

12. Often Arabist writers put pressure on American intelligentsia not to get information from anti-jihadist sources. For an example see Abul Jobain, Ahmad, *Islam Under Siege: Radical Islamic Terrorism or Political Islam?* (United Association for Studies and Research, 1993). Ahmad writes: "In the case of the Sudan, the media readily prints information provided by opposition groups such as the SPLA rather than gather information themselves." *The 9/11 Commission Report,* op. cit., "Adaptation—and Nonadaptation," p. 71.

13. Arguments developed in Phares, "Blinded by Convention," op. cit.

14. Sperry, Paul, "The Wahhabi Corridor," *Infiltration: How Muslim Spies and Subversives Have Penetrated Washington* (Nashville, TN: Nelson Current, 2005), p. 174.

15. See Emerson, *American Jihad,* op. cit., "Appendix A: Current and Recent Militant Islamist Groups in the United States," p. 178; "Appendix B: Current and Recent Terrorist Front Cells and Groups with Direct Association with Terrorists," p. 180; "Appendix C: The Terrorists' Support Networks," p. 183; "Appendix D: A Brief History of Islamic Fundamentalism," p. 221.

16. See Kushner with Davis, *Holy War on the Home Front,* op. cit.: "Media," p. 109.

17. For example author Husain Zohair portrays the Islamists as "revolutionaries," "puritanical Muslims," and "emulators of Prophet Muhammad and his pious companions." At best he defines them as "zealous promoters of the five pillars." Husain, *Global Islamic Politics,* op. cit.: particularly "The Meaning of Islamic Revivals," p. 4; "Revolutionaries," p. 45; "Puritanical Muslims," p. 64.

18. *Taqiya* is a religious-political method used initially by Shiites against Sunnis in the seventh century to "dissimulate" their identity. Later on it became a tactical concept to conceal one's identity or ideas for survival, used by Druse or Ismaelis. Modern fundamentalists, including Sunnis, use it as a mean to infiltrate enemy environment.

19. See for example Lewis, *Islam and the West: A Clash of Civilizations?* op. cit.; Esposito, John L., "The Islamic Threat: Myth or Reality?" p. 188; "Islamic Organizations: Soldiers of God," p. 119.

20. Depending on how jihadism is explained, students can develop their talents. See for example a recent analysis of what jihad is. If instructors legitimize the phenomenon historically, they would contribute to a misunderstanding of the movement in its contemporary forms. See for example Cook, David, *Understanding Jihad* (Berkeley: UCLA Berkeley, 2005): "Crystallization of Jihad Theory, Crusade and Counter Crusade," p. 49; "Jihad during the 19th Century: Renewal and Resistance"; "Radical Islam and Contemporary Jihad Theory," p. 93.

21. On the failure of Middle East studies in America, see the focused research by Dr. Martin Kramer, *Ivory Towers on Sand: The Failure of Middle Eastern Studies in America* (Washington, D.C.: Washington Institute for Near East Policy, 2001), especially "The Beltway Barrier," p. 84. Also Pipes, "Jihad: How Academics Have Camouflaged Its Real Meaning," op. cit.

CHAPTER THIRTEEN

1. New terrorism studies should be developing "jihad projections" as a parameter for counterterrorism strategies. See for example Sageman, Marc, Understanding Terror Networks (Philadelphia: University of Pennsylvania Press, 2004).

2. Note another projection published by Dr. Richard Clarke during winter 2005. My own virtual projection, developed as of 2003, is based on the assumption that 9/11 did not occur in 2001. See Richard Clarke, "Ten Years Later," *Atlantic Monthly,* Jan.-Feb., 2005; "2005: Return to the Homeland Battlefields," p. 61; "2006: Mobilizing the Home Front," p. 66; "2007: Iran and Saudi Arabia," p. 70; "2008: Election Year and Virtual War," p. 72; "2009: 'Nuke Squads' and the New Draft," p. 74; "2010: Using Our Own Chemical Agents Against Us," p. 75.

3. Ye'or, *Eurabia: The Euro-Arab Axis,* op. cit., projects close developments: "The Political Component: The Arab Conditions, p. 53; "The Economic Component: The EEC's Conditions," p. 56.

4. In Phares, Walid, interview, "Iran Nukes and Jihad Networks in the U.S.," Radio America, September 26, 2003.

5. "Sentences Come Down in 'Virginia Jihad' Case," Associated Press, June 15, 2004.

6. In Arabic, a "*Ghazwa*" means a "military raid." Al Qaeda and other Salafist militants use the term *Ghazwa* when terrorist attacks are mounted against an enemy inside *dar el harb,* or infidel lands.

7. These levels of casualties have been advanced by a number of al Qaeda leaders. Sulaiman Abu Ghaith, al Qaeda spokesman, made several threats against the mainland United States, including on October 14, 2001, via an audiotape aired on al Jazeera (op. cit.).

8. View in comparative analysis with the nonexistence at the projected time of a homeland security structure: See *The 9/11 Commission Report,* op. cit.: "Immediate Responses at Home," p. 326.

9. Read in a comparative perspective with real preparation after 9/11 to situations that already occurred. See *The 9/11 Commission Report,* op. cit.: "Wartime," p. 325.

CHAPTER FOURTEEN

1. See *The 9/11 Commission Report,* op. cit.: "Preparedness as of September 11," p. 278.

2. See Keller, Tony, and Speed, Elizabeth, "Functional Issues: Whither Jihadist Terrorism," DND Policy Group, Canadian Defense Ministry, 2003 assessment, http://www.forces.gc.ca/admpol/ eng/doc/strat_2003/sa03_15_e.htm.

3. See for example Kepel, Gilles, *The War for Muslim Minds: Islam and the West* (New York: Belknap Press, 2004).

4. See Pipes, Daniel, "One Year Later: Militant Islam," *Washington Post,* September 11, 2002.

5. "Symposium: The War on Terror: How Are We Doing?" *FrontPage Magazine,* June 18, 2004.

6. See author's article, "*Wahabi vs. Wahabi,*" *FrontPage Magazine,* June 8, 2004.

7. On the subject, see Spencer, Robert, *Onward Muslim Soldiers: How Jihad Still Threatens American and the West* (Washington, D.C.: Regnery Publishing, 2003): "Jihad in Eclipse Resurgent," p. 213.

8. See Durie, Mark, "What Is Happening in Indonesia?" in Spencer, ed., *The Myth of Islamic Tolerance,* op. cit., p. 264.

9. For an expanded analysis of the jihadist war plans in south Asia see Dahlby, Tracy, *Allah's Torch: A Report from Behind the Scenes in Asia's War on Terror* (New York: HarperCollins, 2005), particularly "Holy War," p. 11; "Battle of Wills," p. 125; "Jihad Everlasting," p. 283.

10. See "Saudi Wealth Fuels Global Jihadism," October 27, 2003, *Insight on the News* (a newspaper of News World Communications): www.insightmag.com/news/2003/11/11/ World/Saudi.Wealth.Fuels.Global.Jihadism–538588.shtml.

11. See *2004 Strategic Forecasting,* "The Phenomenon of Jihadism," http://www.lcwatch.com/ special109.shtml: "The [Salafist] movement away from formal organizations by making training lessons available in the public domain has allowed the jihadist movement to sustain itself and tap into the grassroots of society. This bodes ill for the security of foreign companies in the kingdom—and the future of the Saudi monarchy."

12. See short analysis by the author: "The Saudis must define who they are. If they fight bin Laden today but maintain Wahhabism as a state doctrine, they will be preparing for the next al-Qaeda. But if they distance themselves from Wahhabism and engage in reforms, they could transform the kingdom into a constitutional monarchy where Islam would thrive. The emirs must denounce jihad as a form of international relations. But can a branch cut its own roots? If the Saudis do so, we can trust them as allies in the war on terrorism." *Time Magazine,* Sunday, September 7, 2003.

13. On these European structures, see the detailed book by Kohlman, Evan, *Al Qaida's Jihad in Europe* (Oxford: Berg, 2004).

14. See Phares, Walid, "al Qaida's Bombing of London Is the Rupture of a Status Quo," "The Situation with Tucker Carlson," MSNBC, http://www.msnbc.msn.com/id/8503399/>http:// www.msnbc.msn.com/id/8503399/.

15. See Sperry, *Infiltration,* op. cit.: "Law Enforcement Infiltration: Congress and the FBI," p. 135.

16. See *The 9/11 Commission Report,* op. cit.: "Planning for War," p. 330, and "Phase Two and the Question of Iraq," p. 334.

17. Phares, Walid, "The New World Disorder," *The Lebanese American Journal* (November 2001).

18. I made this analysis public in February of 2003 through the lectures at the Lifelong Learning Society at Florida Atlantic University and through interviews on MSNBC, Fox News, and radio shows. See, for example, Phares, Walid, on Fox News, August 6, 2004: "Only after 9/11 [did] the jihadists [become] subjects of interest in the U.S."

19. Osama bin Laden's audiotape on February 11, 2003, aired on al Jazeera, http://news.bbc. co.uk/2/hi/middle_east/2751019.stm.

20. Phares, Walid, "Osama Targets Iraq," *FrontPage Magazine,* January 7, 2004.

CHAPTER FIFTEEN

1. Muslim liberals or dissidents do not escape the persecution. Like Salmon Rushdie, author of the highly publicized *Satanic Verses,* Irshad Manji drew significant threats from the jihadists after the publication of *The Trouble with Islam* (New York: St. Martin's Press, 2004). See Kepel, Gilles, *Allah in the West: Islamic Movements in America and Europe,* translated Susan Milner (Pala Alto, CA: Mestizo Spaces/Espaces Metisses, Stanford University Press, 1997): "From Gang Warfare to the Army of Allah," p. 49.

2. See Kepel, *Allah in the West,* op. cit.: "From Gang warfare to the Army of Allah," p. 49, "When Did We Stop Thinking?" p. 48.

3. On the issue of infiltration of U.S. national security, see the frightening book by Sperry, *Infiltration: How Muslim Spies and Subversives Have Penetrated Washington,* op. cit. The data and revelations in the book warrant a serious governmental investigation.

4. I developed these analyses in the media as of early 2002 on MSNBC, Fox News, and later on various forums on Radio America, radios ABC, CBS, and Radio Canada; see also Gertz, *Breakdown,* op. cit.: "The FBI: The Decline of Domestic Intelligence," p. 83.

5. Phares, Walid, "Homegrown Jihadists," *FrontPage Magazine,* October 14, 2003, also on MSNBC.

6. Intelcon, National Intelligence Conference, February 8–10, 2005, Arlington, Virginia.

7. On the subject, see the postings of the CounterTerrorism Blog, a newly formed outlet founded by Andrew Cochrane.

8. Al Qaeda was successful in Madrid after the March 11, 2004, strikes but not entirely successful after the London July 7, 2005, bombings.

9. See Emerson, Steve, and Pipes, Daniel, "Terrorism on Trial," *Wall Street Journal,* May 31, 2001.

10. BBC World News, "Gunman Kills Dutch Film Director" (Theo Van Gogh), November 4, 2004.

11. Professor Heykal, mentioned earlier, was hired in at least three cases in which Salfis were charged.

12. See Pipes, Daniel, "Wife Tells Court: Islamic Law Made Me Do It," June 15, 2003, http://www.danielpipes.org/blog/24; also Weblog, CAIR's Legal Tribulations, June 27, 2003, http://www.danielpipes.org/blog/32.

13. Pipes, Daniel, "The War on Campus," *New York Post,* September 17, 2002. See Emerson, Steve, "Jihad in the Academy," *American Jihad,* op. cit., p. 109.

14. See Emerson, "Jihad in the Academy," *American Jihad,* op. cit., p. 109.

15. De Atkine, Norvell B., and Pipes, Daniel, "Middle Eastern Studies: What Went Wrong?" *Academic Questions* (Winter 1995–96). Also Pipes, Daniel, "Defund Middle East Studies," *New York Sun,* February 24, 2004.

16. For example, UC Berkeley received five million dollars in the late 1990s from the King Fahd Foundation to build a Middle East studies center; Arkansas University also received millions of dollars from Saudi funds and many other campuses, programs, and centers have been showered with gifts from Wahabi institutions. See the extended research by professor Martin Kramer and Dr. Daniel Pipes in their several books and articles, particularly in Middle East Quarterly.

17. Note for example how an argument is created after 9/11 to distinguish between the bad Salafist and the good Salafist. In short an attempt to save the credibility of most radical Islamists from the deeds of a few. This effort will only blur the vision of the educated public. See for example Esposito, John L., *Unholy War Terror in the Name of Islam* (New York: Oxford University Press, 2002), "The Making of a Modern Terrorist," p. 3; "Where Do We Go from Here?" p. 118. Mideast expert Martin Kramer writes on the attempts by Michigan University history pro-

fessor Juan Cole to mislead the American public on critical issues such as the war on terrorism and the real threat of jihadism. See for example http://sandbox.blog-city.com/juan_cole_noble_enterprise.htm.

18. For example, in his book *Islamic Threat: Myth of Reality,* Esposito systematically attacks Lewis's multidecades' work, projecting it as one of the reasons for past U.S. failures. However, Professor Esposito, who blames "the West" for Islamic fundamentalism, served as an advisor to the Foreign Service in the 1990s, precisely during the time of ultimate U.S. foreign policy failure toward the rise of jihadism. Professor Cole, the current president-elect of MESA, concentrates his criticism on experts who warn about jihadism, such as Pipes and Huntington. This year he went as far as saying that my analysis of homegrown jihadism was playing a "sinister role."

19. Kramer, Martin, Ivory Towers in the Sand: The Failure of Middle Eastern Studies in America, op cit., "The Cultivation of Irrelevance," p. 104.

20. The question is then how to review highly qualified expert opinions projecting the war on terror, if past analyses were based on pre-9/11 academic failures. See for example Clarke, "Ten Years Later," *Atlantic Monthly,* op. cit., "2011: What We Might Have Done Differently," p. 76.

21. The criticism of MESA's "Arabist" policies were the subject of ten years of lecture series and panels organized by the Florida Society for Middle East Studies based at Florida Atlantic University. (1994–2004).MESA was also accused of obstruction of academic material relating to the Jihadi persecution of Middle East minorities, by the academic and congressional panels held by the Coalition for the Defense of HumanRights in the Muslim world Washington, a umbrella organization representing 42 US-based ethnic and religious groups including: Coptic, Assyrian, Sudanese, Lebanese, Berber, Hindus, Humanist Muslims, etc.

22. See "Workshop on Terrorism Studies," SWOT, College of William and Mary, July 18–19, 2005.

23. See Kaplan, "A New Species?" *The Arabists,* op. cit., p. 305.

24. See Muhammad, Elijah, "The Black Muslim in America," *History of the Nation of Islam* (Atlanta: Secretarius Memps, 1993), p. 45.

25. One of the most confrontational subjects between the jihadist lobbies and the U.S. government is profiling. The pressure groups constantly attempt to weaken the concept as a prelude to eliminating it. See Kushner with Davis, *Holy War on the Home Front,* op. cit.: "Profiling," p. 121.

26. The jihadi recruitment within ethnic communities is generalized in the West. For example in the wake of the London bombings on July 7, 2005, see O'Neil, Sean, "Islamic Cleric Declared War on Britain Six Months Ago," *Times (London),* July 12, 2005.

27. See Pipes, Daniel, "Pentagon Jihadis," *New York Post,* September 29, 2003.

28. See Pipes, Daniel, "Islamists Infiltrate Law enforcement," January 24, 2005, http://www.danielpipes.org/blog/400.

29. See Roy, "*Globalized Islam,* op. cit.: "Where Are the Muslim Reformers?" p. 29; "Muslims in the West," p. 100; "Western-born Second-Generation Jihad," p. 315.

CHAPTER SIXTEEN

1. See the voluminous work of Fregosi, Paul, *Jihad in the West: Muslim Conquests from the 7th to the 21st Centuries* (Amherst, NY: Prometheus Books, 1998).

2. See Baer, *Sleeping with the Devil,* op. cit.: "In the War on Terrorism, You Lie, You Die," p. 187.

3. See Clarke, Richard A., Aga, Glenn P., and Cressey, Roger W., *Defeating the Jihadists: A Blueprint for Action* (New York: Century Foundation Press, 2004).

4. For comparative perspective see *The 9/11 Commission Report,* op. cit.: "Terrorist Entrepreneurs," p. 145.

5. Al Jazeera, Associated Press, AFP, June 22, 2002.

6. "United States, What's New?: The Nuclear Posture Review," *The Economist,* March 16, 2002, and Global Security.com, March 15, 2002.

7. New authors suggest that today's fundamentalists are extending a historic line, not deviating from it. They argue that the threat of modern expansion is real. See Bostom, *The Legacy of Jihad,* op. cit.

8. See "Zarqawi Says Katrina 'Beginning of the End' for US," AFP, September 4, 2005; also "'Allah's Soldier': Islamist Bloggers Hail Katrina," Trabelsi Habib, AFP, September 4, 2005.

9. To illustrate the danger posed by future jihadists, read the injunction by the al Qaeda spokesman: "US interests are spread throughout the world. So, every Muslim should carry out his real role to champion his Islamic nation and religion. Carrying out terrorism against the oppressors is one of the tenets of our religion and Shari'ah." Suleiman Abu Ghaith, October 10, 2001 (calling on Muslims to join holy war), BBC-TV.

CHAPTER SEVENTEEN

1. Only a joint effort by western and Arab Islamic democratic governments to counter jihadism can diffuse mounting tensions leading to a clash of civilizations. See Huntington, Samuel P., *The Clash of Civilizations and the Remaking of World Order* (New York: Simon and Schuster, 1996).

2. For example, see discussion of Islamic law and the war on terror in "Muslim Scholars Condemn Terrorists," Associated Press, July 28, 2005 and analysis in Phares, Walid, "The American Fatwa," *Washington Times,* August 8, 2005.

CONCLUSION

1. See Phares, Walid, in an interview by NPR International, San Francisco, entitled "Mideast Politics and Terrorism," May 14, 2003.

2. AFP, Reuters, September 4, 2005. See also Phares, Walid, "Jihadists: Allah Punished New Orleans," in CounterTerrorism Blog, September 2, 2005; also "Katrina, an al Qaida Soldier," in Lebanonwire, September 4, 2005.

3. See Phares, Walid, "Katrina, al Qaida Member?" FDD Blog, September 4, 2005. The APSA Convention took place in Washington, D.C., on September 2–3.

4. Analysis initiated in an op-ed: Phares, Walid, "Al-Qaida: Is It Gaining or Withering?" *Townhall,* September 20, 2003. Will this mean that al Qaeda lost all of its cards and is in retreat? Not at all: the neo-Wahabi movement is still on the offensive, even though many doors have been slammed. An ideological entity that recruits endlessly will wither only when its beliefs are abandoned by a wider enlightened community, and that is the real challenge on the war on terror.

5. See for example the author's examination of new tactics: Phares, Walid, "The Long Planned 'Spontaneous' Riots," *FrontPage Magazine,* May 19, 2005.

INDEX